OUR GEORGE

A Family Memoir

Barbara Best is a sister of the late George Best. Like her famous brother, she has always been passionate about sport, excelling at both hockey and netball in particular. Barbara left Northern Ireland at the height of the political unrest to work as a manageress in a South African hotel, returning to her home country in 1981 when she took up a post in local government. Since 2007 she has worked full-time on a voluntary basis for the George Best Foundation. Barbara has three children and two grandchildren and she lives in Belfast with her husband, Norman.

OUR GEORGE

A Family Memoir

BARBARA BEST
with Lindy McDowell

PAN BOOKS

First published 2007 in Ireland by Gill & Macmillan Ltd

First published in Great Britain in hardback 2007 by Macmillan
and in paperback 2009 by Pan Books
imprints of Pan Macmillan Ltd
Pan Macmillan, 20 New Wharf Road, London N1 9RR
Basingstoke and Oxford
Associated companies throughout the world
www.panmacmillan.com

ISBN 978 0 330 47175 6

9 8 7 6 5 4 3 2 1

A CIP catalogue record for this book is available from
the British Library.

Index compiled by Cover to Cover
Typeset by Make Communication
Printed and bound in the UK by
CPI Mackays, Chatham ME5 8TD

Visit www.panmacmillan.com to read more about all our books
and to buy them. You will also find features, author interviews and
news of any author events, and you can sign up for e-newsletters
so that you're always first to hear about our new releases.

To my lovely mum who, like her much loved and missed son, left us all far too soon. I hope that, together once again, you both have found peace in each other's loving embrace.

CONTENTS

ACKNOWLEDGEMENTS

The decision to write this book was not an easy one. In fact when it was first suggested to me, I baulked at the idea. Despite the overwhelming media attention which George attracted in his lifetime — not least in his final years — ours has always been an intensely private family. Indeed the first full newspaper interview I gave was only after George's transplant, when he was back on the drink again and attracting intense criticism.

What I wanted to explain then was that behind the headlines was a real human being whose family loved and cared for him deeply. George was losing his battle with alcoholism — the same disease that had blighted the life of our beloved mother. But we, his family, knew just how fiercely he had struggled against that disease.

In a way this book is an extension of that interview. It is not just our family's tribute to a dearly loved son and brother but also, I hope, a book that will give some real insight into the life of the Belfast boy who became one of sport's great icons. It tells about his upbringing and the family values that shaped him and remained with him.

But it is not a book that sets out to make excuses for George. It acknowledges his faults as well as the constant pressures with which he lived.

It was our sister Carol who came up with the title for this book. Our George was always what we called our big brother to differentiate him from our uncle George who was almost the same age.

But it also sums up exactly what this book is about. It is not a book that charts the career of a footballing legend — that has been comprehensively done elsewhere. Instead this one is about the boy and the man as we, his family, knew him.

This is a book, quite literally, about our George …

In theory it sounded simple to write this book, but in practice it was to be such an emotional journey.

I would like to thank Lindy McDowell not just for her friendship, but for the emotional support which she has given to me over the past two years and above all for her absolute professionalism.

I believed in my heart that I had a different story to tell and it was from the heart that my thoughts and words came.

I would also like to express my sincere thanks to …

Dad, who even though he has been through so much in the last two years, parted with so much important information, my brother Ian and my sisters Grace and Julie, but in particular my 'big sister' Carol, who has supported and encouraged me every step of the way.

Mum's side of the family, her brother George, her sisters Georgie and Joan and nephew Louis, who all have their own fond memories of our George.

My own children Steven, Jenny and Paul who haven't had much of my time recently.

The staff of Nettlefield Primary School as well as the ex teachers from Lisnasharragh Secondary School for their invaluable contribution.

George's long-time friend Robin McCabe who brought many laughs when they were really needed, and for his continued friendship with the family.

Edel Patterson and Joan McCoy from Castlereagh Borough Council who helped me to fill in the memory lapses in the days following George's death.

Debi, Keith, Caron and Mphatso for their inspiring stories.

Alex and Anita, who so often arrived with tissues and broad shoulders for me to cry on.

Finally, to my husband Norman, without whose love and support I wouldn't have managed to finish this book. You knew how difficult it was for me to put my thoughts on paper, but always found the right words to encourage me to fulfil my dream.

Barbara Best McNarry
July 2007

| SAYING GOODBYE

D r Akeel Alisa came into the room and stood silently for a moment beside us. As he did, two nurses, John and Yvonne, were already taking their places on either side of George's bed. The tension was unbearable. We knew what was coming now.

Akeel dropped his head very slightly and then said softly: 'I am so sorry that I have to do this.'

He bent over George, checked for a heartbeat and gave a barely perceptible nod to Yvonne. In a gentle voice, she explained to us that she was now switching off the machine. And with that it was finally over.

Through the utter devastation that I was feeling, the one thing that struck me most and will stay in my memory always was the silence. That damned silence. After such a long time listening to a machine 'breathing' for my beloved brother, suddenly the room was utterly, unbearably quiet.

It was finally over.

Outside, the news would, within minutes, be relayed to the media and fans who had been keeping their own long vigil for days, in some cases, even, for weeks. George Best, the world's greatest and most complete footballer, was dead.

He would be mourned by so many people in so many ways. By the faithful fans who remembered his genius on the football field and the glamour and excitement he brought to the Beautiful Game. By the world's great sporting legends, many of whom would grieve at the passing of a man who, for all his faults, had been a good friend. By the media for whom his colourful personal life and long battle with alcoholism had provided countless headlines down through the years. By the women who loved him. By people all across the globe whose lives he touched even in some small, distant way.

But as I stood there, watching my brother's life ebb away, I knew that none would mourn him more than those of us gathered around his bedside. His family and friends. To the outside world, he was George Best, football's first and greatest superstar. But to me he was my beloved GB, the brother who at the age of just fifteen had left our home and our family in Belfast.

Over the years, during the good times, the bad times and the downright terrible times my feelings for George had never wavered. Certainly at times he saddened and frustrated me. But I always cared so very deeply for him. And now I was having to say goodbye.

Beside me was my husband Norman who down through the years had built such a close and trusting bond with George. Most of George's closest family were there with us too — our dad Dickie, George's son Calum, our oldest sister Carol and her husband Allen, our younger sisters, the twins Grace and Julie, with Julie's husband Pete and our youngest brother Ian. Also by George's bedside as he slipped away were Phil Hughes and Denis Law, two of his long-time friends.

Norman put his arms around me. But somehow I just couldn't let go and cry. I stood there numbed by sorrow and silence.

Outside, the media were already clamouring for news, but for the moment they could wait. The world might have lost George Best, sporting legend. But inside that room we had lost something more precious still. Between us we had lost a son, a father, a brother and a magical, loving, irreplaceable friend.

We had lost our George.

—

I had been worrying constantly over the last two years of George's life. Okay, so that's an understatement. I'd been worrying about George's drinking for decades. But in those last two years of his life, in particular, my concern for my brother's health had understandably grown.

It was no secret that he was drinking again despite his liver transplant and, as time progressed, drinking a scary amount. It had reached the stage where I had become consumed with the fear that not only could the worst happen at any time, but that we, his family, would hear about it in the worst possible way. On the news. My concern here wasn't solely for George himself. Our father Dickie was in his eighties. What would it do to him to hear in such a brutal way that something terrible had happened to his son?

George's drinking in the aftermath of his liver transplant operation in 2002 had inevitably attracted intense media coverage. But it wasn't just the constant news stories about our George that I had to deal with. The US president wasn't exactly doing a lot for my nerves either. At the time, the headlines were dominated by America's war on terror and I remember feeling a kind of terror of my own each day as I'd listen to the morning news.

The newsreader would invariably begin the bulletin with: 'George Buh — ' and for that awful split second my heart would race as I waited for what came next.

'...Bush,' the newsreader would continue. And then I could breathe again.

I always thought that the newsreader was going to say George Best. I always automatically expected that it would be bad news about our George. Even today, I still get that awful heart-stopping feeling if I hear George Bush's name on radio. It brings it all back.

In September 2005, it had been via the radio that we had had the first serious inkling that George's health was deteriorating, and deteriorating badly. Our sister Carol had been listening to an interview with both George and Rodney Marsh. As she listened to George's voice, she said, she was immediately struck by the feeling that he didn't sound well — he didn't sound, as we say in Northern Ireland, at all like himself. She talked to her husband Allen about it and later mentioned it to Norman and myself. I had also heard the interview and I had to agree. Although initially I'd tried to dismiss it, alarm bells were now starting to ring. George had sounded very weak and, to all of us, a little bit hoarse.

Over the following weekend, Phil Hughes, George's friend and agent, phoned to say that George was indeed sick and in bed. An appointment, he explained, had been made with Professor Roger Williams at the Cromwell Hospital in London for Tuesday, 27 September. But on the Monday, Phil phoned again to say that George had already been admitted to the Cromwell.

Of course, at this stage, while we were concerned, we hoped that it was something that a short spell in hospital would sort out and that George would be out and about in no time.

Sadly, of course, despite every human and medical effort, George was never to leave that hospital again. Less than a week later, at midnight on Sunday, 2 October, George was admitted to the Cromwell's Intensive Care Unit.

Norman and I were then in the south of France, at our holiday home where George had spent so many happy and peaceful times with us. We had been trying to get our garden in order before winter set in. I remember it was one of those glorious, sunny mornings when the whole world seems idyllically peaceful and beautiful. We were both out in the garden having breakfast when the phone rang.

Phil, who was terribly upset, was breaking the news that George was now very ill indeed.

At first, probably because we were so shocked at the news, there was a degree of confusion. Norman had spoken to Phil and, for whatever reason, thought that George had suffered a heart attack. I telephoned Carol to tell her this so that she could let Dad and the rest of the family know. A few more phone calls were made and we realised that, in fact, George hadn't had a heart attack.

Meanwhile, Norman and I were trying to book a flight back to London straight away. We couldn't get flights for that day, but were able to book seats directly, or so we thought, from Girona in Spain for the following morning. We were desperate to get to London as quickly as possible but when we arrived at the airport it seemed to be far busier than usual. Because of industrial action on the French side, all flights leaving France had been suspended. At first, we didn't give this too much thought as we were flying from Spain and so assumed we wouldn't be affected. But of course, we still had to fly over French airspace.

The delay that followed seemed to last forever and, even when we were finally allowed to board, we had to sit on the plane for another two hours. Finally we arrived at Stansted from where we made our way straight to the hospital. Every minute in that long, long day had seemed like an eternity.

Phil, though, had kept us up to date during our journey. He had left for home about half an hour before we finally made it to the hospital as he had been there all day and was emotionally drained.

We arrived at the Cromwell with luggage in tow and were directed to intensive care. My stomach was in knots. I was so nervous about seeing George in ICU as I know it can be such a daunting place. But nothing could have prepared either of us for what we were about to see.

Norman and I were shocked to the core at the state George was in. And it's not as if we hadn't seen him very ill in the past. We had been with him immediately after his liver transplant when he hadn't exactly looked a picture of health. But this was something altogether different. He was so thin, he was a most terrible colour and he was having extreme difficulty even in breathing. At this stage, he had only a few drips and tubes attached to him and although this was hardly shocking in the circumstances, it was still a great worry. He just looked so terribly frail and ill. When first admitted to hospital he had been described as suffering from 'flu-like symptoms' but it was obvious this was something much more serious.

And yet, typical George, even at this point, he was getting into bother with the nurses. He kept taking off his oxygen mask despite their orders that he keep it in place.

Ros Hollidge, who by then had been George's partner for approximately two years, was at his bedside when we first arrived but she left to give us a bit of private time with him.

It was truly heartbreaking to see the difficulty George had even trying to speak. We did most of the talking, just bringing him up to date with what was happening at the house in France. At the same time, we were trying to gauge the severity of his illness.

His mood at least was quite upbeat and he wanted to know all about the new bathroom we were having built in France. He tried so hard to chat to us but it very quickly became apparent that it was just exhausting him. We stayed for only about forty-five minutes. It was by now very late and we knew that we had a couple of days ahead to spend with him. It was better that we left to let him get some rest. As usual, I gave him a kiss and a hug before we went.

One thing that will stay with me forever is that just as Norman and I got to the door to leave, George called out: 'See you tomorrow, darlin'.'

When I think now of the sheer effort that it must have taken for him just to call out those words, it breaks my heart. I am so sorry that I didn't go back and give him another hug. But little did we know at this stage that the number of times over the next few weeks that we would be able to chat to George or to hug him and hold him would be so very few.

Norman and I left the hospital that night desperately worried. It was very late and we still had to find a hotel. But even when we eventually found a room, and even though we were both shattered, sleep didn't come. Despite trying hard to be positive, we both had to admit to each other that we felt a deepening sense of foreboding.

That night was to be the start of eight long weeks for family and friends. Many journeys were to be made not just by Norman and myself but by the rest of the family from Belfast and from Poole in Dorset where my brother Ian lived. Denis Law, Dave Sadler and Alan Platt were also to become frequent visitors, travelling from Manchester to London to be at George's bedside.

Any family who has been in a similar situation will recognise the pattern. There's the constant tiredness, the never-ending worry. You seem to hover between despair on one hand and sudden surges of hope. We felt all of those things in the weeks that followed.

But I think that that night as we left the Cromwell, both Norman and I already knew in our hearts that this was the beginning of the end. Even though we were occasionally to snatch at signs of hope in the coming weeks, it would be fair to say that that feeling never really went away.

We spent the next two days at the hospital speaking to the nursing staff and particularly to the doctors, Professor Williams and Dr Akeel Alisa, trying to glean as much information as possible to take back with us to Dad in Belfast. Those two doctors, as everyone knows, had become George's friends as much as his physicians. To him they were the Prof and Akeel and that's how we came to know them too.

It was so difficult to understand everything we were now hearing, especially as there was so much information to digest.

We spent as much time as possible with George but he was often very weak and receiving a lot of treatment from the nursing staff. It was just a case of going in and out of the ICU when we could.

Already many get-well messages and cards were starting to arrive at the hospital and I spent some time reading these to him. I thought that it was really important to keep George's spirits up. Although he wasn't able to speak much, his eyes, those famous twinkling blue eyes, were still the same. They could speak volumes about the mood he was in.

I remember on one occasion during those first couple of days having a long chat with one of the ICU nurses, Anne Marie, who was originally from South Africa. We had plenty to talk about as I used to live there and had spent three weeks there in 2002, for my fiftieth birthday. I had booked to go back for Christmas that year. Anyway, we were chatting away while Anne Marie was just gently massaging George's feet and legs as he dozed. Our chatting must have been disturbing him for all of a sudden his eyes opened wide.

'I'm sorry, George. Are we keeping you awake?' asked Anne Marie.

He just rolled his eyes heavenward as if to say, 'Of course you are, you stupid women!'

We got the hint and I left to give him a bit of peace. As I say, those eyes could speak volumes!

It was with a heavy heart and considerable reluctance that we flew back home to Belfast. The next two weeks were extremely difficult for the entire family. We regularly kept in touch with Phil for medical updates but sadly the news was never very positive. Each day, George continued to become weaker, and our fears for him grew. On a couple of occasions, he had hallucinations, and would insist on calling Phil or Ros to come and take him home. He said that he wasn't getting any peace and quiet as all of the staff were so noisy. He claimed that the doctors and nurses were having parties, dancing and drinking all night. As George himself might have said, probably wishful thinking on his part!

Norman and I flew back to London from Belfast towards the end of October. Phil had said that George was eating very little so I decided to bring him over a little treat from home. There was no problem in deciding what to bring. Ice-cream from Desano's.

Desano's is an institution in Belfast. As the name suggests, the family who own the business come originally from Italy and they make ice-cream which, in my opinion, nothing in the world comes close to equalling. George just loved it too. So I bought the largest tub possible, wrapped it in layers and layers of paper for insulation, and packed it with ice blocks into a cool bag. When we arrived at the hotel in London, I put it in the fridge until I got myself organised for the hospital. But then, on the way out of our room, I was rushing so much I almost forgot it.

'Oh, George's ice-cream,' I called to Norman.

But Norman didn't move. Gently he said to me: 'Sit down, Barbara. I need to speak to you.'

Of course, by that stage I had realised that George was very ill, but even so, it took a few minutes to take in what Norman was now trying to tell me. Phil, it seems, had phoned earlier in the day to say that there had been a serious setback. George's condition had deteriorated badly. Norman had tried to protect me by keeping this from me as long as he could. But now that he was forced to break the news, I still couldn't really bring myself to accept what I was being told. I even insisted on taking the ice-cream with me to the hospital. In a way, I was still clinging on to hope. But in my heart I now knew that hope was melting away.

As soon as I talked to Phil at the Cromwell, I was in no doubt about how terribly ill George was. He had started to develop severe complications, including internal bleeding. By this stage, he was also heavily sedated.

I remember talking to him, hoping that he could somehow hear me, trying to reassure him. I told him that I had brought him ice-cream all the way from Belfast and that he had better get well and eat it. But even as I was saying this, I knew he was not going to get well.

The next couple of days were very difficult. Norman and I had to go to France on urgent business. The medical staff reassured me that it was okay to go. So we aimed to make it there and back to London within twenty-four hours. I was inconsolable on the flight over to France. My great fear was that George might die before we got back.

It brought back heartbreaking memories. My Mum died in 1978 as I was on my way back from Belfast to my then home in South Africa. I wasn't able to get back for her funeral and for that I can never really forgive myself.

Now I feared that history was about to repeat itself. Especially when we found that our plans to come straight back to London had been scuppered. It was the half-term break and we couldn't get seats on any flights back despite having at least six airports in France and Spain within four hours' drive from our home there. It took almost three days. Three interminable days. I just wanted to be back with George.

Phil was still keeping us up to date. Meanwhile, my sister Julie, her husband Pete and my brother Ian had all travelled to London so that

George always had some of the family with him. We also wanted to ensure that Phil had support.

Julie recalls, 'Carol had explained to me how ill George looked. However, this did not prepare me for the shock I felt when I first saw him in the ICU. I suppose part of me still expected to see my handsome big brother, but as I entered the room, the person I saw in the bed looked so ill that it frightened me.

'George looked so frail that I didn't even know if I should approach him or not. After a few moments I went to his bedside and kissed his forehead. He opened his eyes and attempted a half-smile.'

Typical of George even when he was ill, he still retained his sense of humour.

Julie says: 'Although George's hair had been gradually greying in recent years, it now seemed completely grey and sparse. His beard had grown and it too was grey. He reminded me very much of Dad so at one point during a visit, I whispered to him, "Do you know who you look like?"

'"Chris Bonnington?" he joked.'

Finally Norman and I managed to get a flight back to London. Norman had to return to work in Belfast but I was able to get leave from my own work to stay on. During this time, I stayed at George's flat in Chelsea.

In the flat it was heartbreaking to see that all of his worldly possessions were now sitting packed in a few cartons. Was this all he had left? I wondered. It seemed so pathetic, so very little to show for a life. And yet, as I will explain later, amazingly many of his prized possessions would eventually turn up after his death.

I remember George telling me shortly after he left Champney's Forest Mere, the health farm where he had stayed for practically the last two years of his life, during his separation and subsequent divorce from Alex, that he didn't think that he would ever get back to live in his flat in Chelsea. Perhaps even then he knew in his heart that the state of his health was beyond recovery. Anyway, he was right: he never came back to the flat that was his home.

During those next few days while I stayed in London, George rallied a bit and we were able to talk to him a little. Yet he was so very weak and barely audible. Phil, Ros and I now spent as much time as possible with him, trying to coax him to eat little bits and pieces.

Phil and I were to get into trouble a couple of times during those days. Once we had gone off to Sainsbury's to buy George some fruit. He seemed to enjoy bananas, small oranges and definitely ice-lollies, so we stocked up on all three. When we got back, George nodded that, yes, he would love a banana. He attacked it with great gusto. It was such a relief to see him eat something that Phil and I just stood with huge grins on our faces watching him. But that was short-lived. To our horror, we suddenly realised that actually he was choking on the thing.

His assigned nurse that day, Kirsten, had to step in to remedy the situation and we got a right telling off. We both felt terrible but even though it was serious, I had to laugh. I could just imagine the headline — Bestie Finished Off By Banana!

After that incident, all food was removed. It was a shame as Julie also would have gone off to Sainsbury's to get George ice-lollies. Any flavour except orange! She would bring him back a Calippo and hold it up for him to eat. He would hang on tightly to her hand and wouldn't let her take it away until he had finished the lot. He must have been so very thirsty.

There was another occasion when Phil again got into trouble for his well-intentioned efforts to help.

George's lower legs were encased in special massage pads but, dear love him, these were very tight and were causing him great discomfort. For George to complain was very unusual but after quite a while, bearing in mind that he could hardly speak, he managed to signal to Phil to switch the pads off.

Phil did as George requested, but once the nurses discovered what he'd done, he got another telling off. I know it might seem a bit of a strange thing to say, but compared to what we were all to go through over the next few weeks, those couple of little things brought a bit of light-hearted relief to what was otherwise such a difficult time.

One morning during that stay, I received a very early call from George's night nurse in the ICU. George had been very distressed and had become very fearful during the wee small hours. She and I talked about his condition.

It was the day I was due to fly home and although I didn't really want to leave him, George had improved a bit so I was feeling reasonably content. However, Hilary, the nurse who had phoned me, suggested that if it was in any way possible for me to stay on, it might be a good idea. I would never be able to get that time back, she said.

But still I went back home to Belfast. I had things to sort out, I explained.

But now, of course, I wish that I had taken her advice. Now I know that she was right.

It was around this time that I first met Joyce. She was the nurse responsible for staying with George during the times when he was receiving dialysis. I remember going into the little private section where George was and she would be sitting there, quietly reading. We spoke very briefly but I got an immediate feeling about her. She exuded such calm. I knew that there was something special about her. It was during the last few days of George's life that it would become apparent that she was indeed a very special person.

Statistics show that the longer a person remains in intensive care, the less chance there is of a good outcome. There are exceptions, of course. I remember going out for a quick lunch with Ros one day, and she tried to boost my spirits (and probably her own, too) by telling me about a close relative of hers who had been in intensive care for almost as long as George and had been given little or no chance of survival. And yet miraculously he had got better. That gave me a momentary glimmer of hope.

Obviously we had become more deeply worried as time went on. Yet, remarkably, George rallied again and, despite everything, he was considered well enough to leave intensive care on 9 November. He was understandably really pleased and, of course, we were all delighted. And yet I still found it very hard to raise my spirits and be positive. Deep down in my heart, I knew that it wasn't looking good.

Even on days when I spoke to Phil who would try to be buoyant and who would relay how George was eating little bits of food or how there had been some minor improvement, my sense of optimism was equally minor. The reality was that George was eating only tiny amounts and there was little or no improvement in all of the test results which were coming back.

And then, sadly, he suffered another serious setback and had to be taken back down to intensive care. He was typically stoical about it.

'Okay, Prof. Let's go back downstairs,' was all he said when Professor Williams broke the news.

But we were all absolutely heartbroken. And once again the family trips to London started.

Throughout George's illness and especially during the final weeks of his life our other great concern was for our dad, Dickie.

He was eighty-six years of age, and the worry about George's illness, together with the gruelling travel between London and Belfast, was, understandably, taking a heavy toll on him. But our dad is a remarkable man and, as so many times in the past, he showed his true grit. The way he saw it, his son was ill and nothing was going to stop him from visiting.

Initially, in the very early stages, he was content enough that the rest of us had managed visits and were able to keep him up to date. But as time progressed, he really wanted to go to London himself.

The first trip he made was with Carol, Allen and Grace, flying over to London and back in the same day. This would have been emotionally draining for any parent, but imagine what it was like for Dad at his age.

During this time, on top of the worry about George, he also had to deal with the constant attention from the media asking for interviews and inquiring about George. Even when he was back in his own home in Belfast, the pressure was constant.

For the rest of us, travelling back and forth, juggling family life and work commitments, was exhausting both mentally and physically. We all got to know the airports very well, in particular Belfast City Airport which poignantly enough was the same airport that was to be renamed in memory of George only a few months after his death.

On Friday, 18 November, the worst week of our lives began. I was in work on night duty when, at 4 a.m., I received a distraught call from Phil saying that he was on his way to the hospital. George's condition had suddenly deteriorated.

I phoned the hospital, and was immediately connected to the doctor who was looking after George. 'Should we come over?' I asked. The reply — a simple one word: 'Yes.' I left work and came home to organise flights immediately.

I had spoken to my sister Carol, who would call the rest of the family and make arrangements to fly over that evening with her husband, Allen.

At this stage I had already braced myself for the worst-case scenario. I knew now that there was no way that George was going to make it, and I was determined that no matter what, this time I was staying by his side for as long as necessary. I had ignored Hilary's advice once. But not this time. I knew that I had to be strong for whatever lay ahead.

I am a great believer that nothing happens by chance, and it was while we were waiting to board our flight that we met Adrian Donaldson, the Chief Executive of Castlereagh Borough Council. Little did we know at that stage just how significant that meeting with Adrian was to be and of the enormous role that the council was to play over the next couple of weeks. On reflection, I believe it was meant to happen like that.

Norman and I went straight to the Cromwell Hospital to be met by the most heartbreaking sight. George was now totally sedated. He really was a shocking sight with so many drips, tubes and monitors attached to his body. The little bits of him which were visible were extremely bruised. I will never be able to erase that image from my mind.

I had prepared myself for the possibility that he wouldn't survive the next twenty-four hours. But typical of George he was to astound us all by surviving for another week — the most traumatic week of our lives.

The doctors and staff of ICU worked non-stop with him. George was never left unattended. The week that followed was to show to us the absolute dedication of the medical team. The cliché is to call nurses 'angels'. But, however trite it might sound, to our family that's exactly what that entire medical team were. Not just in terms of what they did for George himself, but what they did for all of us as a family. Simple little things mattered so much — even the details such as making sure that George never had so much as a dirty mark on his gown. They were amazing, every single one of them. Their dedication and professionalism were to shine through during the last forty-eight hours of George's life. I really cannot find enough words to express our gratitude to them all.

At first when confronted with the deterioration in George's condition, I simply didn't know what to do or say when I was in the room with him. I just tried to talk as normally as possible to him. Norman and I would talk about the time that he had spent with us in France, about all the people who had been asking for him, telling him that we were there with Phil and that Carol and Allen were coming. Just anything really.

I tried to keep my tone reassuring and natural as if nothing untoward was happening. I didn't cry or break down. I was so afraid of frightening him with talk of death. I was determined during the next week that all of us should be wary of discussing anything negative in front of him. Even though he was heavily sedated, I was acutely aware that he might be able to hear us.

One day, Phil was particularly upset. I can't remember what sparked it off as there were so many things. I took hold of both his arms and said firmly: 'Phil, it's his time to go.' I immediately regretted that so much, as I had broken my own rule about saying anything that I thought might distress George. What's worse, I only succeeded in making Phil even more upset. I can only hope that George didn't hear it. And yet I honestly don't think that he himself was afraid to die. He used to say that it was just like switching off a light. All the same, that scene is one of those now etched in my mind. And it was not my only regret.

I desperately wanted at this stage to let George know that I loved him, something which I had never told him. But somehow, I just couldn't say the words. Instead, I just quietly leaned over him and thanked him. I thanked him for being my brother, thanked him for all of his kindness to me and thanked him for being who he was.

We all have regrets and 'if onlys' in our lives, and the fact that I didn't tell George that day that I loved him will always be one of mine. And yet I think he knew anyway.

When George had started to drink again after his liver transplant, I wrote to him. It was a very personal letter, most of which I prefer to keep that way. But I did tell him how proud I was of him for achieving so very much. I told him not to be hard on himself for what he saw as his failings.

I hope that from the tone of my letter he knew how I really felt about him. I hope that by having the courage to speak at his funeral I made up a little bit for never actually telling him what I had never managed to say outright...

How very much I loved our George.

Chapter 2 ∾

| DEATH OF A LEGEND

My sister Carol and her husband Allen had arrived from Belfast on the Friday evening and the pair of them, along with Norman and myself, now spent the weekend in ICU, sitting by his bedside talking to George or simply holding his hand. I felt that it was important always to have that physical contact so that he would know we were with him.

Carol and Allen, who are both devout Christians, would spend time praying with him or reading the Bible. All of us were coping in our own different way. Carol, who was the closest to George in age in our family — there were seventeen months between them — drew her strength from the Lord. Although Carol always has her own Bible with her, she had found one which had been left by George's bedside. It had been sent to him by Christians of Mitcham Baptist Church in Surrey. Chapters which had been underlined included Psalms 23, 46, 91 and 121. Deeply moved by the kindness of whoever had sent the Bible and all of those people who were praying for George, Carol decided that she would read each day from the passages marked.

Late one evening, Carol and I took a break and went to the hospital canteen for a cup of tea, leaving Norman with George. Norman was leafing through the Bible when a nurse came in and asked him if he was a Born Again Christian. He said that although he wasn't, his sister-in-law Carol was. The nurse then explained that it was she who had left the Bible, that she had also been reading and praying with George and, at times when he was able, he had prayed with her.

It turned out that this was Joyce, the same nurse I mentioned earlier. As I said, she just seemed to have such a presence about her. Carol was delighted to meet her. She and Joyce are both firmly of the belief that

George was Saved before he died. In Carol's words: 'George accepted the Lord on his deathbed, he trusted the Saviour, welcomed Him into his heart and he is now in heaven.'

Even now, Carol and Joyce still keep in touch. Joyce still works in the Cromwell Hospital.

Ian, our youngest brother, had driven up again from Poole in Dorset and Akeel asked if he could speak to us all in the office. Phil had just left, and Calum was at his flat in London. I got in touch with both and when they arrived we went to see Akeel. We were all expecting him to say that this was definitely the end. We were all prepared for that. Instead, he said that he had promised George that he would do everything in his power to help him and that was exactly what he was now doing, even though some of the treatment might be considered very radical.

I must say that I was totally taken aback. I remember catching Carol's eye and I think that she was probably thinking the same thing as me: no way can George survive this.

Later I spoke to Phil privately and apologised for having upset him a couple of days previously by telling him it was George's time to go. Now here we were with, suddenly, a renewed glimmer of hope.

As I've said, that week was to be the most traumatic time of our lives. Allen, Carol's husband, had to fly back to Belfast. Carol had been due to go with him, but she decided to stay on.

We were acutely aware throughout this period that we were not the only family going through such a long and difficult time in the same hospital unit. As so often happens in such circumstances, gradually other people who had been complete strangers but who were in the same terrible position as ourselves now became our friends. We were to spend many hours in each other's company, helping each other, trying to keep everyone's spirits up.

There were two families, in particular, we became close to. Dave Prebble was there with his three daughters, Emma, Sarah and Jane. And Javid Lotia with his daughter Suroor and daughter-in-law, Michelle. Dave's wife Bridget and Javid's wife, Masuma, were also patients in intensive care. I had seen Dave during a previous visit to the Cromwell as Bridget was in ICU for quite a long time. But it was during that last week that we got to know him and Javid and their respective families so well.

Everyone was just willing the other families' loved ones to pull through. We would keep each other up to date on progress, drink endless cups of tea and coffee together, and the smokers would take it in turn with Phil to go to a little area at the back of the staff canteen for their nicotine fix. Every day, someone would bring in little bags with bits and pieces to eat, although most of the time I wasn't really hungry. Two of Dave's grandchildren, Sophie and Daniel, had each made a card for George. These cards were put on George's bedside locker which is where they remained until he died.

We all tried to be as upbeat as possible, and every now and again I would read out some of the emails which by this stage were arriving in great numbers at the hospital, together with the hundreds of get-well cards and letters. In particular, one of the emails we received at this time I will always remember, as, despite the circumstances, it gave us such a great laugh.

It came from a chap called Michael who told us that even though he himself hadn't seen George play, his dad had skipped school to watch United beat Benfica at Wembley. He also said that George had gone out with his mum who lived in Chorlton-cum-Hardy, the same area where George had boarded many years ago with Mrs Fullaway. He ended the email by saying, 'kinda hoping I am your love child!' I wrote to Michael after George died to thank him for his support and for cheering us all up.

Another message that stood out came in a get-well card from a young boy called Kyle Reid who lives in Belfast. Kyle, who was only eleven at the time, told George all about the team he played football for and about how he supported Manchester United. He said that he was George's number one fan and really wanted him to get well soon. He finished by asking George to wish him luck as he was sitting a really important exam in school on 25 November. It's a date which I'm sure he will always remember.

Kyle struck such a chord with me that I kept his card on one side. I don't really know why I decided to, but it would become clear the following week when we buried George. Once again, I believe that things don't happen by chance.

One other very moving get-well letter came from a six-year-old boy called Daniel who wrote:

I would like to give you my best wishes on getting better because
football wouldn't be the same without you. Besides, I would like to
meet you and show you my ball skills I copied from your video.

I'm only six but I think you were the best player in the world, so
could you please get well. I would pop in to say hello but my Mum
and Dad say that I have to go to school as it's football practice today.
In the meantime could you please sign my card so that I can put it
in my bedroom and can pray for you to get better soon.

I was so deeply moved by that.

Sadly Dave's wife Bridget passed away only a few days after George.
Javid's wife Masuma recovered. We still keep in touch with both
families. Dave came over to Donegal in May 2006 with all his family to
scatter Bridget's ashes, and Carol, Allen and I drove from Belfast to
spend an afternoon with them.

Javid returned to Karachi in Pakistan once Masuma was well enough
to travel, and we still chat occasionally. He rang on Christmas Day to
wish us a Happy Christmas and has invited us to holiday with him and
his family at any time.

Even though it was such a traumatic time for everyone, I consider it
a privilege to have met such lovely people. People really do establish a
special bond when faced with common adversity.

On the evening of Monday, 21 November, it was decided to try to bring
George out of sedation. The thought of this just frightened the life out
of me because although George was attached to so many pieces of
medical equipment, at least he looked peaceful. I dreaded to think what
was going to happen.

Gradually, bit by bit, George started to waken up. It obviously took
many hours for the sedation to wear off, and, when it did, it was so
heartbreaking to watch. First Professor Williams and Akeel had to
ascertain that George's brain hadn't been affected in any way. The Prof
and Akeel both spoke to him and George clearly responded, opening
his eyes when he heard his name. He was able to nod when he was
spoken to and once again it seemed it was his eyes which did the talking
for him. Everyone was truly amazed.

At one point, the Prof said to us: 'I don't know what to say except that he is still alive. It is in the Lord's hands.'

We went outside into the corridor of ICU. Akeel was visibly moved and I just threw my arms around him and thanked him so much. But that sense of elation soon subsided as Norman reminded me very gently not to get too built up on this small improvement.

At first, I was angry at him. But deep down I knew that he was right. I was just so desperate for George to survive.

Carol and I went in and out to see George, talking away to him. I really can't remember what I said as it was so heartbreaking to watch him trying to respond. He looked as if he was in pain. He looked very distressed. Carol and I both now knew that there was no possibility he would survive this. His organs were failing and infections were constantly setting in. Even if he did survive, we asked ourselves, what would his quality of life be?

Dad arrived on the Tuesday with Grace and Pete and Julie. To me it seemed as if George knew to stay with us until Dad arrived. At least Dad got a bit of time with him while he was still conscious. He took George's hand and spoke to him. George seemed to be well aware that Dad was there and, every time that Dad spoke to him, he moved his head to signal that he had heard him, and on a couple of occasions he squeezed his hand.

Carol was also there. When Phil came in, Carol said, 'Look, George, Phil's here.' Phil took his hand but got a bit upset and withdrew it. George stretched out to take his hand again. Ian and Julie were there, too.

Very soon after, George became so distressed that he had to be sedated again. And that was how he remained until that awful moment when the machines were finally switched off.

Carol was due to fly back home on Wednesday, 23 November, and was so unsure what to do. It really was a juggling act for everyone with work and family commitments. I travelled to Victoria station with her and even as we said a tearful goodbye at the station, I think that we both knew deep down in our hearts that we would see each other sooner rather than later. George's condition was obviously deteriorating and, despite our hopes and prayers, we knew that he was fighting a losing battle

I returned to the hospital where the rest of the family, together with Phil, were still keeping vigil. It was my prime concern that George would not feel fear and that he would know that he was surrounded by people who loved him. It was quite late when we left the hospital that night. Any fleeting optimism which we had previously felt had all but disappeared.

It was a restless night for us, expecting at any minute the dreaded phone call summoning us back to the hospital. The call didn't come. But the news first thing in the morning was the inevitable — it was now only a matter of time. I immediately phoned Carol so that she could make arrangements to return. I was alone at the hotel, as Norman was attending a meeting in another part of London and had left the hotel very early. I had to get in touch with him and tell him to come to the hospital straight away. And then I headed once again to the Cromwell.

It is funny how it's the little things that stay with you. I remember standing outside the hotel desperately trying to hail a taxi which, given the number of taxis around in London, should have been an easy task. Yet on this occasion it seemed to take an eternity. Eventually I was on my way with every second dragging and panic setting in that I wouldn't get there on time.

I was the first one to arrive. And while the staff didn't say it outright, it was all too evident that George had so very little time left. My beloved brother was dying.

Distressed and devastated as I was, I knew that my first priority was to protect my elderly father. The media would know by now that it really was only a matter of hours. All hope had now gone. But I didn't want Dad having this relayed to him by the press who were camped en masse outside the hospital. I wanted to break it to him myself.

Over the years, our family has at times had a difficult relationship with the press. When George was in the headlines, often for not the best of reasons, we sometimes had to deal with very aggressive intrusion and inaccurate reporting. In previous days, Dad had been hassled by some of the media, with some of the more persistent ones following him along the road outside the hospital despite his pleas to be left alone. One girl had come up to him in a shop near the hospital. Assuming that she was a genuine and concerned fan, as she seemed to be, he talked about George's condition and how the family was coping. Next day, this appeared as an 'exclusive interview' in a newspaper.

That morning, I was determined to head off the press pack before they got to our dad. Feeling utterly distraught, I now went outside to talk to them, something which I wouldn't have contemplated doing during the previous difficult two months. While our family had some considerable experience of the press and how they operate, I had little experience in dealing directly with the media. In fact, as I went out that morning, while I may have known what I wanted to do, I didn't know how to do it. I wasn't sure who to ask for or what I was going to say. But I was determined that I wanted Dad left alone.

So, with as much authority as I could muster, I approached what seemed like ranks upon ranks of journalists and cameras.

'Excuse me,' I called loudly. I couldn't think what else to say to get their attention.

A hush descended. Dozens of eyes focused on me. But nobody spoke.

'I need to speak to someone in authority, please,' I said.

They all just looked at me blankly. Nobody moved or said anything.

I had no idea what to do now. In desperation, I mentioned the first news organisation whose name came into my head.

'Can I please speak to the representative from Sky News?' I asked.

A female reporter whose name I never found out stepped forward. I talked to her and asked her to speak to everyone else. Please, I said, could they show my dad, who was by now en route to the hospital, some respect and compassion. As yet, I told her, he was not aware of the latest tragic news.

'You all know by now that it will be only a short time. But my dad hasn't been told that yet and I want to break the news to him myself when he gets here,' I explained.

Even while I was speaking to her, out of the corner of my eye I could see that Dad had now arrived with Grace, Julie and Pete. I left the reporter and rushed over to them. I put my arms around Dad and hugged him tightly and quietly told him the terrible news. We all had a bit of a cry together. Then, having composed ourselves, we started back towards the hospital door.

I sometimes regret that I told Dad in that way. Basically I told him there in the middle of the street that his son was now dying. But I was so concerned that he would hear it from one of the press instead of one of his family.

And yet, for once, I needn't have worried. Those journalists gathered outside the hospital that day showed Dad the same respect they might have shown their own fathers. I will never forget the absolute silence as we walked back through that sea of cameras. Not one lens was turned our way. Many cameras were actually very pointedly lowered towards the ground. Not one person spoke. Nobody took a single photograph. Some of the reporters nodded at us as we went past. You know — that knowing look of sympathy.

I will always be grateful to all of them — grateful that in those couple of minutes when it mattered more than ever to our family, but in particular to our elderly dad, we were given our privacy.

Dad didn't find out that I had spoken to the press until months afterwards and he thanked me when he found out. But thanks weren't necessary. It was just something that I knew I had to do. I had to protect him. At that point, I didn't even think that we had twenty-four hours left with George. I was sure it would be a couple of hours at the most.

Professor Williams and Akeel had been with George earlier in the morning. After their visit to George's bedside, they returned to the waiting room. Akeel asked a relative of another patient if she would mind giving the family a few moments alone in the family waiting room. Professor Williams quietly and tearfully told us that nothing more could be done and it was now really just a matter of hours.

To see a man who has been described to us as 'a man of steel' so visibly moved was very difficult. Both the Prof and Akeel had truly become more than his doctors to George. They had become real friends.

George was, as the Prof was to say memorably to the gathered media, 'coming to the end of the long road of his ill health.'

Professor Williams added: 'The situation is that, medically, the intensive-care team and everybody concerned have managed to cope with pretty well all the complications except the one that's happened again during the night, which you know about, this bleeding.... That is now affecting the lungs and other parts. There is really no return from that situation. It's just not possible to recover from that episode he had during the night.

'He is still alive, he is still having standard medical care and treatment, but I have to tell you that his hours are numbered ... I can't be precise as to time but it is the final stages of this illness and I am afraid he could die at any time over the next twenty-four hours. I would be very surprised if he survives another twenty-four hours.'

George, he stressed, was not in any pain.

'I don't want to go into medical details.... He is not conscious or aware. I think we are all very upset.'

Back home in Northern Ireland, Carol and Allen now faced a mad scramble to get back to London. On arrival at the airport in Belfast, they found the queues so bad that they were concerned that the check-in would close before they reached it, and so, completely out of character for them, they jumped the queue!

They apologised and Allen explained to the check-in girl who they were.

'Oh my God,' she said and whisked them straight through.

Carol told me later, 'At that point, I would have flown the plane myself if I could.'

Norman and I met them at Earls Court station and together we made the short, five-minute walk back to the Cromwell for the last time.

It was now lunchtime. In the previous twenty-four hours, George's condition had deteriorated so dramatically that no one thought he could survive much longer. But at 8 p.m. we were saying goodbye to the day staff, telling ourselves that it would be all over long before they returned in the morning. And in the morning there we were still, saying goodbye to the night staff.

For weeks, the band of media, fans and interested onlookers had been steadily growing outside the hospital. Now, in these last few days, the size of the crowd was just crazy.

Old friends were arriving to bid a last farewell to George. Denis Law, who had already been for a number of visits, arrived a couple of days before George died and stayed with the family at the bedside to the very end. Alan Platt was there too but sadly he had to leave just before George died.

When George first joined Manchester United, Denis Law and he were simply team mates. Denis was a few years older. At the time, it would have seemed a big gap. However, as they both grew older, the difference in ages became unimportant. They became and were to remain firm friends. George often went to Portugal to stay with Denis and his wife Diane and their family. Denis is a great character.

He was one of the first, along with Alan Platt and Dave Sadler, to visit George shortly after he had been admitted to the Cromwell. Norman and I had just arrived and were walking towards the hospital when we met them all just leaving. There were great hugs and kisses all round. 'How are you, my darling?' asked Denis.

'I'm great. What about yourself?' I replied. There followed a couple of minutes of pleasantries before Denis asked, 'Anyway, what brings you to London?'

Norman and I looked at each other and burst out laughing. Denis obviously knew the face, but couldn't make the connection; when the penny finally dropped, he was mortified. Talk about a smoothie! Needless to say, he recognised me on subsequent visits.

Sir Bobby Charlton also visited. Despite what has been written about their relationship when they were younger, Sir Bobby and George had become good friends over the years and we were all deeply touched by his visit. George had great admiration for Bobby as a player and once said of him: 'Just to be on the same pitch as Bobby was a great pleasure. I've never seen anyone go past players as easily as he did. He just glided past.'

Milan Mandaric, the then owner of Portsmouth, had also travelled to London to see George. He is such a lovely man and I know George had great respect for him. That George's son Calum has the middle name Milan is a reflection of the esteem in which George held him. They first met when George was playing in America and I know that over the years Milan remained a loyal and close friend as well as a staunch supporter.

All those who came to the hospital were very obviously deeply moved.

Throughout this time, Calum called in as much as he could to see his father. Each time he was faced with the usual barrage of cameras and questions. Without doubt, it was an extremely emotional and difficult time for him. His mum, George's first wife, Angie, had flown in from the States early on during George's stay in hospital and visited him along with Calum. George and Angie had married in 1978 and Calum was born on 6 February 1981 (the anniversary of the Munich air disaster). They subsequently divorced in 1986.

For all of us watching George hold on and on, it was very harrowing.

Because he had been in intensive care for so long, I was prepared for his death. I found a strength from somewhere during this period although that's not to say I found it easy. But somehow I got through George's final hours.

Dad remained his usual dignified self. He sat at the right-hand side of George's bed. Every now and again, I would look at him. He was watching his son in the last few hours of his life and was obviously struggling at times to keep his composure. Yet he was determined not to distress George in any way. Occasionally Dad would lean over to speak softly to him. He told us later that he had whispered in George's ear, 'Just let go, son. Just let go.' He was comforted that George wasn't in any pain.

Throughout this time, the staff at the Cromwell, from the management to the canteen staff, couldn't have done enough for us. Every one of them was so compassionate and so kind. During that last, long night of George's life, Susie, in particular, was a tower of strength to us all. We were given a suite for privacy and, up until late in the evening, we took it in turns to go in and sit with George.

The staff worked with him, making sure that he was comfortable, changing his gown and so on. All we could do was to sit and watch and wait. We were transfixed by the monitors. We had been told that George's blood pressure would just keep dropping until his heart would finally stop. We couldn't tear our eyes away from those monitors. At times, his blood pressure would rise and, absurdly, I would get a glimmer of hope. But then we would realise that each time the staff worked with George, this was putting his blood pressure up slightly.

It was at around midnight that Pete, my sister Julie's husband, told us that Alex, George's ex-wife, had turned up unexpectedly at the hospital reception and that she wanted to see George.

Now, it has been reported that Alex had been prevented from seeing George by his family. What really happened is that quite early on during George's illness, Phil and I had had conversations about Alex visiting. I was left in no doubt whatsoever by Phil that George had made it plain that he did not want Alex to see him. But when she rang Phil to ask if she could visit, Phil told her that the family wouldn't allow it. Later he explained that he had put it this way to her to spare her feelings!

Anyway, as time wore on, and George became weaker and weaker,

Ros and I had gone for lunch one day and discussed the situation. Ros was concerned that it might be thought that she was influencing the decision to keep Alex away and we agreed that day to speak to George himself, who although weak at that point, was still quite alert. I was present when George was asked if Alex could come to visit. I can categorically say that his reaction was a definite no. We felt therefore that we could only carry out his wishes.

On the morning of the day before George died, however, Norman and I again spoke to Phil about it. Even though it was clearly not what George wanted, we were still uncertain what to do. Phil didn't think that it was a good idea so we didn't push the matter. But I couldn't stop thinking about Alex and wasn't really surprised that she had turned up that night at the hospital.

Norman went up to talk to her. She was with her friend Julie and was dressed in a pyjama-style grey tracksuit. She was in a distressed and dishevelled state and was crying and begging over and over again to be allowed to spend a few last moments with George.

Norman said that he wasn't in a position to make that decision by himself and came back down to ICU to speak to the rest of us. Carol, Norman, Phil and I now talked the matter over.

Personally I had really mixed emotions. I was angry that she had turned up, yet at the same time, I was also glad. My anger was down to the fact that it had been widely reported that Alex had said she wouldn't shed a tear if George died and I didn't know at the time that she denies ever saying this. But nevertheless, she had spent twelve years of her life with him. I cannot understand some of the things that Alex has said and done over the years, but I have always believed that George loved her and she loved him. Not only that, but she had stood by him and looked after him through some very difficult times. It isn't easy living with an alcoholic.

Now, as we stood there trying to decide what to do about her, one of the staff who was passing and had overheard us, stopped.

'What harm will it do at this stage?' she asked simply.

George was now unconscious. What harm, indeed, would it do, while it could give Alex some comfort?

Carol, Norman and I went back up to the reception area to speak to her. Carol explained that she could come in on the condition that she left the hospital quietly through a back door afterwards and didn't speak to the press. 'If you do,' said Carol sternly, 'I will never speak to you again.'

At the time, with emotions running high, it obviously wasn't funny. But looking back, we had to laugh. There was Carol, standing in reception, wagging her finger at Alex, warning her of the dire consequences of going to the press. As Carol said later, 'I'm sure she was bothered whether I ever spoke to her again or not!'

We took Alex down to intensive care where Calum was at his dad's side. Calum had been dozing before Alex came in and now looked up as if he had seen a ghost.

We all stood back to let her have some private time with George and it really was quite a heartbreaking scene to watch.

Afterwards, Norman, Carol and I took her back up to the reception area and ensured she left by a side door away from the cameras.

Before she left, Carol and I both hugged her. Despite George's wishes, I still think we did the right thing. I truly hope that seeing George for that last time made his death a bit easier for Alex to bear.

The night wore slowly on. Calum went back to the suite for a sleep. Outside, meanwhile, the hospital was providing hot drinks for the ever-expanding media corps and the legions of onlookers now waiting for news. And indoors during that long night the staff continued to provide us with support and any practical help that they could.

Dad and Denis took naps in the waiting room. I remember Denis commenting (while rubbing his back) that life wasn't fair. At 6 foot tall, he had to sleep in a chair while Dad, at just about 5 foot 4 inches, had commandeered the settee!

Norman and I went upstairs to rest for an hour, but couldn't relax so came back downstairs again. Carol also stayed with George.

Morning dawned and still he clung to life. Bit by bit, George's blood pressure was falling and his heartbeat becoming more erratic. Dad, Phil and Carol maintained their vigil on George's right-hand side. I was on his left. The rest of the family, with Denis, now began to drift in. The morning staff, including the nurses, John and Yvonne, came on at eight o'clock.

I think that it was about 11 a.m. when John looked in through the screens. He nodded to us and said that we should get everyone together. We looked again at the monitor. It was now much lower.

Someone ran to get Calum who was still sleeping. He came and sat alongside me. I just sat with my hand on George's chest. With Calum, I held George's left hand. Phil held his right. Dad sat quietly watching.

Carol lifted her Bible and started to read Psalm 23 while, one by one, each member of his family and his friends in the room now spoke quietly into George's ear and said their final farewell.

But I didn't do this. I simply said quietly, 'I have nothing to say to you except to tell you that you know how I feel.' Norman was totally devastated. But still I didn't cry.

I have no idea who said what to George, and to this day it's something we've never discussed. It is too private.

At about 12.45, I felt a strange rumbling sensation in George's chest. I frantically looked up at Norman. He just shook his head. Then it happened again.

Akeel was there now, with John and Yvonne. Akeel was visibly distressed. His words, 'I am so sorry that I have to do this', will stay with me forever.

At 12.55 p.m. George was pronounced dead.

As a child, I'd always thought the saddest day of my life was that day when George left home at just fifteen. It paled into insignificance compared to this one. I truly felt my heart was breaking.

For a few minutes after the machine had been switched off, I stood there. Then I walked out into the corridor and finally let the tears flow. Norman held me tightly. We stood there for some time comforting each other.

When we had all composed ourselves a bit, we decided that it would be better to face the press sooner rather than later to get that ordeal over with. And so, barely half an hour after George died, we went out as a family group to make the statement they had been waiting for. Again, my priority was to deflect attention from Dad. So hastily I scribbled out a statement which we would make as a family.

Inevitably, as soon as we emerged from the hospital, the cameras started flashing wildly. But again the media gathered there were quite respectful. One cheeky chap had decided, however, that he would crawl on hands and knees through the throng and try to get his questions in first. 'Dickie, Dickie,' he called.

Once again, my protective instinct kicked in. The moment he spoke to Dad, I snapped at him: 'Excuse me!'

When I think back on it, it is quite funny how I silenced him and watched him scurry back into the little space from which he had emerged.

I then made a brief statement, thanking in particular the thousands and thousands of people who had sent cards, emails, flowers and messages of support. I said that our family had drawn such great comfort from this.

Calum stood alongside Dad. Ian placed a protective hand on Dad's shoulder.

When I had finished speaking, Dad also spoke to the throng, asking that as a family we now be left in peace to grieve. It was, he said, 'just a human request'.

But even as he spoke I was aware of the challenge that now lay ahead. News stations were already broadcasting the news globally. Throughout the world, tributes to George from statesmen, sportsmen, friends and fans were already being paid. Prime Minister Tony Blair, who was attending a Commonwealth Heads of Government meeting in Malta at the time, described him as 'probably the most naturally gifted footballer of his generation, one of the greatest footballers the UK has ever produced'.

'Anyone who has seen him as a football fan will never forget it,' he added.

In Dublin, Taoiseach Bertie Ahern, himself a great Manchester United fan, said, 'He was one of the best players the world has ever seen. He was quite simply a football genius.'

And most poignantly, in Belfast, grieving fans were already laying a carpet of shirts and flowers outside our dad's home, the house where George and the rest of us grew up in Burren Way in the Cregagh Estate.

We knew that so many people would want to pay their respects to the man they regarded as the greatest footballer the world has ever seen. How would we ever organise such a large-scale funeral? And at that stage, we had no comprehension of just how large it would be.

For my dad, though, it was now a simple situation. George would be brought home to Belfast to be buried, as he had always wanted, beside our mum who had loved him so much. Our dad, as I have said, is a determined man. But for any man in his eighties to watch his son die, his beloved first-born son, is such a terrible thing. To have to go through that nightmare with the world watching from the sidelines is harder still.

Throughout his life, Dad has faced great tragedy and hardship but, like George, he is not a man who has ever complained about his lot or who will lie down under pressure. All of us in our family have always had the utmost respect and admiration for Dad and for the tremendous courage and dignity which he has shown down through the years. Our respect for him only increased during those last, awful weeks of George's life.

All his life, Dad worked hard to provide for and care for his family. In the past, he has had to put his own ambitions on hold to ensure that we came first. He did so willingly. His own upbringing, values and interests were reflected in the family he reared. His love for sport — for football, in particular — was to inspire and encourage George on his path to greatness. But, above all, it was Dad's unfailing love and support which marked his relationship with George — a love and support that never wavered even through the most difficult times.

In terms of height, Dad is certainly not a big man. In one nasty and needlessly cruel newspaper report of George's funeral, a journalist was even to describe him as 'absurdly small'. But what that commentator obviously never grasped is that there are other measures of the stature of a man than his height. In terms of the sort of man he is, in terms of integrity and character and sheer guts, our dad is not 'absurdly small'. In those terms, the terms that really count, he is a giant.

| MUM AND DAD

Our dad, Dickie Best, was born on 19 November 1919, the first of three children to James (Jock) and Mary Best. As a young child of about two and a half, Granda Best had been taken to Scotland with his mum and dad who wanted to find work. They decided to return home a number of years later, but it was agreed that Granda Best would stay on and live with an old aunt as this enabled him to serve his time in the Clyde shipyard. Granda later came back to Belfast, intending to stay for just a short holiday but during this time he met our granny and fell in love.

They married on 31 May 1918 — in fact, on the day I married my first husband, they were celebrating their fifty-fifth anniversary.

Dad was born during bleak times in Belfast. Thousands of its young men had been killed or maimed in the Great War which had just ended. Those who returned came back to a city sliding into economic depression. The heavy industries through which Belfast had consolidated its reputation at the turn of the century were in trouble. Not least among those facing this post-war slump was the great Harland and Wolff shipyard where the legendary *Titanic* had been built only seven years previously.

Throughout the harsh Depression years of the 1920s and the 1930s, work was hard to find — even for those who had skills and a trade. Our grandfather was a shipwright by trade. He worked in Harland and Wolff and for a lesser-known Belfast shipbuilding firm, Workmans. He was also an ardent trade unionist, determined to defend the rights of working men who laboured long, gruelling hours in jobs that were often dangerous and ill paid. But standing up to the bosses and refusing to compromise his principles cost him dear. At one point, he was out of work for a period of seven years. Dad says that once the bosses got him out of the Yard, as Harland and Wolff was always known locally, they made sure he was kept out much longer than he otherwise would have been.

There's little doubt that our grandfather would have found life easier — and would have been better paid — if he had been prepared to give up his union activities. But he wouldn't be bought. My dad, as I will describe later, shared the same principles. For Granda's family it inevitably meant considerable hardship. But difficult as those times were, they helped shape the man Dad became. People may have had nothing in those days, he says, but they had pride and they had self-respect.

'We didn't have very much,' is how he puts it. 'But what we had was kept clean and tidy. You were taught manners and you were taught respect for people.'

That is exactly how we were brought up as well. We hadn't a lot but we knew the difference between right and wrong. Respect was instilled in all of us from an early age, and the number of times when any one of us would have defied Mum or Dad would have been very few and far between.

The part of East Belfast where my father grew up has changed a lot in recent years, with streets of two-up, two-down terraced houses where the shipyard workers and their families used to live giving way to new housing development and apartment blocks. But much of the area still retains its character. Then, as now, what epitomised such streets in Belfast was the strong sense of community.

In the Depression years, unemployed men used to hang around in the streets — there was little else for them to do. From his childhood, Dad recalls games of marbles, the sing-songs on the street corners at night but most of all the games of street football: 'Many of the men, most of the men, would have been out of work. Part of the thing they did was a kick-about in the streets with an old ball.'

Dad would join in the men's games. Even though he was small, he was a skilled player, able to use both feet and absolutely fearless. Those early street kick-abouts were the beginning of his lifelong love for the game of football. As he got older, he would play through a series of youth, church and amateur leagues.

But football wasn't the only love in his life. When he was twenty-one, Dad met our mum, Annie Mary Withers, at a dance in the Willowfield Unionist Hall on the Woodstock Road in East Belfast.

Mum was born on 13 December 1922. Her parents were George and Elizabeth Withers. George was a stone mason and plasterer by trade and Elizabeth the local post mistress in the town of Saintfield just outside Belfast. It was at their home in Main Street that Mum was born. She was the second of six children and, when she grew up, her own family of six children would, like her mother's before her, also include twin girls.

In 1936, Granda was left a house and shop by his Aunt Mary and, when Mum was about thirteen, they moved to Donard Street in East Belfast. The shop sold mainly sweets and Granny made her own ice-cream and candy apples. Mum followed in her footsteps, as I can remember that at Halloween she also made candy apples, the likes of which I have never tasted since.

The night when Dad first met Mum was a classic case of their eyes meeting across a crowded dance floor! Dad even remembers vividly what Mum was wearing that evening: a white dress with a sailor collar trimmed with red piping and five-inch stiletto high-heeled shoes which Mum always loved to wear. I have never seen anyone else walking or even running so elegantly in stilettos!

Our mum always said that what attracted her to Dad first was his big brown eyes.

Dad says, 'She caught my eye immediately. But I didn't think I stood a chance because I was only a little titch. I didn't think she'd be interested. But obviously I was wrong!'

That night, Dad and a friend walked Mum and her older sister Margaret home. Dad spent more time talking to Margaret and Mum spoke more to Dad's friend.

Dad recalls that over the next couple of weeks on the way home from Hugh J. Scott's in Ravenhill Avenue, where he worked at the time, he had to pass Mum's house in Donard Street. Quite often, Mum would be standing at the door when he passed and they used to catch each other's eye but never spoke. Eventually my mum asked him why he didn't speak to her any more. Dad replied, 'I didn't think you'd be interested.'

Mum said, 'Well, you might be wrong.' And the rest, as they say, is history.

There is quite an interesting story which Dad tells about that period — around the beginning of the Second World War. Just about seven months before Mum and Dad met, a bomb landed in the shop window at Granny and Granda Withers' house. The entire area was cordoned off, but Dad recalls how he and his friend Bobby Stewart on their way back from work decided to take a closer look. They actually crawled underneath the window to see!

Granda Withers who was in the Home Guard at the time was unaware of the incident at the house until he returned home to find that his family had gone. On asking the neighbours, he discovered that his wife and children had been evacuated to the country. When Granda heard this, he walked the whole way to Saintfield just to satisfy himself that they were all okay. Our Aunt Georgie remembers how blistered and bleeding his feet were after such a journey by foot.

Meanwhile, little did Dad know that the girl he was to marry so soon after that incident lived in the house where he'd risked his life just to get a close-up look at a bomb!

In 2005, the *Belfast Telegraph* published a supplement to commemorate the sixtieth anniversary of the end of the Second World War. A man called John who lived in Roslyn Street, close to Donard Street, remembered the incident of the unexploded bomb and wrote a piece that appeared in the supplement. He wrote:

> It was lucky for the people who lived there, because if it had gone off, it would have killed everyone in the house. The people who lived there were called Withers.
>
> Many years later I remember remarking that if the bomb had gone off that day and killed them all there would have been no Geordie Best, for one of Mrs Withers' daughters was to become Mrs Best, his Mum.

Mum would have been about twenty at the time she met Dad. She was a beautiful young woman with thick, wavy, dark hair and sparkling eyes. She worked in Gallaher's cigarette factory at the time. She was also very sporty and was a great hockey player. She played for a club called Queenspark, and went for trials for the International team, but with the onset of war, no international matches were played.

She had to put her playing on hold for a while when George was born shortly after her marriage, but in later years, she did go back to playing hockey. Carol thinks that she played a bit while she was expecting her, and later on, as soon as George was big enough, she used to take him along to her matches. While she was playing, he was quite happy to kick his ball along the sidelines until the game ended.

On one occasion before they were married, Mum and Dad wanted to go to Dublin together for the weekend but of course Granda Withers would never have approved of this, so Mum told a wee lie and said that one of Dad's sisters was also going. A short while after they came back, Granda just said to Dad, 'Well, did your sister have a good time in Dublin?' leaving Dad stammering, 'Yes, she did.'

Obviously Granda knew rightly that there was no sister there and just wanted to let Dad know that he knew.

Mum and Dad were married on 30 June 1945, just before the war ended. Mum was twenty-two and Dad was twenty-five. Rationing was tight at the time, but my mother wore a lovely blue suit with a knee-length skirt and a jaunty little black hat with a veil. Her bouquet was the old traditional bouquet of red roses.

They managed to go on honeymoon to Dublin, which was quite exciting as money was so short, and Dad recalls that when they came back they had just thirty shillings to their name (about £1.50 in today's money) to start off married life.

Their first home was a wee terrace house at number 18 Jocelyn Street, Belfast. They rented from July 1945 until June 1946 but it was expensive and our Granny Withers suggested they move into the attic in her house. This wasn't exactly palatial accommodation but it didn't cost them anything so they were able to save some money for their future. And it worked out well for them as Dad got on well with his in-laws.

Times were difficult in those post-war years, of course, but when my father looks back, he remembers a much gentler, kinder era than we know today.

'Technology and economic advances may have changed the world for the better in some respects,' he says. 'But back then people didn't live in fear of being attacked. You could have left your door unlocked. People helped each other. Society may have advanced in some ways. But in others, I think, it has gone back.'

On a Sunday, he and Mum and their friends would go over the

bridge towards Belfast city centre to the steps of the ornate old Custom House where people would gather and promenade. There would be hawkers selling their wares there, and speakers addressing the crowds. On other evenings, there was the cinema to go to, or the dance halls.

Belfast today is a very different place from what it was back then. In recent years, it has seen dramatic development with the opening of stunning new pubs, restaurants and hotels. But Belfast has always been a city where people knew how to enjoy themselves. It is a sociable city where people have always enjoyed sport too — and idolised the many great sports men and women it has produced.

Dad at this time was working as an iron turner in the shipyard where Granda Best had worked for just over forty years. Like his father before him, he became a committed trade unionist. He was also a member of the Orange Order — he is a Past Master in that Institution and in the Royal Black Preceptory. And when George himself was small, he was in the junior Order and used to carry the strings of the banners of the local lodge on the Twelfth.

Mum wanted a family straight away, and Dad recalls how she used to say to him, 'If I'm not pregnant next month, I'm going to leave you.' After six children, I'm sure she felt like saying, 'If I *am* pregnant next month, I'm going to leave you!'

In any case, the threat obviously worked as, eleven months after Mum and Dad married, on 22 May 1946, George was born in the Royal Maternity Hospital in Belfast. He was named after our Granda Withers. (Just to confuse matters, Mum's youngest brother who was actually born after our George was also called George. And we have an auntie Georgie!)

Our dad recalls how George walked at ten months. 'That was probably remarkable of itself. But George was also fascinated by a ball, any ball. He seemed to know instinctively it was for kicking whatever size, whatever shape.'

One day, Dad watched as George, who was then about fifteen months old, kicked a football around the garden. Dad was so struck by his balance and his concentration that he rushed in and got his camera, an old Kodak box camera, which he used to record the scene. The grainy black-and-white photograph shows the toddler George, his head down over the ball, totally concentrating, even at that age looking so natural with the ball.

That picture is now very much a part of George's history. That old family snap has been reproduced time and time again in newspapers and books throughout the world. It's the first ever picture of George Best demonstrating his footballing skills to the world.

Dad and Mum had their name down with the Housing Trust for a home of their own and eventually, in January 1949, when George was about two and a half and Carol — who was born on 28 October 1947 — was just fifteen months, they moved into Burren Way in the Cregagh Estate.

That is the house that all of us were raised in and which Dad still lives in to this day. Dad has the original rent book which shows the princely sum of fourteen shillings (70 pence) per week for rent.

Cregagh is built up now with high-rise blocks of flats and new developments. But back then, the house they were moving into was the first in the street to be ready for occupancy. The builders handed each house over to the tenants as it was ready, and ours was first.

Mum and Dad moved in with hardly anything — a table and four chairs, a bed and cots for Carol and George. But it didn't matter as they were so happy to have a place of their own. Dad recalls that it was a bit strange at night with only one house in the street lit up. On the opposite side of the street, there was just grass and he says that on a summer's evening you could see the rats running up and down — they came from an old farm nearby.

Right from the start, Burren Way was always a friendly street. We had good neighbours, both Catholic and Protestant, and we all played together and mixed together. There was never any sectarianism or bigotry in our family — we were all raised that way and, as everyone knows, George like the rest of us did not give a toss about what anyone's religion was.

Carol recalls, 'Ours was a happy, carefree childhood. George and I shared a bedroom in those early days which was the normal thing back then. There wasn't much money, but we never noticed. Playing together, fighting together. Mum was boss over us two. When things got out of hand, she used her hand on us to put a stop to the nonsense.

'I always said that I got the worst because George could move so quickly to get out of her way that by the time Mum got to him, she was tired out!

'She was very strict with us. Bed early and no lights on at night. We would be called in from our games in the street. We used to plead, "Just a little longer, Mum", but the argument always fell on deaf ears. We just went in as we were told. Many a time we would sneak out of bed to watch and wave at all of our friends who were still playing in the street, feeling really sorry for ourselves especially in the summer with the long evenings. Then we'd hear Mum's foot on the stairs and we would scramble back into bed. She had seen our friends waving back at us.

'She was firm with us. If you were asked to go on a message, you didn't say no. Well, you might have tried but in the end you still had to go.'

I recall on one occasion one of our neighbours criticising Mum for bringing us in so early during the summer, but Mum left her in no doubt that her interfering was not appreciated, adding, 'I prefer to know where they are in the evenings.'

Our strict upbringing never did us any harm, and, to this day, I would never argue with Dad or cheek him back. The respect which we all have for him is immense.

George played football every chance that he got. He joined the local Cregagh Boys' Club near our home. That was his first football team. At first, they met in the Community Centre at Greenaway, just around the corner from where we lived. Later they moved to a purpose-built centre in Ladas Drive, just a five-minute walk away.

The changing room the boys used (if you could call it that) was cold and spartan. It was at the top of our street and was a storeroom below one of the houses. It was always known to us as 'Jack's Stores'. No one knows who Jack was but it was used as a storeroom for lawnmowers or paint and was really grim, especially in winter when it was so cold.

Robin McCabe, a lifelong friend of our family, recalls that it had one door, no windows and just a couple of old wooden planks for the boys to sit on to change. The walls were just cold, grey cement, but George and his friends didn't seem to notice or mind. All they wanted to do was play football.

Robin remembers how he used to come down to our house after school to do homework with George. They used to drink tea with Mum who always had the teapot on the stove and they would listen to records on the radiogram. He says that George, whom he remembers as always being clever, used to help him out with homework and sometimes even

Baby George and Dad. This extremely rare photograph of George as a baby was taken in 1946 outside Granny and Granda Withers' house in Donard Street, Belfast.

Granda and Granny Best, Jock and Mary, with a photo of George in the background.

Mum's parents, our Granny and Granda Withers, Elizabeth and George.

Mum in her hockey kit. She was a great player, and when George was small she'd take him along to her matches. He'd kick a ball around on the sidelines while she was playing.

War bride: our beautiful mum on her wedding day, 30 June 1945.

Mum and Dad on honeymoon in Dublin, July 1945.

An eye for the ball: at only fifteen months, George was already showing signs of footballing skill!

Big brother: George and Carol as kids.

Classmates: schoolboys from Nettlefield Primary School. George is seated on the bench, second from left.

A glowing report: George's end-of-term report from Nettlefield Primary School, December 1953. Overall 'excellent', conduct 'excellent' — and even a 'vg' in needlework!

A poignant last letter to George from his beloved Granda Withers.

18 Ward.
B.C.H.

Dear George,
I was very very pleased to receive your lovely letter. It is grand to think that you remember me, especially in prayer. Thanks to both you and David for your prayers and I hope that both of you will continue to pray throughout your whole lives, so that you will be kept close to the Saviour from whom all good things come.
Cheerio
& God Bless you both.
Your Loving Granda-dad.
x x
o o

Cregagh Boys' Club football team. George is fourth from right, in the front row.

Could do better: a poor report for George from Grosvenor High School in 1957, reflecting how deeply unhappy he was there.

Grosvenor High School, Belfast

REPORT FOR   AUTUMN   TERM, 1957

Name   Best, G.   Age on 1st September, 1957   11 years   3 months

Form   II A   Average Age of Form on 1st September, 1957   11 years   6 months

	Section of Form	Pupil's Percentage	Average of Section	REMARKS ON PROGRESS AND INDUSTRY
DIVINITY		53	64	Fair.
LATIN				
GREEK				
ENGLISH		59	63	Satisfactory.
HISTORY		45	60	Hard work needed
GEOGRAPHY		39	59	Well below standard.
FRENCH		60	89	must do better
GERMAN				
SPANISH				
ARITHMETIC		51	66	
ALGEBRA		50	72	must reach a higher standard
GEOMETRY		46	66	
TRIGONOMETRY				
PHYSICS		30	65	Very weak. He must work much harder.
CHEMISTRY				
BIOLOGY				
ART		60	52	Satisfactory.
MUSIC				Fair.
DOMESTIC ECONOMY				
WOODWORK				
PHYSICAL EDUCATION				Good

ATTENDANCE	LATENESS	CONDUCT
Absent 6 days	Late 2 days	satisfactory

This is much below II A standard.

Prefects at Lisnasharragh Secondary School, 1960–61. George is in the third row from the front, fourth from left.

9 Aycliffe Ave,
Chorlton,
M/cr 21.
Wednesday 3·15.

Dear Mum & Dad,

~~~~~~~~~~ Sorry I haven't written sooner. I've just come in and am going to watch England v Brazil.

Before I forget Sheff Wed beat us 2·0. in Youth Cup.

I went to see the 1st team play Arsenal on Mon. night. We were robbed. Denis got another two ~~fabuld~~ fabulous goals especially his second. An overhead scissors kick. He got another but the ref said offside. The full back and keeper were stood on the line. He also hit the bar with a fantastic shot from about 40 yards. Did you see Germany vs Brazil on Sunday. What about Peles goal. I didn't think

he played very well. Germanys Shcultz played very well.

I'm sorry but this is all for now the match has just come on.

All my love,

George xxxxx

P.S. Excuse writing paper. Sorry I haven't been sending money home but I've bought a Mac for Saturday as my other is finished.

xxx

Letters to home: a series of treasured letters from the young George in Manchester to our mum and dad in Belfast.

a little bit of copying went on by Robin, just so that they could get out to play football all the quicker.

During the summer months, George and Robin played in a summer league that was held in a place called Leadhill. The matches used to start at seven in the evening, but Robin had a paper round to do as he was saving for a bicycle at the time. George used to help him out so that the paper round was done quicker and Robin wouldn't miss out on playing. Although he didn't get paid for this, once Robin had enough saved for his bike (a Triumph Palm Beach), George was allowed to use it too to deliver the papers to the faraway houses on what is known as South Bank in the estate.

I wonder how many people realise that it was wee Geordie Best who used to deliver their *Belfast Telegraph* or the 'Ulster' (the local weekend sports paper) to their house.

When the paper round was finished, the boys used to run the whole way to Leadhill, about five miles away. It's hard to imagine many of today's children being so dedicated.

Sometimes they would be accompanied by a couple of girls. George's first girlfriend was called Liz and Robin's was called Margaret and after the games they used to say 'goodbye' behind the garages in the Downshire Estate where the girls lived.

When the Cregagh Boys' Club was playing, Mum would send Carol up at halftime with kettles of hot Oxo in winter, and sliced oranges when the weather was a bit milder. She also used to take her turn in washing the team's football strip which was a daunting task.

Robin remembers that the jerseys were so rough, it was like wearing old cloth flour bags, but that didn't deter Mum from doing the job properly. Bearing in mind that we didn't have a washing machine in those days, Mum had to wash all the strips by hand using the old-fashioned washboard (which my sister Carol still has). She was so fussy about the strips, even down to making sure that when they were hung out on the line, all of the socks were pegged facing the same direction. Sometimes if the jerseys were really muddy, she would boil them but she had to make sure that the collars were not submerged in the water as they were red and the dye would have run out onto the white shirts.

Many a time when George came home, he was so dirty that Mum would have to hose him down outside, then send him straight up to the bath.

Dad didn't go along to watch many of George's games. He remembered that when he was a boy himself, he hadn't wanted his own father to go along and watch him play — he thought it put him off. Similarly George made it clear that he'd prefer our dad to stay away. George said it made him nervous if he knew Dad was watching.

I remember watching him play on a number of occasions in the 'big field', as it was known, at the top of the street. On one occasion, I was stupid enough to run behind the goalpost when a goal was scored. I never realised that a football could travel so fast and it knocked me clean out. I often wonder was it George who scored the goal. Anyway, I had had enough of that so didn't go back to any more games. That is, of course, until many years later when I was privileged to watch him in slightly grander surroundings!

But Dad spent hours with him coaching him in the sport they both loved. Dad had played in various leagues when he was young and had eventually been spotted by a scout for Glentoran, the famous East Belfast side. Later he'd signed for Cliftonville which is based in North Belfast. He played a couple of trial matches, but with a young family he couldn't afford either the time it took travelling across the city to training sessions and matches or, more importantly, the money he would lose since he'd have to forgo the chance of doing overtime at work.

As always, Dad decided that the family came first, although he continued to play in various leagues right up until he was thirty-seven. On the pitch his favourite position was left back. He was known as a tough wee player, agile and quick. He could use both feet too. These were skills that he now passed on to George.

Did he recognise even in those early days the extent of the gift his son had been born with? He remembers people saying to him back then, 'That wee boy of yours is going to be a footballer.'

And no wonder. You never saw George without a ball at his feet. In fact, he was seldom without a ball at all; he even took one to bed with him as a child.

Dad encouraged him to practise with either foot against a gable wall where we lived. He'd target the top half of the wall with his right foot, the bottom half with his left foot and then he'd reverse it. He played football with his friends at every opportunity but when his friends had long given up, George would continue perfecting his skills by himself.

He would use the kerbstones as a target for the tennis ball and was so precise that he was able to hit the edge of the kerb and make sure the ball came straight back to him. He also used the knobs on garage doors as a target, such was his precision. He just lived to kick the ball, and, more often than not, Mum or Dad would have to go and call him to come in home as it was getting dark.

Dad showed him how to trap the ball sideways, under his foot. But as he says: 'George didn't take much teaching because he had that basic skill. And the most important thing of all — he had balance. He could have turned on a knife edge. He'd drop the right shoulder and go left or drop the left shoulder and go right. When the game demanded it, he could have gone past at about a 30-degree angle, still in control. And he did it at pace as well so that once he went past a player, he was away, he was clear.'

George was small and skinny but he tackled anyone and anything. On the football field, he was unbeatable. But back at home he was about to learn that he wasn't a knockout in every sport!

One evening, when he was about eleven and a half, and Carol was ten, the pair of them decided to have a go at boxing. For a few minutes, they jumped around swinging their fists at each other like the boxers they'd seen on television. Suddenly Carol threw a punch — a great left hook. George went down. He was out cold! Carol was horrified. She thought she'd killed him. Fortunately, though, the only real injury was to George's pride. Needless to say, once our parents found out, that put paid to the boxing.

When she recovered from her shock, Carol didn't let George forget about it for a day or two. It was, she says, a left hook Barry McGuigan himself would have been proud of!

I was born in our house in Burren Way on 22 October 1952, exactly five years after Carol — so I was six and a half years younger than George. As with so many working-class families at that time, money was very scarce. Mum didn't work full time during our younger years but she used to be a home help for an elderly lady, and later she took a job at Ulster Creameries.

Even though money was scarce, we were all given our pocket money on a Friday when Dad got paid. It usually started with 3d and increased according to age with the maximum amount of 2/6d (which would be about twelve and a half pence in today's money).

It was a brave one who would have asked for money during the week, but I would have been considered to have been a little bit pushier than Carol and George, and I remember one summer evening when the ice-cream van came round running in to ask Dad for sixpence to buy the three of us an ice-lolly. Dad just gave me one of his looks which strongly suggested that I take the matter no further.

There was never any spare money for birthday presents, and parties were unheard of. Although our meals were basic, there was enough to go around. Potatoes and vegetables were always part of a meal, with sausages, vegetable roll or mince. Stew was always made on Wednesdays with a big slice of plain bread broken into it to fill us up.

Dad had a small vegetable patch and, in the summer, we had fresh berries such as strawberries, blackcurrants and gooseberries. Supper before bed was lovely plain bread toasted, spread with real butter. No matter how little money there was, Dad insisted on butter and liked it spread right to the edges of his toast. George loved his toast, too, and every time that he came home from Manchester, the first thing that he wanted was tea and toast. He always said that nothing could match the toast which was done on our old gas cooker, especially as we toasted it on only one side. I suppose this was done to save money, but I must admit it was very good.

George used to say that back with Mrs Fullaway, his landlady in Manchester, the toast was done on both sides and he was always too shy to ask for it any other way.

One of his favourite haunts on his visits home was Eddie Spence's fish and chip shop, and he would always make a beeline for it at the first opportunity, for a fish supper. Like Desano's ice-cream shop, Eddie's is famous in Belfast and is still going strong today. It's now operated by the third generation of Spences. In fact, the original Mrs Spence celebrated her 108th birthday just before Christmas 2006.

Mealtimes in our house were always a family affair, except the evenings when Dad worked overtime. Unlike children of today, we were never offered a choice of food. The meal was set in front of you and no would have dared say, 'I don't like that!'

On one occasion, I didn't eat all of my food and I remember George saying, 'You'd better eat that or Mum will kill you.'

His warning fell on deaf ears and I was just scraping it into the bin when Mum caught me red-handed. She was furious with me for being wasteful and I went to bed with a sore backside, which George thought was hilarious. I was really indignant at the time, but it taught me a valuable lesson as today I hate to see waste. In fact, I often think of that incident with guilt as I know how hard Mum and Dad worked to make ends meet.

If we needed anything extra for school, it was always a last-minute scramble to get it, but Mum somehow always managed. Dad was an extremely hard worker and our needs were put first. On occasion, he would have lined his leaking shoes with cardboard to see him through until he could replace them and I remember him mending shoes on an old lathe which he made himself and which he still has to this day.

Those days may have been lean, but Christmas was always exciting and magical for us. We got a fraction of what children get today, but all the same we did well and got lovely surprises. George, of course, was easy to buy for — football boots, football, football strip and football annuals. It would have been rare for him to have asked for anything else. But on one occasion he did want a bicycle which Mum and Dad managed to get for him. However, not long after he got it, he damaged it quite badly.

Bud McFarland from the Cregagh Boys had asked him to go on a message and even though Dad had forbidden him to go out on it because the roads were really icy, he went anyway. Bud was kind enough to pay for the damages.

Carol and I got the usual girly things like dolls and annuals like the *Bunty* and *Judy* and either Oor Wullie or the Broons. I was always a bit of a tomboy but one year Carol and I each got a bride doll — one blonde, one brunette. A dog chewed the hair off Carol's and I left mine outside in the rain and the face melted. So for me that was the end of the girly toys. After that it was train sets and cowboy outfits.

Christmas was always so happy, and each year Mum and Dad would hide our presents in the big, old wardrobe in our bedroom. I remember trying to pull the wardrobe door open wanting to have a sneak preview; the wardrobe door ended up very buckled.

On Christmas Eve, we would all get up in the middle of the night to see what Santa had brought. It was so bitterly cold in the house back then as we hadn't the luxury of central heating. And I recall that the winters seemed much colder anyway. Sometimes it was so cold in our bathroom that we had ice on the insides of the windows. The three of us, George, Carol and I, used to huddle in the big bed together with the woollen blankets pulled up to our chins, trying to keep warm. Selection boxes were opened and eaten with our apple and oranges before tiredness overcame us again.

Christmas dinner was always a grand affair with lovely treats like dates and ginger cordial. And we didn't sit down to eat until about three o'clock as football came first — Dad used to go to the final of the Steel and Sons Cup.

In later years, one great advantage of George playing for United was the fact that we had a huge hamper sent over by the club. It was always so exciting to get the turkey, ham and lots of really luxurious food which we couldn't afford.

Like any normal children, we bickered. Carol and George did it quite a lot as he often teased her. Name calling was standard. He called her 'foghorn' while she called him 'skinny rake'. After one such argument, he chased her upstairs and, to escape, Carol locked herself in the bathroom. But, to both their dismay, she got locked in. The door had become wedged on the linoleum on the floor and, when she eventually managed to get out, she was so upset that George ending up giving her a hug and trying to calm her down. He probably thought it better than getting on the wrong side of Mum!

I was always a bit of a torture as a child, telling tales and quite often being a brat. Carol maintains that by the time I was born, Mum had mellowed quite a bit and that I got nowhere near the punishments that she and George got. This is something that I strenuously deny!

One evening, Carol and George were in bed and were really playing up, quarrelling and generally misbehaving. As a result of their fighting, a very old and thin and well-used pink hot-water bottle burst and smeared Mum's lovely white cotton sheets in pink rubber.

'Please don't tell Mum,' George begged but I hurtled downstairs quicker than you could say 'water bottle'.

Mum was sitting in front of the fire knitting and, in my most sanctimonious voice, I said, 'Our Carol and George have made a terrible mess of the sheets.'

'You just stay there,' Mum said before racing upstairs where punishment was duly administered.

I stayed put with a smug grin on my face which was soon wiped off when Mum came back down and gave me a few smacks as well. 'That's for telling tales on Carol and George,' she said.

When I went back upstairs, it was George's turn to be smug and very pleased that I hadn't got away with it.

George, as everyone knows, was such a skinny little thing. On occasion, he took full advantage of this, especially when Mum was in pursuit, and he used to disappear under the big bed where she couldn't get at him. However, her patience was much better than his!

Dad seldom had to hand out punishments as Mum generally had the problems sorted before Dad got home from work. In any case, all Dad had to do was give us a look which said, 'Don't go there!'

We didn't have a television when we were very young, but a neighbour called Mr Harris did. In fact, he was the only one on the street who did. George learnt very quickly to play outside Mr Harris's house when there was a football match on, and sure enough he would be brought in to watch the match.

We did eventually get our own TV. Carol recalls on one occasion Mum and Dad were out and our TV went on fire and black smoke was coming out of the back of it. Carol asked George to crawl in underneath to switch it off, but he wasn't terribly brave and wouldn't do it. They had to run across the street for a neighbour who came to the rescue, carried the TV out into the garden and threw a bucket of water over it. As Carol says, the miracle wasn't just that they weren't either burnt to death or electrocuted, but the fact that Dad later got the TV fixed and it went for years after that!

The incident also shows that George was never very technically minded, a trait which was to continue throughout his life.

Even as a child, though, he was always a bit of a character with a great sense of humour. He wasn't entirely squeaky clean either. Back in those days, Mum used to keep sixpences in a big empty bottle. The neck was too narrow for them to fit in, so she had it filed to make sure that they did go in. George every now and again used to 'borrow' some of these sixpences. I have vague recollections that to get them out he used to slip a knife into the bottle and balance the sixpence on it and then slowly slip it out of the bottle.

He also used to collect stamps and would go to the local shops to have a look at the collection. He would 'accidentally' knock the stamps onto the floor, apologising profusely while picking them up again. Somehow he never managed to return the number that had fallen — one usually ended up in his pocket.

Our uncle George, who, as I mentioned earlier, was actually younger than our George, recalls a great story from the stamp-collecting days. He was also quite a keen collector and had been proudly showing his stamps to our George, who took a great interest, asking the usual questions about their origin and so on.

'How much did you pay for them?' asked our George.

'Oh, about one penny, or one and a half pence each,' was the reply.

'I tell you what,' said our George. 'I'll buy them for two pence.'

Uncle George, who has always been a very successful business man, readily agreed on such a great deal, as in some cases he would be making 100 per cent profit.

'Can I pick as many as I want?' asked our George

'Go ahead,' said Uncle. Our George picked out a substantial number of stamps and then, with a straight face, handed over two pence.

Uncle George looked puzzled until he was reminded that the deal was to buy 'them' for 'two pence'. By 'them' George meant a job lot!

He laughed all the way to the bank.

As children, we were always very excited by family holidays. Harland & Wolff shipyard used to close for the first two weeks in July — known in Northern Ireland as the 'Twelfth fortnight'.

We used to go to the local seaside resorts of Groomsport, Millisle or Donaghadee and hire either a caravan or a little wooden holiday home. Even though there wasn't much money, we had such great fun, with the beach being the main attraction. We generally had meals in the holiday home, but every now and again we got a treat of fish and chips.

Mum used to enjoy going in to the local resort of Bangor in Co. Down and playing Bingo which she loved.

Occasionally during the summer, we would go on a day trip to Bangor. Once there, we would swim, play mini-golf and visit the amusement arcades. To save money, we would take sandwiches for lunch, and in the afternoons we would get a treat of candy floss, a candy apple or an ice-cream. Generally in the evenings we ate in one of the many chip shops along the front before we made what seemed to be an endless journey back home to Belfast again. They were such fun days and the three of us would arrive home and fall into bed exhausted from all the healthy sea air.

One of the last family holidays that we had with George would have been in about 1964, the year after he signed professional for United. Mum and Dad had rented a lovely house overlooking the sea in a little place called Ballyholme just about a mile and a half from Bangor.

There was great excitement, not just because we were going on holiday, but because George was coming back from Manchester to join us. We had a lovely time together. In the evenings, we would all go in to Bangor and walk along the promenade and enjoy the long summer evenings.

One evening, George and I had gone into Bangor on our own. True to form, he was always on the lookout for a pretty girl, and it didn't take too long for him to become friendly with a crowd. He really wanted to join them, but he had a twelve-year-old sister in tow. Much as I really wanted to spend more time with him, I was wise enough to take the hint. I reassured George that it wasn't a problem and, having made arrangements with the girls, he agreed to walk me back to the holiday home. Actually, we practically ran back, and as soon as we had our house in view and he was happy that I was safe, he was away like a hare back to Bangor.

Carol recalls that George brought one of his girlfriends called Sue, who came from Warrington, on that holiday, as she can remember the two of them going for a midnight swim. I can only assume that Sue had gone back home when George met up with this new crowd.

He was well known for his escapades with women but, in fairness to him, it was often the girls who threw themselves at him. Carol can remember the girls calling at the house when we were growing up and asking Mum could Carol come out.

Then, as soon as she appeared, they would ask her, 'Is George in?'

Sadly family holidays which included George ended shortly after that Ballyholme trip as he was visiting home less and less.

As I mentioned earlier, Granny and Granda Withers came from Saintfield and, even though they moved to Belfast, Granny always remained a country girl at heart and for a long time had a brilliant little cottage in the countryside close to her home town. I just loved going to that cottage, although as we had no car, it was a two-bus journey to get there.

Mum used to love getting off the bus when we arrived. The first thing she always did was to take deep breaths and say, 'Smell that fresh country air,' while we were all holding our noses and retching at the whiff of the manure.

The cottage had no mod cons. There was a big black range for cooking and only one electric light. At bedtime, we had to take candles to light our way. There was also a dry toilet and no running water. But we didn't care about that. Imagine the fun of going with our big white enamel buckets to collect water from a well that had frogs jumping about in it. And it was the nicest water that I have ever tasted!

Mealtimes were always a big family affair, with everyone bringing food along and putting it in the middle of the table for all to share. It was the new potatoes that we loved best. They were boiled, and then piled into a big white enamel bowl with a pound of butter beside them, and everyone got stuck in. I think that George must have loved them just as much as I did because he used to have competitions with Uncle George and Louis to see who could eat the most. George usually won. I believe that the record was twenty-three potatoes! Hard to believe considering that he was such a slip of a thing.

The days were full of 'adventures' — walking along the country lanes to collect wood for the fire, visiting the nearby Jamesons' farm, picking berries from the hedgerows and walking to the one and only shop for miles around to buy fresh milk and the occasional treat of sweets.

The boys used to roam around the countryside and fight in the barn at the back. On one occasion, Uncle George and our George had been out and about and decided to have a race back to the cottage. They both set off but Uncle George decided to cheat and took a short cut. However, he got quite a surprise to find that he was way too late and George was already sitting at home by the time he got back. George just didn't like to be beaten at anything he took on.

At the end of the break, we were always so sad to leave and, more often than not, had to run like mad down the road to catch the last bus back to Belfast.

You can imagine the excitement when, a few years after George went away, we got our very first car. It was actually also George's first car, a dark green Austin 1100 which he had bought from fellow footballer David Herd who ran a motor business. Dad recalls that, typically for George, it had lots of extras. Even to this day I still remember the registration number: HTB 860B.

George had come back to Belfast with the car to sit his driving test having already failed it once in Manchester — the reason stated was that he was 'too confident'.

He then gave the car to Mum and Dad.

Just recently I was speaking to a retired police officer who as a young chap was stationed at our local police station in Castlereagh. He remembers giving George his first driving offence warning in that wee car. Apparently George had driven the car up to the local shops with no accompanying driver before he had actually passed his test. But he gave the policeman his usual impish grin and got away with it.

Once George signed for United, the trips to the country also stopped, probably in about 1964 or 1965. George tried to get home as much as possible at the start of his playing career. But by the time he was eighteen, he was already being pursued by the press, and on more than one occasion when he was trying to surprise us with a visit home, the press would spoil the surprise by calling at the house to tell Mum and Dad that he was on a flight from Manchester to Belfast.

But fame and media attention were, of course, a long way away back in those glorious days of childhood.

Although no pressure was ever put on George or, in fact, on any of us with regard to school exams, nevertheless Mum and Dad were keen for George to do well academically. In 1956, he sat what we called the 'qualifying' exam — what came to be known as the 11-plus. If he passed, it would mean that he could go to a grammar school.

However, around the time that George was due to sit the exam, his beloved Granda Withers became very ill with cancer.

I remember Granda Withers as a very stern but loving man and George was very close to him. I was only four when he died but I remember him well. He was a deeply religious man who ensured that Sundays were spent worshipping the Lord, and we were marched to church on the Ravenhill Road where he had his own pew. Back then, playing games on a Sunday was forbidden but we would have been allowed to go for an afternoon walk.

Sadly Granda died on the morning of the exam itself, but Mum and Dad decided that it was best not to break the news to George until after the exam was over. They didn't want to distress or distract him. It must have been very difficult for Mum to keep her grief from George that day but she was determined to give her first-born son every opportunity to succeed.

Carol recalls that as he left the house that morning, George had no inkling of the tragedy. He was in an optimistic and determined mood. Our grandfather had encouraged us all to do well at school and had great hopes for George. George adored him and was determined not to let him down. 'Granda will be so proud of me if I pass this exam,' he said as he set off. George had written to Granda when he was ill in the Belfast City Hospital and Granda replied to him. The letter is a treasured family possession. It reads:

Dear George,
I was very pleased to receive your lovely letter. It is grand to think that you remember me, especially in prayer. Thanks to both you and Carol for your prayers and I hope that both of you will continue to pray throughout your whole lives, so that you will be kept close to the Saviour from whom all good things come.
Cheerio and God bless you both.
Your loving Grand-dad

On the day he died, Mum and Dad took Carol and me to see Granny and to help out with getting the funeral arrangements started. When we arrived home later that day, our house was in darkness. All the doors were lying wide open and, for a few heart-stopping minutes, our parents couldn't find any sign of George.

And then they discovered him. He was sitting in a darkened corner of the room, crying his heart out. Sadly he had found out before Mum had a chance to tell him herself. On his way to school that morning, he had gone into our local shop, Allens, to buy himself a new ruler and pencils for the exam, and the owner had said to him how sorry he was to hear about his Granda Withers.

He had had to go ahead and sit the exam with this on his mind, so it was even more special when George passed the exam. Mum and Dad were very proud of him. A new era was now opening up in his life.

And he was so full of hope for the future the first day our mum and dad saw him off to his new school. But little did any of us know then that it was all going to end in tears. Or that in a roundabout way it was to bring George closer to the sport he loved. And to his discovery by the man who would change his life.

Chapter 4 ∾

'I THINK I'VE FOUND YOU A GENIUS'

When Mum and Dad moved to the Cregagh Estate in January 1949, George was two and a half years old. Although the local Cregagh Primary School was just around the corner, Mum and Dad had decided to enrol George at Nettlefield Primary School as it was close to my Granny Withers' house. George started Nettlefield in the autumn term of 1951.

It was a bit of a family affair, as my Mum's twin sisters, Georgie and Joan, her brother George and her nephew Louis all went to the school as well. It was a little strange for George as he had an uncle who was younger than him at the same school at the same time. Uncle George was born in February 1947. And that explains why we called George 'our George' — so as not to confuse him with our uncle.

When George attended Nettlefield, he had to travel by bus, and Dad recalls how he used to dribble a tennis ball from our house to the bus stop and then, when he got off the bus, he dribbled the ball all the way to school. This process was reversed at the end of the school day. Needless to say, the tennis ball was very bald.

Uncle George and Louis remember that during the time at Nettlefield School, he did the same thing when they went back to Granny Withers' for lunch. George never stopped to eat properly. That was just wasting precious football time.

Quite often in the playground, George and another lad called Jim Heron would captain two teams and pick their players. Louis never seemed to be on the same team as George and remembers on one occasion the humiliation of losing something like 16-0 with George scoring every single goal. Louis told me: 'Even in those days, George's ability was so apparent. I used to check George's shoe to see if there was a piece of string attached to it and the tennis ball. When he was hitting a target, he was so precise that it was just like a yo-yo effect.'

George was a happy, contented pupil and, most unusually, his attendance card even had a comment to this effect.

In September 1957, after he had passed the 'qualifying', George won a scholarship to Grosvenor High School. Grosvenor in Belfast is still one of the city's premier grammar schools. Today the school buildings are situated in the east of the city. Back when George won a place in the school, though, it was based close to the city centre, on the Grovesnor Road. From the beginning, it was fairly clear that George was having difficulty settling at the school. His attendance card from Nettlefield Primary School shows that he was a bright intelligent pupil who took a keen interest in class work. But now he was missing football. His new school had a range of sports teams and activities. But no football.

Rugby was the main sport at Grosvenor and George was quite good at it. He played on the wing and, because he was fast and fearless, he was a popular player. But his heart just wasn't in the game. Even though George loved to watch all sport and indeed excelled at many, he had football in his veins and quite simply it was the only game he wanted to play. Worse still, he now found that his new school expected him to attend for Saturday-morning rugby training, which meant that he was missing games with the Cregagh Boys team. But an even greater problem he faced had nothing to do with sport.

Although the dark years of the Troubles still lay ahead, the sectarianism for which Belfast is still infamous was rampant. Children and young people from both sides would target those seen as belonging to 'the other side'. George was regularly attacked on his way home from school. To get back to our house, he had to pass through a predominantly Catholic area. The blazer he wore immediately identified him as a Protestant, and the Catholic boys would throw stones at him as he ran past. He was small and frightened and an easy target. He was miserable in his new school and terrified coming home from it. Eventually it all became too much for him.

George didn't talk to anyone at school or in the family about his problems. In fact, this was to be the pattern throughout his life as he was to remain a very private person who didn't discuss his problems much with anyone. What he did do was start to play truant or 'mitch off' as it's known in Northern Ireland.

My Mum's sister, Aunt Margaret, lived in the Cregagh Estate not far from our house but she was out working all day. George used to leave for school as usual, then go to Aunt Margaret's where he knew there was nobody in, and hide his schoolbag behind her bin which was in the porch. He would then play football all day or just wander around aimlessly. Then in the afternoon he would nip back for his bag and be off home as if he had spent all day behind a school desk.

Our cousin Louis caught him one day, but instead of the usual ball at his feet George was practising sparring, wearing a very familiar pair of boxing gloves. The gloves belonged to Louis, and George, because he was such a skinny thing, had managed to climb in through a small window at Aunt Margaret's and 'borrow' the gloves.

It was Carol who eventually spilled the beans to Mum and Dad about George's truancy. She candidly admits that she was delighted when she discovered his guilty secret.

Like so many siblings, Carol and George used to fight and argue a lot and because of this they were often sent to bed early. On one particular family holiday to the local seaside resort of Groomsport, they spent so much time bickering that Mum, who took no nonsense, had them in bed more times than they were on the beach!

So now it was sweet revenge for Carol that she could get her own back by telling tales. However, if and when circumstances dictated, she and George would definitely have stood up for one another too. And in the long run, of course, she did George a great favour by revealing what he was up to.

It was very apparent from George's school reports from Grosvenor just how much his academic work had suffered. He was in the 'A' stream in his first year. But the three reports from the autumn of 1957 and spring and summer of 1958 certainly did not carry 'A'-stream marks or comments. With Art being the only exception, every subject was below the class average, and in some cases way below.

For example, one history result shows a mark of only 26 per cent. The one subject where he came close to the class average was English. His work attracted teacher comments such as 'Careless', 'Must make more effort', 'Must work harder', 'Makes no effort'. The headmaster had commented: 'Not up to the work of the form, much below "A" standard, and progress still very modest.'

However, what is most significant is that on each report, the number of days absent from school is recorded. During the first term, it was six; by the second term, that had more than doubled to thirteen — confirmation of just how miserable he was becoming. It may not seem that much to some but it was unusual for our family. I wouldn't have had that number of days off during my entire school years.

But now that his secret was out, for the first time George was able to tell Mum and Dad how truly unhappy he was at Grosvenor. As it all tumbled out, Dad and Mum reassured him that, if it made him so miserable, they would not force him to go to his new school. Dad recalls that the board of governors at the school were not too impressed by George's truancy and were going to remove the scholarship from him anyway. The headmaster at the time, a Mr Moles, came from the Shankill Road in West Belfast, a working-class estate very much like the Cregagh. Where he grew up, football would have been played rather than rugby, too, so he was sympathetic to George's plight and was very supportive. Mr Moles would have been prepared to fight George's corner, but Mum and Dad had made the decision and they transferred George to Lisnasharragh Secondary School which was close to our home.

Our parents may have been firm with us. But when it came to it, they would never have forced any of us to do something that made us blatantly unhappy. This would be reflected later when a homesick George would return home from Manchester after only a couple of days. Again, no pressure whatsoever would be put on him to do something that clearly made him unhappy. As with his decision now to leave Grosvenor, that decision would be made by George alone. Mum and Dad wanted what was best for him and let him decide.

Right from his first day in Lisnasharragh, George was a changed boy. His work improved dramatically. He worked harder and, before leaving the school, he held the position as head prefect. And, of course, once again he was back playing the football he loved so much.

Lisnasharragh had been opened only a few years when George joined it. Many of his teachers were young men and women just starting out on their teaching careers. There was a great enthusiasm and sense of camaraderie in the school. His teachers from that time remember him fondly. What is telling is that he stands out in the memory of every single one of the teachers he came in contact with back then. As one of them puts it, 'As a teacher you remember the bad pupils. But you remember the good ones too.' And George they remembered for all the right reasons.

Rennie Meneely taught him English and Maths. He recalls the boys being asked to write about their ambitions for the future. George wrote: 'When I grow up I want to be a professional footballer. I would love to play for Manchester United.' Little did he know that his childhood dream would be realised sooner rather than later. At the age of seventeen, and just a few short years after writing those words, George was to sign professionally for one of the greatest football clubs in the world.

On 14 September of the same year, he played his debut match against West Bromwich Albion. It was to be the start of a glittering career with Manchester United. During his time with the club, he played a total of 466 games, scoring 178 goals, the first of which was against Burnley on 28 December 1963.

As a schoolboy, George had also dreamed of playing for his home country, Northern Ireland, and shortly after his debut with United, on 15 April 1964, he proudly pulled on the green jersey for the first time against Wales who were defeated 3-2. George didn't score in that game but he was to slot in his first goal for Northern Ireland on 14 November 1964. He went on to win thirty-seven caps for Northern Ireland and score nine goals.

Rennie remembers those prophetic words of his so well because they were part of a project in an exhibition in the school at the time and were pinned on a wall for some months afterwards.

George did well at English — he did well at almost every subject. He was a voracious reader — he remained so throughout his life — and he was interested in just about everything. He had an extremely high IQ and I remember him telling me once that he was a member of MENSA, but had applied under a pseudonym as he was a bit shy about using his own name. He loved crosswords and trivia and didn't like anything to get the better of him. On one occasion, during a conversation in a pub, no one could get the answer to a particular question, so George hailed a taxi and returned to his flat in Chelsea to check the answer in a book and then made the journey back to the pub. I think that the fare was about £100 at the time. Every now and then, our dad would get a call from George if he was stuck on a particular crossword clue. And George would often say to friends, 'Don't worry. I'll ring our dad. He'll know this one.' More often than not, he was correct, as Dad is also very intelligent and very well read. And he too has a great love for crosswords.

At Lisnasharragh, pupils did not sit outside examinations. But Rennie remembers entering George and a couple of other boys in a national essay competition. George was one of the winners and was awarded £25 in vouchers which, as Rennie points out, was big money in those days.

George excelled at art too. His art teacher was Roy Murray. 'I remember George as quite a spindly little boy,' says Roy. 'But on the football pitch of course he was magical, even back then. We used to have games where the teachers and some of the pupils would play and he'd take possession of the ball and he'd be challenging you to try to take it off him.' He remembers George as 'an extremely well-mannered boy and very bright and keen'.

Many of George's paintings and drawings — carefully signed with his trademark G Best — along with the work of other pupils, were kept in a store in the school. Sadly the store was broken into at one stage and the entire contents trashed. Everything was dumped afterwards, so none of George's work survived. But Roy is adamant that he had a real talent.

Oddly enough, while he was good at sport in general, George wasn't anything special at gymnastics. Bill Davey who taught him PE recalls that: 'He wasn't as interested in gymnastics. But the one thing you couldn't help but notice was that he had this superb sense of balance.'

His teachers also remember that even back then he had an impressive dress sense.

'I'd describe him as dapper,' says Roy Murray. 'His clothes were always immaculate.'

His teachers recall George coming back to the school several times to see them after he'd been signed by Manchester United.

Says Roy: 'I remember one visit when he came back wearing this very striking light blue suit. He was starting to make his name by that stage but he still struck me as very young and inexperienced. He was as always, tremendously polite and respectful. There was no boasting with him. He just seemed so pleased to be back to see everyone.'

George is remembered at Lisnasharragh as a shy, self-effacing boy. Jim Hewitt who taught him Maths and Religious Education (RE) recalls that at the beginning, when a teacher spoke to him, he was so lacking in self-confidence, 'he shrivelled.'

Jim says that when he started his first year in teaching in 1958, he got to see George's raw talent as he played for his football team, and even then he shone out like a lighthouse. Jim adds that he often commented over the years that teaching a class full of George Bests would have been paradise.

George quickly settled in. Many of his old friends went to the school and, despite his shyness, he also made new friends quickly.

Back then, Lisnasharragh had almost 1,000 pupils, both boys and girls. Teachers recall, however, that classroom romances were few and far between. Later in life, George may have become as famous for his romantic exploits as for his football, but as a schoolboy he knew where to draw the line. All the pupils at Lisnasharragh did.

Says Roy: 'There was a line across the playground, and, at break-time and lunchtime, the girls stayed on one side and the boys on the other. The fascinating thing is the line wasn't actually drawn across the playground. It was an imaginary line. But everybody knew where it was and to keep on their side of it!

'George wouldn't have been seen then as someone the girls chased after. Frankly none of them was. My abiding memory is of this bright, quite shy, well-mannered boy. The way I'd sum him up to other people? If as a teacher you had thirty pupils like George Best in your class, you would have been happy.'

George seldom broke the rules at Lisnasharragh, but on occasions he got into trouble just like any other schoolboy.

There was the time that it was claimed both he and Robin had 'mitched off' school to attend the final selection for the Northern Ireland Schoolboy team. Robin, however, is certain that both sets of parents knew that they were attending the trials which were held at playing fields on North Road in Belfast.

But it was to be a story with a sad ending as Robin recalls. Imagine two young boys who have faced massive competition to get to the final selection only to have their dream shattered with one single phone call. Neither boy had missed a single pre-selection game. And competition was stiff, especially from other schools in the area like Orangefield and

Ashfield, which both had some great players and probably double the number of boys entered compared to Lisnasharragh.

However, George and Robin did well and were in the final group of twenty boys who took part in an intensive residential two-week coaching course at Orangefield. They then attended the final selection event at North Road playing fields in Belfast. Suddenly one of the coaches called out, 'Best and McCabe, please come forward.'

They were really nervous, obviously not sure what to expect, but no doubt hoping that they were two of the lucky boys.

Far from it. Instead, they were told that the organisers had just received a phone call from their school saying that they didn't have permission to be at the trials and on that basis they could no longer be considered for the team. They were devastated. Robin says that they cried the whole way home. He recalls that his mum and dad went to our house that night to talk the matter over and that they were so incensed that his dad decided to go to the school and have it out. The following day, he missed work from the shipyard, which in those days was a very brave thing to do, as it was a case of no work, no money.

Mr McCabe spoke to Mr Barbour, the headmaster, who was adamant that he knew nothing about the call and that it certainly hadn't come from him. Robin's dad went on to explain that it was such a shame for the school as it was very likely that the boys would have been selected. Not only had their dreams been shattered but the school had also lost out on a bit of reflected glory. It was never discovered who made the phone call, but I wonder does that person ever think about it now.

It is ironic that in the same year, on 13 March 1961, at Ulidia Playing Fields, Cregagh Juniors played a friendly game against the selected Northern Ireland Schoolboys' Team which Robin and George had lost out on. It was designed to give the Schoolboys a bit of practice. Unusually, Dad did go to the game that day, getting a special pass out of work to do so, although George didn't know that he was there until afterwards.

Dad remembers that George played a great game that day even though Cregagh lost 2-1. And Robin is fairly sure that George scored the goal that day.

Despite this disappointment, nothing was ever going to keep George from playing football. He was now playing for Lisnasharragh as well as

Cregagh Boys. The school did not take part in a competitive league but there were plenty of 'friendly matches' with other schools in the area. Robin remembers that the school team was not very good at all and it would have been normal to be beaten by as much as 10-0. The head boy at the time was Terry Lynas and Robin suggested to him that if he made George a prefect as quickly as possible, then George would come to play for the team, thus increasing their chances of winning.

Jim Hewitt recalls one match when Lisnasharragh were playing Dunlambert High School, a large boys' school and one of the top schools at football at the time. 'We were playing Dunlambert at Grove Park and after about half an hour when I was walking up and down the line, all I could hear was — "Who's that wee number eight playing for Lisnasharragh?" Of course it was George. He was brilliant — even in those days.'

Although Dad supported George in his playing and encouraged him to practise regularly, he never put any pressure on him to excel. As Dad rarely went along to watch George play, because he knew it made him nervous, there was little indication to the rest of us in the family that George was already showing signs of his great skill at the game.

George excelled at many sports. As I mentioned before, he was good at rugby. And my Uncle George and cousin Louis who grew up with George recall an occasion when they all got together for a game of cricket. The wicket was chalked against the door of a local garage and the game began. George was batting first and an hour and a half later, no matter how hard they all tried, they were still trying to bowl him out!

If he wasn't kicking his tennis ball around, he was twirling it endlessly on the end of his forefinger. He played tennis very well too, and on one occasion Dad was approached by a coach called Mark McCormack who thought that George had potential and might want to train professionally. Also, in later years, George was approached by an American football team who were interested in signing him as their 'kicker'.

Mind you, to interest George, the sport didn't necessarily even have to have a ball. Uncle George told me of the time that he had made himself a javelin. It was a work of art and he was very proud of it. It had a bamboo cane for a shaft with a nail in one end and feathers in the other to make it go further. Our George, true to form, was always able to throw it further than anyone else.

Surprisingly, the only sport which George wasn't comfortable with was swimming. In fact, he couldn't swim. I have often thought about this and although I never spoke to George about it, I wonder if he had a fear of the water. In 1956, during one of the family holidays to Groomsport, the two Georges had been playing on the beach with a friend of theirs who decided to go in for a swim. Bit by bit, the young lad got out of his depth with the tide carrying him further and further out to sea. Uncle George remembers running for Granny, who in turn alerted a neighbour. Together they ran to the beach with an Alsatian dog which tried to reach the child, but sadly he was carried too far out and drowned. His body was washed up a few hours later in a bay just around from Groomsport. Carol remembers the incident very well and can recall running for Mum and being so incoherent that Mum thought that something had happened to our George.

Meanwhile, George was already catching the eye of various talent scouts. Just weeks before he went over to Manchester United, a scout from Leeds United came to Belfast and asked Hughie 'Bud' McFarland who ran the Cregagh Boys' team to arrange a match so that he could watch George play.

Bud set the game up. But after about fifteen minutes the scout made it clear that he'd seen enough. He was off. Bud stopped him on his way out. 'Where are you going?' he asked.

'I've seen enough,' said the Leeds scout, 'That wee lad's far too skinny and too light. He'll never make it.'

For years after that, Bud used to rib that scout about his decision that day. He never let him forget the day he turned down George Best.

Only a few weeks after that débâcle, George finally left school. Dad had a couple of jobs lined up for him. One was with the *Belfast Telegraph* as a compositor, and the other was with a printing firm which I believe was called Clellands and was based in Durham Street in Belfast. When George went off to have the trials for United, it was agreed with both companies that in case George didn't make the grade at football, the apprenticeships would be held open for him until he was seventeen and a half. This was also agreed with Sir Matt Busby.

At this time, Bob Bishop was the local scout for Manchester United, having just replaced Bob Harper who had died. Bishop was from East Belfast also and was very dedicated to the game and the young lads who wanted to make it their career. The two Bobs — Bishop and Harper — had worked with a club called Boyland and they were sending Eric McMordie, who was a couple of years older than George, across for a trial with Manchester United. Bishop was looking for some other boys to send across to England with him and he asked Bud McFarland at Cregagh Boys if he knew of anyone. Bud, who never had any doubt in his mind that George was something special and always enthused about him to anyone who would listen, suggested that Bishop come along and take a look at the young teenager.

In one of the games that Bishop subsequently watched, George was up against a team of players at least two years older than he was. Bishop was stunned by what he was seeing. In a now famous message to Matt Busby, he declared: 'I think I've found you a genius!'

But first he had to convince the genius's father to let the boy move to Manchester. Today it's almost impossible to convey what a big step that move was back then. Although Manchester is just under an hour away by plane, back in the 1960s working-class families like ours could not afford air travel. Until that point in his life, George had never been outside Northern Ireland. None of us had. He had never been on a boat or a plane. Manchester might just as well have been on the other side of the world. And he was only fifteen — a very young fifteen too, compared to the teenagers of today. He was still in short trousers. In fact, Mum bought him his first pair of long trousers for that trip to Manchester. We had no phone in our house so if George wanted to get in touch with us, he would have to write a letter.

As I say, today it is almost impossible to convey how daunting a prospect that move to Manchester was. But George, who lived and breathed football, was determined that it was what he wanted to do.

Bob Bishop came to see Dad and Mum and talked it over with them. Dad wasn't happy about the idea. But he said that if it was what George really wanted, he wouldn't stand in his way. If George had decided not to go, there would have been no pressure put on him by either of our parents. Mum was even more reluctant than Dad to let her first-born child go away. But she too knew that it was something he desperately wanted to do. So she agreed.

I distinctly remember the day on which George was due to leave.

Although he was nervous, he was also excited. But what I remember is the terrible sadness and just wanting the minutes to go so very slowly. There was a terrible gloom all over our house. Mum had to go down the Cregagh Road to get some new clothes for George, including those new long trousers. That night, after he'd left, I thought my heart would break as I thought of my big brother so far away. I couldn't imagine when I would see him again. It was as if there had been a death in the family — as if our family had been broken for ever.

Mum and Dad were inconsolable. Our dad told us years later that they both lay in their bed that night and cried. The only comfort they both clutched at was that this would be a golden opportunity for George. It was what he wanted to do. And with a big, internationally renowned club like Manchester United, he would obviously be well looked after.

On this last point, little did they know how very wrong they were.

| ON HIS WAY

M um, Dad, Carol and I, together with Eric McMordie's brother, John, travelled with George and Eric to the ferry that would take the pair of them to England that evening.

Carol remembers George being really excited. 'I can see him to this day standing on the deck of the boat looking down at us before it sailed. For the rest of us, but in particular for Mum and Dad, it was a very sad occasion. So much so that my Mum over all of the years that followed and all the visits home by George never went with him again to say goodbye. She found it too heartbreaking.'

When Dad and John waved goodbye to the boys, they confidently believed that they would be met at the other side by representatives from Manchester United. The club had led both our families to believe that the pair would be met and chaperoned at the other side.

They weren't. The two lads who had never even been out of Belfast on their own before now found themselves alone in a strange city. They arrived at the Liverpool ferry terminal early in the morning. They too had believed that they would be met by someone from the club as soon as they arrived. When nobody showed up, they discussed what to do and decided to make their way to the local railway station. It was the obvious place, they reckoned, where anyone who had missed picking them up at the ferry terminal would head.

Once there, the pair of them, still lugging their suitcases, wandered around the station for a while hoping that there might be somebody there. But it soon became clear that they were on their own. There was nothing else for it then but to buy train tickets to Manchester station and make their way to the club from there.

Again it's hard to convey to people today just how unworldly most young teenagers from that era were compared to today's kids. I don't think that up until then George had even been in a taxi before. What is both sad and shocking is that our parents never had any inkling that the two boys were left on their own on the other side. It was two or three years later, in fact, before George told Dad exactly what had happened. It wouldn't happen these days to young lads going to trials, but to this day, it haunts Dad.

If our parents and indeed Eric's family had thought for one moment that the boys would be left to make their own way to the club once they'd got to the other side, they would never have allowed the pair to travel unaccompanied.

So why was there no one there? Dad believes that the club didn't want family members around when the trials were taking place. He also suspects that leaving the boys to make their own way may have been part of the club's plan to test their mettle — to see how they could use their initiative and cope on their own. Then again, maybe it was just straightforward thoughtlessness.

Whatever the reason, George and Eric's introduction to their new career was hardly welcoming. Once they'd made it to Manchester station, and there was still no sign of anyone waiting to collect them, the boys decided to hail a taxi. Fortunately they both had enough money on them to afford the fare.

They asked the taxi driver to take them to Old Trafford. He was confused and brought them to the cricket ground instead. The boys explained that they were in the wrong place. They were going for trials with Manchester United, they told him. The taxi driver looked them up and down — particularly George, this small, shy, skinny kid.

'Yeah, of course you are,' he said in a tone that actually said, 'I've got a right pair here.' But he got them there in one piece.

And it was to be for an extremely short stay. Already feeling homesick, disheartened and deeply unhappy, the boys famously spent only a day and a half at the club before deciding they'd had enough.

Dad was at home the morning George returned. It was the summer break from his job in the shipyard. It was early morning and our mother was getting ready for her own work — she had a part-time job at the Ulster Creameries which was based on the Castlereagh Road, just a five-minute cycle ride from our house.

Dad was in bed, having a cup of tea, when he heard the knock at the door. Then he heard a familiar voice.

'That's George!' he said incredulously.

He pulled on his clothes and bounded down the stairs. And sure enough, there was George, tired and a bit shamefaced, standing on the doorstep.

'What happened?' asked Dad. 'What are you doing back?'

'I was homesick' said George quietly.

'Don't you worry about it,' Dad reassured him. 'Homesickness could happen to anyone. It's nothing to be ashamed of. Many a grown man gets homesick.'

Both he and Mum were, of course, delighted to see their boy back again. Later in the morning, when Mum had gone on to work and George had been fed and had some sleep, Dad had a bit of a talk with him.

From his pocket George produced a crumpled note from Joe Armstrong who was the chief scout at Manchester United. There was an address in Stockport and a phone number to contact. We didn't have a phone in our house at the time, so Dad went up the road and called him from a phone box.

Joe Armstrong explained that the club was desperately disappointed that the boys hadn't given it a better chance. 'This has never happened before,' he told Dad.

Dad said that he could understand why the club felt let down but that there wasn't a whole lot he could do about it. But then Joe added that the club had seen George play and what they'd seen had impressed them very much. They would still like him to come back for another trial.

Dad explained that if that were going to happen, it would be entirely up to George. He couldn't — he wouldn't — force the boy to go back against his will.

'If George goes back,' Dad stressed, 'it will be of his own accord. I won't be putting pressure on him.'

On the way back home, Dad bought a newspaper. Back at the house, he made a cup of tea. Then he settled down at a small folding table in the living room to read his paper — or at least pretend to read it, while George sat fidgeting nervously in the corner.

Dad deliberately never mentioned the phone call, waiting for George to raise the subject, as he knew he would.

Eventually George could stand the suspense no longer. 'What does Mr Armstrong say?' he asked.

Dad didn't even lower his paper. 'He says they're disappointed in you and they don't want you back.'

Out of the corner of his eye, Dad noticed that George's expression had suddenly changed. All morning, he had seemed relieved, glad to be back home again. Suddenly he looked deflated, disappointed. It was as if his pride had been hurt. It certainly didn't seem to be the answer he'd been expecting.

After a few minutes' silence, Dad, pretending that he was still reading the paper, remarked casually, 'They do want you back, you know.'

Instantly George became animated. 'When?' he asked. 'I really want to go back.'

Dad put the paper down. 'George,' he said, 'this is not something you can rush into a second time. You weren't happy the first time. You've got to think about it this time. Give yourself a while, think it over.'

But George was adamant. 'I really do want to go back' he insisted. 'What do I have to do?'

'You'll have to write a letter,' Dad explained.

George mulled it over and later in the day asked Dad if he would help him to write the letter.

Dad wrote it out, George signed it, and Dad put it in an envelope and addressed it. Then he gave the envelope to George. 'This is your letter,' he said. 'And it's up to you entirely if you want to send it. I want you to take your time and think about it. If you do send it, we'll back you all the way. But if you decide not to, it makes no difference. Whatever you do, you have our support. But it has to be your decision.'

George took the letter from him. It wasn't mentioned again that day.

The next day, with Dad still off work on holiday, he decided to take us all to the seaside at Bangor in Co. Down for a day out. This was a big treat for us all and we were in high spirits as we set off. The sun was shining, it was a lovely day and I remember feeling happy because my big brother was back and we were all so pleased to see him again. I remember hoping selfishly that we could just get back to normal again and that maybe Mum would try to talk him out of going back to Manchester.

We were taking the train to Bangor, which in itself was an adventure. Bangor is only about thirteen miles from Belfast but it took a while to get there as, first of all, we had to get a bus just to get to the train station. We were headed for the bus stop all laughing and joking together when George suddenly said, 'Hold on, I've forgotten my letter.'

He ran home quickly to get it and tucked it in his pocket. As soon as we got to the railway station in Bangor, George crossed over the road straight for the post office and posted his letter. My heart sank. He'd made his mind up. He really did want to give Manchester another go.

Dad was a bit concerned that it seemed that United had not asked Eric to go back with George. But he was to learn later that Eric had, in fact, been asked back too. But Eric had declined the offer as he had been badly homesick and didn't want to leave his family again. However, a few years later, he did move to Middlesborough, where he played for several years. He also played for Northern Ireland. I remember as a child thinking Eric an extremely handsome, well-mannered lad, and, in fact, I had a bit of a soft spot for him. George and Eric remained friends over the years and it was great to see him again when he travelled to London to participate in the second *This is Your Life* programme that featured George.

Within a few days of that day-trip to Bangor, George got a telegram from the club, telling him to collect a pre-paid ticket at what was then Aldergrove Airport, for the flight to Manchester.

It was like a re-run of his first departure. Again, there were tears and goodbyes. This time, though, there was little doubt that George was determined to make it work. Dad travelled with him on the bus to Aldergrove which is about thirty miles outside Belfast. He went with him as far as the Departure lounge and then stood and watched as the plane climbed into the air and disappeared through the clouds. In every sense, George was now on his way.

At the start, he used to write home, not just to Mum and Dad but also to Robin. On a couple of occasions, even Granny Withers got postcards from him. Mum, who couldn't get used to George being away, looked forward so much to those letters. But like most fifteen-year-old boys he wasn't a great letter-writer so they were often short and usually about football. Still, in the days when telephones were few and far between, that was how we kept in touch.

It may seem incredible that a number of those letters have survived for all of these years (between forty-four and forty-six years) but that is some indication of how precious they were to our mother — and still are to our family. Unfortunately only one letter has a date so I have tried as far as possible to put them in the correct order.

Dear Mum & Dad,

Sorry I haven't written sooner. I've just come in and am going to watch England v Brazil.

Before I forget Sheff Wed beat us 2-0 in Youth Cup.

I went to see the first team play Arsenal on Mon. night. We were robbed.

Denis got another fabulous two goals especially his second. An overhead scissors kick. He got another but the ref said offside. The full back and keeper were stood on the line. He also hit the bar with a fantastic shot from about 40 yards. Did you see Germany v Brazil on Sunday? What about Pele's goal? I didn't think he played very well. Germany's Schultz played very well.

I'm sorry but this is all for now. The match has just come on.

All my love,

George xxxxx

P.S. Excuse writing paper. Sorry I haven't been sending money home but I've bought a Mac for Saturday as my other is finished. xxx

The following letter was sent to Mum when she was in hospital in 1963, when she was expecting the twins, Julie and Grace.

Dear Mum,

Well how are you feeling? O.K. I hope. I've just written to Dad. Well I'm on again tomorrow night. Hope I play as well as last Wednesday. I suppose Dad's up and down every night to see you. Hope Carol & Babs are looking after the house. I suppose Mrs Beirne is in and out doing her little bit. It's a nice day here. It's been very hot this last few days. How's Gran keeping? Send her my love and tell Dad to send my love to Gran and Granda. I'm sorry I'll have to close now but I've just realised I've no stamps and I'll have to rush to the shops before they shut.

All my love,

Your loving son,

George xxxxxx

Feb. 1963

Dear Mum & Dad,

Well I've played at last. I played inside left for the Youth Team yesterday against Oldham A. We drew 1-1. I played very well. I helped to get our goal. I chased a through ball and as the keeper came out I hit it over his head and ran round him. As it bounced I headed it towards the top corner of the net and the flipping full back punched it out. Denis Walker scored the penalty. I felt rotten. We should have won easy. We had ninety per cent of the play. I see the first team should have won yesterday.

It's a lovely day here. The sun is shining and it's very warm. I think I'll go for a walk when I've posted this. How are Carol & Babs. If you see George tell him I'm sorry I forgot about his birthday. I got the Arsenal badge from Julie.

I've enclosed £1. Hope it helps a bit. I'm going tomorrow to town with Willie Anderson (Youth team right winger) to book for a show on 4 March. It should be good. Joe Brown & Susan Maughan are in it.

Well, I think this is all the news for now.

All my love xxxxx

George xx

P.S. They signed Sadler on Tuesday.

Dear Mum & Dad,

Well, what about yesterday. I suppose you know by now. I've enclosed some cuttings from 'The Pink'.

I nearly died when the boss called me into his office and said I was playing. I was talking to Harry Gregg before the match and he said the boss was going to play me last week.

It was a fabulous experience coming out of the tunnel before the match. The left back was a madman. He nearly broke my flipping ankle. I've been to the ground for treatment this morning. (He was only an international.)

It's a beautiful day here. There's nothing much to report. I had a great chance of playing tomorrow night but now I'm injured I've had it.

It's great to see your name in all the papers over here. I'll close now. Love to the girls.

Your loving son,
George xxxxxxx

Dear Mum & Dad,

Received the 'Sunday Post' O.K. I'm just getting ready to go to Everton. You said in your letter about Harry Gregg's article. Well, I haven't seen it so if you send it over and let me have a look, I'll send it back. My ankle is coming along fine. I should be fit for Saturday. I got a letter today from the fellow I met on the boat when I was going to London for Julie's party. He congratulated me for Saturday. He lives in Randalstown.

It's great here when you've been in the first team. I've just got a lift home from the Y.M.C.A. by some fellow I don't even know.

I've enclosed a cutting from *The Evening News*. Imagine my name beside 'The Menaces'.

I think this is all for now. I've got to report at 5.15 at the ground.

Love to girls.

Your loving son,
George xxxxxx

Dear Mum & Dad,

Well we done it! We won 3-0. It was fabulous! Steve said the crowd think I'm another Johnny Berry. I started on the left wing but switched with Willie Anderson. I laid on two of our goals. Everyone was very pleased. They said I was the best forward. It was a great feeling playing in front of such a big crowd. The noise kept buzzing in my head. SMASHING!

We play Sheff. Wed. now in the quarter-finals (away). I'm just going to the ground to get my wages. I think I've earned them. I'm dead beat. Maybe if I'm lucky Joe will give me something extra (Bonus?). Wilf Maguinness told me after the match he had put my name forward for Ireland's Youth team. Well there's really not much to say. I just wanted to let you know how we went on.

Love to Carol & Babs.

Your loving son,
Garrincha George
xxxxxxxxxxx
xxxxxxxx

Dear Mum & Dad,

Just writing this before I go to the ground for a flu injection. Well, the first team had their first defeat last night. Steve and Graham went. Steve says they need me back. I went to Old Trafford last night to see the reserves. They beat Blackpool 2-1. The Boss said I could either watch the reserves or go to Blackpool with him, but I didn't fancy the journey to Blackpool. Everyone here has been congratulating me. Some girl phoned yesterday to congratulate me. I didn't get a chance to ask her name.

I've just received a letter from Mr H.L. Sant the personnel officer from the Manchester Ship Canal Co. to congratulate me. He was at the match on Saturday. I still haven't got over it all. People have been stopping me in the street to ask me how my ankle is.

It's still a bit stiff but the swelling's gone down. I'd better close now or I'll be late for my injection. I'm going to see Bury play Cardiff tonight and the club are taking me to see Everton v Milan tomorrow night.

Love to the girls,
Your loving son,
George
xxxxxxx

As a mother myself, reading those letters after all these years, what strikes me first is how typical they are of a teenage boy. I can't help smiling at how consumed George was with football — he talks of little else! But it tugs at my heart, too, when I think of my mother reading those letters, scanning them for news of what her boy's new life was like. They must have been so very, very precious to her.

Apart from his talk about football and the first indications of how he was being noticed by his bosses and the team's fans — 'Some girl phoned to congratulate me' — he doesn't exactly give a lot away: 'It's a nice day here' ... 'It's a lovely day here' ... 'It's a beautiful day here.'

But to me the most moving and deeply ironic line is at the end of one of those letters where he signs himself 'Garrincha George', referring to the Brazilian footballer Manoel Francisco do Santos, known as Garrincha or 'little bird'. Garrincha, who is also remembered as Mane Garrincha, was born in 1933 in Brazil where he is still regarded as second only to the great Pelé. Like George, he was a forward, and, like

George, he was lauded for his skills at ball-handling and dribbling, his ability to shoot effectively with both feet and to turn at great speed.

But it was in his private life that the parallels really strike. Garrincha, too, had major problems with alcohol. He was married twice but his name was associated with many women. The last years of his life were plagued with marital, financial and drink problems. He died aged just forty-nine from cirrhosis of the liver. And although he was regarded by some as a forgotten hero, his funeral drew tens of thousands of fans and stars from the sporting world. His other nickname is on his gravestone.

'Here lies one,' it reads, 'who was the Joy of the People...'

When I think of my teenage brother back then comparing himself to a footballer whose life would in many ways mirror his own, I can't help feeling moved.

After George left, life at home carried on as normally as possible. Carol left school at fifteen and had a couple of short-term jobs before going to work in Gallaher's cigarette factory just as Mum had done before her. We laugh about it now as Carol remembers how, before she left school, friends were talking about what they were going to do when they left. The usual jobs were mentioned: hairdresser, nurse, fireman and so on, except for Carol who announced, 'I'm going to work in Gallaher's.'

I also left school at fifteen. Like George, I'd also passed the 'qualifying' and had gone to grammar school. I really loved all sport, especially hockey and netball, and I played on both school teams at Carolan Grammar School, but in the end had to choose one as matches kept clashing. I chose netball and was lucky enough to go for the Northern Ireland schoolgirl trials where I got down to the last twenty.

I was average academically so struggled to get the grades to get me into PE college which is where I wanted to go to become a PE teacher. I couldn't understand why I needed all of the academic subjects to teach PE, though, so, just two months after my fifteenth birthday, I left school. Mum and Dad didn't try to stop me. In those days, very few people, particularly from a working-class background, continued into further education. And it was always more money coming into the house.

Carol remembers that her pay packet was actually handed in to Mum who in turn gave back what she thought was enough for Carol to keep herself. By the time I started work, Mum just told me how much 'housekeeping' money she wanted, and it wasn't negotiable.

Because George was too young at fifteen to sign for Manchester United, the club fixed him up with a sham job with the Manchester Ship Canal, with a wage of £4 per week. He'd sign on there every day, then return to the club for training. The club also fixed him up with lodgings. His new landlady was Mrs Mary Fullaway, a tall thin woman with glasses. She was a motherly, kindly woman who looked after George as if he were her son. She had two sons of her own, Steve and Graham. Graham was married to Olga.

To George, the Fullaways were like a surrogate family. He was quite close to Steve, and together the two of them would go along to the local snooker hall or out on the town. On one occasion, though, they did fall out, as George pinched Steve's girlfriend and took her out on a date. The romance didn't last but the friendship did.

Mrs Fullaway would cover for George occasionally, but she was firm with him, too, providing the stability and discipline he would have been familiar with from home. The club, which had done so little to help George make that initial move from Belfast, didn't exactly put itself out either in terms of keeping our parents up to date with what was happening with their son. In fact, as Dad says, if it had been up to the club alone, he wouldn't have known whether George was alive or dead.

Eventually, after about five months, the club did get in touch and invited Dad over to see George play. Dad had to ask them if Mum could get a ticket too. 'It was as if it never occurred to them that the boy's mother might also want to see her son again,' he says.

For the rest of his life, our dad was to be haunted by doubts about whether he did the right thing in letting George go at such an early age to a city which, while reasonably close to Belfast today, given advances in transportation, back then might as well have been on the other side of the world. George was away from all he knew and loved and was familiar with and Dad has tormented himself with 'what ifs' for all these years. It was a long time, as I've said, before he found out that George hadn't even been met by anyone from the club when he went over. But had he known back then, would it really have made that much difference?

The fact is that George was adamant he wanted to go back for the trial. For George himself, that decision to return to Manchester was obviously a momentous one that took a lot of courage. In his first year, he constantly battled homesickness. But he was determined to stick it out. George himself didn't see it as being about courage, though. For him, it was about achieving his dreams. As he saw it, being apart from his family and everyone he knew and loved was the price he had to pay for realising his ambitions.

And gradually, of course, he began to settle in. He made new friends. He found a new life. As far as his football was concerned, he was always absolutely dedicated. During training sessions, he threw himself into it 100 per cent. And although he didn't tell anyone at the time, after the sessions were over, he would continue to practise out on the pitch. He would take corner kicks, first from the left with his right foot, then from the right with his left foot, trying to hit the centre of the crossbar. He was totally dedicated.

It all paid off in May 1963 when he finally signed for Manchester United. It was three days before the FA Cup clash with Leicester — although obviously George wasn't on the team at that time. He signed in the same week he celebrated his seventeenth birthday.

Dad remembers that he had written to George and had casually mentioned how great it was that United were in the final and it must be great to go to Wembley to see a Cup Final. Imagine how absolutely thrilled he was when Manchester United got in touch with him to let him know that they were flying him over for the game and would also put him up in a hotel. It was even more special as United won the cup.

On the evening of the final, a big celebration dinner had been organised for the Savoy Hotel and Dad was invited along. They told him he'd have to come in by the back, however, as they didn't want the other boys wondering why he was there and why their parents weren't. At the dinner, Dad was introduced to Harry Gregg, a straight-talking, honest man for whom our dad has the greatest respect. Harry is from Coleraine in Northern Ireland, where he played for the local team before going to Manchester. Dad fondly remembers a story that Harry told him many years ago. He was getting over an injury and was training with the youth team. George had also been training and had outwitted Harry who was in goal and had slotted the ball past him into the back of the net. Harry jokingly said, 'Do that again and I'll break your neck.' George just gave him that impish grin and lined up to take another shot. Harry thought that he had read George's mind on where the ball was headed, but once again George had the upper hand and, for a second time, put the ball firmly in the back of the net. Needless to say,

Harry didn't carry out his threat!

Anyway, that evening, as George went off to talk to his mates, Dad got talking to Harry who said to him, 'You make sure that this wee fella's well fixed here.'

Dad asked him what he meant and Harry said: 'He's getting signed, Dickie. You make sure it's all in order.'

'But he's already signed,' Dad pointed out. 'They signed him this week.'

'And you weren't there?'

'No, I wasn't,' said Dad. 'And I feel a bit aggrieved about that.'

'They know they've got a great kid there,' said Harry.

But Dad was already mulling over in his mind why he hadn't been asked to attend the signing of his son who was still a minor. It wasn't until about one o'clock in the morning that he finally got the opportunity to talk to Sir Matt Busby about it.

Understandably since it was late, Sir Matt said that he'd talk to him about it the next day, and they arranged to meet before Sir Matt set off for the train station to Manchester. But next morning, he didn't show up at the appointed time. Apparently he was already on his way to catch the train to Manchester.

Now, as anybody who knows our dad will tell you, he is not a man to give up easily. He told Joe Armstrong that if he had to, he would go back to Manchester himself and have it out with Sir Matt there. In fact, he didn't have to go that far. He made his way to the station in London where he spotted Sir Matt and other officials from the team already on the platform. The problem was that in order to get on to the platform, you needed a train ticket and Dad didn't have one.

For a moment, he says, he considered vaulting the barrier, but he decided that there had to be an easier way. Calmly he walked up to the ticket collector, produced his gold-rimmed invitation from the dinner the evening before and said, 'I'm travelling with Sir Matt and the gentlemen over there. Unfortunately they've gone on ahead but they've got my ticket.'

The ticket collector looked suitably impressed. 'Go ahead, sir,' he said.

As for what he had to say to Sir Matt, Dad is a small man but he isn't cowed by authority and if he feels he has a point to make, believe me, he'll make it!

Sir Matt assured Dad that he was not trying to pull a fast one when he signed George. (For the record, Dad believed him too.)

He added, 'We thought you'd be happy with him signing for the team.'

Dad conceded: 'If George is happy, then I'm happy. I'm just surprised about the way it was done. I thought you should have waited until I was there since he's still a minor. But then maybe some other team was interested and you wanted to get in first?'

Sir Matt didn't answer that one. What he did say was that he had seen something special in George. And it was clear that he was fond of him as events over the following years would prove. He looked after George as if he were his own son.

Dad left the platform that day more at ease in his mind that there was someone at the club who had George's best interests at heart.

About four months later, on 14 September 1963, in a game between Manchester United and West Bromwich, George made his professional debut. He was playing against Graham Williams, the Welsh international, who gave him a bit of a rough time. Years later, after they'd both stopped playing, Graham met up with George and shook hands with him.

'Stand still and let me have a good look at your face,' he said. 'Because when you were playing, all I ever saw was your arse disappearing up the sideline!'

For a while after his not particularly spectacular debut, though, George didn't make much of an impact.

That Christmas, he came home to Burren Way. There was great excitement in the Best household, but it was to be very short-lived, as George was back only a few days when a telegram arrived asking him to return to Manchester. The team had been beaten badly by Burnley and were due for a rematch with them.

It was in that game that George began to make an impact. United turned the score around and beat Burnley 6-1. George scored a goal, as did Willie Anderson who was also playing his debut senior game.

And from then on, George never looked back. He was now constantly on the team. Sometimes, Dad would go over to watch him play. He would meet up with George at the ground to collect his ticket. Sometimes he was lucky, sometimes not, but even if George didn't always manage to get him a ticket, there was always a space for Dad beside Sir Matt Busby on the hard wooden tip-up seats in front of the stands.

Dad remembers one lovely little story about one of his trips. George had given him a spare ticket for a game and had said, 'That will get you a few quid for yourself.'

Dad had put the ticket in his pocket and was heading to his own seat in the ground. A young chap was walking towards him, desperately asking, 'Anyone got a spare ticket?'

Dad initially walked passed him and then he turned back and called to him, 'Are you looking for a ticket?'

The young chap eagerly replied, 'Yes.'

Dad took the spare ticket from his inside pocket and handed it to the young lad who reached into his pocket to give him the money.

'Thank you so much,' he said. 'How much do I owe you?'

Dad just pressed the ticket into his hands and said, 'You owe me nothing. Take it with the compliments of George Best.'

He walked on, leaving the chap with his mouth hanging open. Dad looked back and saw him checking the ticket all over. It was as if he couldn't believe what had happened.

That was typical of Dad. He knew that he could have sold the ticket for a bit of extra money, which always came in useful at home, but that wasn't his style.

What is also typical of Dad is that he doesn't take nonsense from anyone. This is illustrated by another story from George's early career when, again, Dad had gone along to watch a big game. Dad recalls: 'I used to go across when I could to Old Trafford to watch George play and I used to love to come down below the stands to the stalls there and have a cup of Bovril and one of their hot pies.

'I remember one day I joined the queue — there were three blokes in front of me. Suddenly this guy just pushed in right in front of me.'

Dad said to the newcomer, 'Excuse me, but there's a queue here and you're behind me.'

The guy looked at him with contempt and said, 'Oh, you're a foreigner here.'

Dad was enraged. 'A foreigner!' he said. 'I come from a part of the United Kingdom the same as you!'

Hearing Dad's accent, the man sneered, 'Ah, you must be a George Best fan, then.'

'Actually I'm his father,' Dad said.

'If you're his father, I'm a monkey's uncle,' said the man.

'Well, I don't know about your ancestry,' Dad replied, 'but you've certainly got the manners of a bloody monkey and you're not getting in in front of me.'

With that, he gave the guy a massive push. Everyone around them laughed. 'The wee man's right,' the other guys in the queue said. 'Take yourself off.'

And the man had to retreat to the back of the queue.

Dad became quite well known at Old Trafford among the staff, but remembers a couple of occasions getting on the wrong side of the doorman at the players' and directors' entrance there.

One time, he had to collect tickets which George had left for him. He explained to the man on the door that he had to go into the office to collect tickets. He explained who he was and the man replied, 'Sure, I've heard that one before.'

An old friend of George's, Danny Birch, happened to be passing and rescued Dad, leaving the man looking very embarrassed.

On another occasion, Dad had gone to a game with a cousin, Alfie Cousins, an ex-navy man who had settled in Manchester. Sir Matt had left tickets for Dad, but on arrival at the ground, Dad discovered that the tickets weren't where they should have been. He went around to the directors' entrance and asked at the office there. Still no tickets. He explained yet again to a very sceptical doorman who he was, but it fell on deaf ears. 'Can I not just nip up and speak to the Boss?' Dad asked.

But there was no way he was gaining access. Just at that point, Sir Matt walked along the corridor upstairs and spotted Dad. 'How are you, Dickie? Come on up,' he said.

The doorman was very apologetic and, of course, Dad got in and was given seats in the directors' box!

Over the years, Dad got to know the Busby family. Sir Matt's wife Jean was a lovely woman and their son Sandy was always a real gentleman. When my youngest brother, Ian, was born, Mum and Dad, who had such a genuine respect for Sir Matt, gave Ian the middle name 'Busby'. Sir Matt and Jean sent a gift over for the baby. It was a lovely white pram quilt with blue flowers on it. Mum always said that it would be handed to her first-born grandson, who turned out to be my son Steven, and she actually posted it out to me in South Africa. I still have it to this day and for something which is now just over forty years old, it is in remarkable condition.

Because Dad was now going over to the matches on a regular basis, he got to know the other players really well. George would often say, 'Away up and have a cup of tea or a beer with the lads.'

Among the team members Dad met was the great Bobby Charlton. It has been reported on occasion that George and Bobby didn't get on very well. Some may perhaps have seen it as George stealing Bobby's thunder. However, we believe that it was just an age gap, and the fact that their lives were totally different. Bobby was already married with a family and George was just a young guy living a very different lifestyle.

Dad thought at the time that Bobby was 'a wee bit odd in his way', but he makes the point now that Sir Bobby was never rude to him in any way, and he's met him over the years since and they get along just fine. He is by nature a very reserved man and our family, as I mentioned earlier, was deeply touched that Sir Bobby came to visit George before he died.

Dad got on with brilliantly with the rest of the team: Nobby Stiles, Paddy Crerand, Denis Law, all of them. To this day, every single one of them has a deep respect and fondness for Dad.

By now, it was becoming clear to Dad, to everyone really, just what a phenomenal player George was. He made his international debut for Northern Ireland in an away game against Wales. The morning after, Dad bought the *Northern Whig*, a local paper that is now defunct. Writing about the game, the reporter remarked that he couldn't see why people were raving about this young lad Best. He said that actually he couldn't see anything special in him.

The next Northern Ireland match was played at Windsor Park against Uruguay. Northern Ireland were the victors with a 3-2 win, and although George didn't score, he played a blinder! So much for the lad who wasn't anything special.

Understandably, every game at Windsor Park was a big occasion for our family. I used to love going to the games, although I used to get terribly upset if anyone made any sort of negative remarks about George if he wasn't playing well. And I was very quick to tell them so, even though I was generally very quiet. No one was allowed to get at my big brother.

I remember for one of the games being picked up in a big, fancy limousine after I had finished work. I felt really embarrassed, just the same as George would have felt.

In fact, the game that some people say was George's greatest ever was at home at Windsor Park. It was a game against Scotland in 1967 and he didn't even score in it. There was a simple explanation for that, though. He should have scored — he came close seven or eight times — but the Scottish goalie, Ronnie Simpson, who was truly outstanding that night, played his socks off. (And George, of course, famously once played his shoe off, and I think it may have been in that game! It happened when he took a corner kick, his boot came flying off and he left it and went on playing. There's grainy old black-and-white footage of that incident and I never get tired watching it. Even now, when they show it on television, it really reminds me of the unique talent that George had.)

Dave Clements scored the only goal that evening for Northern Ireland. But George put on a display that is still talked about in Belfast. At times, it was as if he was taking on Scotland on his own. At one point, it's said, Tommy Gemmell who was the left back for Celtic Football Club and was playing for Scotland that night, asked the right back did he want to change places with him. It was Gemmell incidentally who scored the winning goal when Celtic won the European Cup.

'I'm bloody sure I don't!' the man replied.

George's amazing performance on the pitch that night wasn't the only memorable thing. George did so many things which he never boasted about or sought recognition for. Malcolm Brodie, the highly respected journalist who was for many years Sports Editor with the *Belfast Telegraph* had spoken to George and asked him if he would sign an autograph for a young lad called John who was very ill and was in hospital. George said to Malcolm, 'I'll do better than that. Call for me tomorrow and I'll go to see him.'

The next day, Malcolm and George arrived to see John. George had a brown parcel with him. He told John that he wasn't to open it until he had left. John was so excited that, within seconds, he had the parcel ripped open, expecting to find sweets and comics. Imagine his sheer delight to find the Northern Ireland jersey from the Scotland match, signed by George. Thirty-five years later, George was appearing on a local UTV show hosted by Gerry Kelly. Malcolm Brodie was a guest in the audience and was telling the story about the incident at the hospital. 'Have you ever spoken to the lad since?' asked Gerry, to which Malcolm replied that he hadn't.

'Just turn to your right,' said Gerry, and there was John Doherty sitting beside Malcolm, with the very jersey which he had treasured for all of those years.

George was very moved and was quite emotional about it. John said to George that evening: 'It's not often that dreams come true but on that day you made mine come true. Thank you, George.'

There was controversy, too, needless to say. There was a famous game where George played for Northern Ireland at Windsor Park against England. Gordon Banks, later Sir Gordon Banks, the legendary goalie, got the ball and was about to field it when George went close up to him. Banks threw the ball or pretended to throw it up one way and then went the other way. But George read it beautifully. He just hooked the ball out of the air, it bounced and George headed it in to the net.

Sir Gordon claimed that he had been fouled. In the *Daily Express*, though, they showed photographs of the action under the headline, 'Who Fouled Who?' For Banks had tried to grab George around the waist to pull him back.

The evening after the game, Dad talked to George about the incident. George explained, 'Dad, I just knew what he was going to do before he did it.'

If he had become a local hero back in Belfast, over in Manchester, George's dazzling performances were winning him national and international recognition and praise. His football skills and pop-star good looks were an explosive combination. The games are now the stuff of legend. Thousands of words have been written about George's skill, his balance, his artistry, his genius. But one of the most touching things for us, his family, is that in all the books written about him he is remembered not just with so much respect for his football skills, but with real affection by so many of the great names he played against.

Our dad has an odd way of summing it up. George took a lot of knocks during his playing career from rival players marking him — often quite literally. As Dad describes it, he took so many blows to the legs that after some games his bruised ankles were 'pure mahogany'. And yet Dad sees this in a roundabout way as a tribute to George. He

says, 'Even the people who kicked him, they respected him. The way I
see it they respected him so much you could say they went to such
lengths to kick him! Okay so you might say that's a contradiction in
terms. But that's the way it always looked to me.'

Along with Bobby Charlton and Denis Law, George was now one of
the stars of the Manchester United team. Off the pitch, with his taste in
fashionable clothes and beautiful girls, he was beginning to get the sort
of attention from the newspapers that celebrity footballers today take
for granted. Back then, though, it was different. Footballers did not
have a particularly glamorous image.

However, the 1960s were revolutionising the world of sport, as a new
generation made its impact. George epitomised the new order. He was
young, gifted and good looking. The beautiful boy of the beautiful
game. His prowess on the football pitch still took priority, but gradually
he was being written about more and more on the news pages too.

And it all began to snowball, of course, after the famous game
against Benfica in Portugal — the second leg in the semi-final of the
European Cup, on 9 March 1966. Sir Matt had told the players to take it
easy out on the pitch, to play it a bit defensively for the first twenty
minutes or so until they felt they'd settled down. As one of the papers
said later, George mustn't have heard him because he scored two goals
in the first seven minutes.

Dad was working that night but he had taken his radio with him
and, when the match had started a few minutes, he nipped into the
inspection hut and switched it on to listen to the commentary. He
couldn't believe what he was hearing. The commentator was going wild
about 'this boy Best' and how he'd turned it into a terrific display in the
opening minutes of the game with two terrific goals. Dad couldn't
contain himself, so he decided to take a chance and sneak out of work
and nip around to Granny and Granda Best's house in Harland Street
to catch the second half on TV. In order to get out of the shipyard, he
had to climb a gate, but unfortunately while making his escape he
landed very heavily on his ankle and hurt it quite badly. Carol
remembers his ankle being really badly bruised and Dad limping
around for a couple of weeks afterwards.

On the way home from the Benfica game, George was photographed
wearing a big sombrero. The Portuguese papers had already dubbed
him El Beatle, and the name stuck. Suddenly his face was all over the

front pages of every national newspaper.

But not every one was impressed. Harry Gregg, who was a good friend to George, told him off about wearing the hat.

'You don't need gimmicks like that,' he told him.

Was George getting carried away with his new-found fame? He was certainly enjoying himself. On the pitch, his skills were magical. Off it, he was leading a charmed life, with fans, particularly the girls, mobbing him wherever he went as if he were a pop star. Despite the adulation, though, George remained self-effacing and down to earth. He was very mild mannered and not at all pretentious. He never expected special treatment.

I remember him telling a story about going out for the evening with a friend who had the very unfortunate habit of snapping his fingers to attract the attention of waiters. George hated such displays and warned his friend that if he did this, he would get up and leave. True to form, when a waiter was called with a click of the fingers, George again warned his friend to stop. But again it fell on deaf ears and the guy did exactly the same thing a second time. By now, George was highly embarrassed so he simply got up and left the restaurant. He also told me that he never liked to be collected in stretch limos.

Uncle George and cousin Louis recall how, during the early years of his fame, George was so patient and understanding with people; they admitted that at times it would have been they who became irritated by the attention. One such occasion was on the day that Mum was buried. After the burial service, the men all headed to the local hotel for a drink. This would be quite normal in Northern Ireland (although George's first wife Angie was quite amazed at this aspect of our culture!).

There was a wedding reception going on at the hotel and the bride approached George to ask him to go outside to get a photograph taken with her. He politely refused, explaining that he had just buried his mum and needed a bit of quiet time with his relations. Most people would have accepted this but she became persistent to the point that Uncle George and Louis were becoming quite annoyed and were about to intervene. But George was able to take it all in his stride and to diffuse the situation without any fuss or further embarrassment.

On another occasion, the three of them were just having a quiet drink when George was approached by a guy who literally pushed a piece of paper under George's nose. Obviously he wanted an autograph but he didn't even have the manners to say 'Excuse me' to the company. Once again, whilst others were amazed by this ill-mannered intrusion, George simply signed the autograph and ambled off.

I remember in later years he was back in Belfast recording a television programme with local presenter John Daly. George, Alex, Norman, Phil and I all went to a well-known local restaurant for a meal. Everyone except George had been served their meal and, in fact, we were practically finished ours by the time George's arrived. We were all feeling really bad, but, true to form, he remained totally unconcerned and just enjoyed his meal when it did arrive. Not once did he complain or kick up a fuss. Even his critics concede that George was never a boastful or arrogant man.

However, for all his success, away from the limelight it was clear that the pressure on him was beginning to build. It seemed that no matter what George Best did, the world would hear about it. His rapid rise to fame was dizzying. People couldn't get enough of him. He was becoming a marketable brand. In today's world, this would seem quite normal but back in the 1960s it was all new.

He loved fashion, he loved girls, he loved cars and he was starting to enjoy the social drinking. He was a young guy with a bit of money and, just like any other young person, he was enjoying himself. Increasingly, however, his life was not his own. Everyone wanted a little piece of George Best. A fan club was started and, at its peak, he received as many as 10,000 letters a week. Advertising firms were queuing up for his endorsement. You name it, people wanted George's name attached to it. There were hundreds of products with his name and signature attached. There was aftershave called FORE with the slogan: 'FORE brings out the BEST in a man.' There were Stylo matchmaker shoes with the slogan, 'Put yourself in my shoes.' The Egg Marketing Board had: 'E for B and George Best.' Back in Northern Ireland, we even had a television sausage ad with the slogan: 'Cookstown are the BEST family sausages.'

Don Fardon had released the pop song: 'Georgie, the Belfast Boy.' Even after all these years, it is still played today. Fashion catalogues wanted George to model their clothes — yet again something that was new and unusual back then. And there was the inevitable series of George Best soccer annuals, published in the late 1960s and early 1970s. In so many ways, George set a precedent. How did he cope with all the clamour, the attention, the demands?

In a way, maybe he didn't. The drinking that was to blight his later life had already started. But in those few heady years in the late 1960s and early 1970s, George could do no wrong in the eyes of the media. Everything football's glamorous new star touched seemed to turn to gold.

For an all-too-brief period, our George had the world at his feet.

9, Aycliffe Ave,
Chorlton - Cum - Hardy,
Manchester 21.
24th February, 1963.

Dear Mum + Dad,

Well I've played at last. I played inside left for the Youth Team yesterday against Oldham A. We drew 1-1. I played very well. I helped to get our goal. I chased a through ball and as the keeper came out I hit it over his head and ran round him. As it bounced I headed it towards the top corner of the net and the flipping full back punched it out. Dennis Walker scored the penalty. I felt rotten. We should have won easy. We had ninety per cent of the play. I see the first team should have won yesterday.

It's a lovely day here. The sun is shining and its very warm. I think I'll go for a walk when I've posted this. How are Carol + Babs. If you see George tell him I'm sorry I forgot about his birthday. I got the Arsenal badge from Julie.

I've enclosed £1. Hope it helps a bit. I'm going to-morrow to town with Willie Anderson (youth team right winger) to look for a show on March 4th. It should be good. Joe Brown + Susan Maughan are in it.

Well I think this is all the news for now.

All my love xxxx
George xx

P.S. They signed Sadler on Tuesday.

---

9 Aycliffe Ave,
Chorlton.
M/cr 21.
Sunday 3·25.

Dear Mum + Dad,

Well what about yesterday. I suppose you know by now. I've enclosed some cuttings from 'The Pink'.

I nearly died when the boss called me into his office and said I was playing. I was talking to Harry Gregg before the match and he said The Boss was going to play me last week.

It was a fabulous experience coming out of the tunnel before the match. The left back was a madman. He nearly broke my flipping ankle. I've been to the ground for treatment this morning. (He was only an International) It's a beautiful day here. There's nothing much to report. I had a great chance of playing to morrow night but now I'm injured I've had it. It's great to see your name in all the papers over here. I'll close now. Love to the girls. Your loving Son,

George xxxxxxx

9 Aycliffe Ave,
Chorlton,
M/c 21.

Thursday 11:15.

Dear Mum + Dad,

Well we done it! We won 3-0. It was fabulous! Steve said the crowd think I'm another Johnny Berry. I started on the left wing but switched with Willie Anderson. I laid on two of our goals. Everyone was very pleased they said I was the best forward. It was a great feeling playing in front of such a big crowd. The noise kept buzzing in my head. SMASHING!

We play Sheff Wed. now in the quarter-finals (Away). I'm just going to the ground to get my wages. I think I've earned them. I'm dead beat. Maybe if I'm lucky Joe will give my something extra (Bonus?). Wilf Maguinness told me after the match he had put my name forward for Irelands youth team. Well theres really not much to say. I just wanted to let you know how we went on. Love to Carol & Babs,

Your loving Son,
Goirtacha George

XXXXX > XXXXX
> X XXY>YY

3 PTAS
ESPAÑA
CORREOS

Dear Gran, Just a few lines before we play to-night. Weather and girls fabulous. Having a smashing time. I'll be seeing you in a couple of weeks. I'm writing this at the tea-table. The match starts in about 3 hours. Give my love to everyone. All my love, George xx

MRS E. WITHERS,

89 DONARD STREET,
RAVENHILL ROAD,
BELFAST,
N IRELAND

N.° 5 SAN SEBASTIAN.
Playa de Ondarreta.
Plage d'Ondarreta.
Ondarreta beach.

'Weather and girls fabulous. Having a smashing time!' A postcard from Spain to Granny Withers.

George with his girlfriend, Kay Williamson, during a visit back home from Manchester United. Kay, who lived not far from us, was a lovely girl.

An early visit back home. George with Carol on his right and Mum on his left. I'm in front, and on either side are Georgie and Joan, Mum's sisters. Sadly, George's visits back to Belfast were to become rare.

The two Georges: Uncle George with our George, in Granny Withers' house, circa 1963.

Outside Granny Withers' country cottage, in the summer of 1963.

Party time! George, bottom right, and Carol, centre, in the green cardigan, at Billy Elliot's birthday party in 1963.

Proud parents: our mum and dad with George, before a match at Old Trafford in 1965. The lady on George's right is his landlady, Mrs Fullaway.

El Beatle: returning from the Benfica game in Portugal, March 1966, in THAT sombrero!

Chapter 6 ∾

I FAME — AND ITS FALLOUT

W hen George left home, it inevitably left a major gap in all our lives. But what none of us realised then was just how much George's growing fame would impact on us all. The twins, Julie and Grace, were born on 1 July 1963, just about six weeks after George signed professionally for Manchester United. George was delighted, and at the start he used to try to get home as often as possible to see them.

A couple of years later, Mum became pregnant again, this time with our youngest brother, Ian, who arrived on 19 July 1966, completing the Best family. Back then, it was a bit more unusual for women in their forties to have children, and Mum was a little embarrassed about it all at first. Carol was given the task of telling George when she went over to visit him in Manchester.

'Any news from back home?' he asked when he picked her up at the airport.

'Yes,' said Carol cheerfully. 'There's going to be another addition to the family'.

All George said was, 'The dirty old man.' Poor Dad.

Going over to see George in Manchester was a great, although rare, treat for us all. Obviously with the rest of us to provide for, it wasn't something my parents could do on a regular basis. Carol recalls that George would have taken her across for Easter. She remembers fondly that, on one occasion, he had booked cinema tickets for her and Mrs Fullaway to go to see a newly released film, and he had promised to treat them both afterwards with a trip to a fancy restaurant, which apparently served the best 'steak Diane' in Manchester. He kept telling them how delicious it was, so that by the time the end of the film came, they couldn't wait to get to the restaurant. He picked them up at the cinema only to break the bad news that the restaurant was closed for the Easter break and that he would just have to drop them back home. Then he said that he had to go out somewhere else, and, even though Mrs Fullaway pressed him a bit, it was obvious that Carol and she definitely weren't invited! So they had to settle for chicken sandwiches in Chorlton-cum-Hardy.

Meanwhile, as George's fame increased, his visits back home became less frequent. In many ways, it's not hard to understand why. For a young man at the peak of his fame, who loved socialising, Manchester and London offered excitement and fun. George was now never out of the papers, pictured out on the town at clubs like Time and Place in Manchester, and Tramps in London, enjoying himself with a succession of beautiful women. Since the Benfica game when he'd been dubbed El Beatle by the Portuguese newspaper *Bola*, the British newspapers had taken up the theme and his face was now appearing regularly not just on the sports pages but on the front pages — and, needless to say, in the gossip columns.

Along with a friend, Malcolm Mooney, he had opened a boutique called Edwardia. His clothes, his lifestyle, his girlfriends — suddenly they were all under intense scrutiny by the media.

And, of course, there was the drink. George's drinking began slowly. He himself used to recall his first drinking 'binge', if you could call it that, during his first trip abroad with a United youth team competing in Switzerland. After a few pints of beer, he had to be helped back to his room where he promptly threw up! But although it was not a major feature of his social life at the beginning (and he never got involved in the drugs that were such a part of the Swinging Sixties), it was inevitable that someone who was spending so much time in clubs and out on the town would find alcohol difficult to avoid. Gradually it became obvious that George was drinking more and more.

At first, as his family, we found the fame and the attention George was receiving all very exciting. In those years of the late 1960s, he was the golden boy of British football. It seemed as if every year brought another highlight. There was that game against Benfica in 1966, the outstanding game for Northern Ireland against Scotland in 1967. In May 1968, he was named both British Footballer of the Year and European Footballer of the Year.

The media attention even back then was phenomenal. When George came back home for a visit, our house in Burren Way was virtually under siege by reporters and fans. When reporters called at our house, as they increasingly did, at first we'd rather naively talk to them freely. Gradually though we were learning to become more wary.

All of us have different experiences of how George's fame and the media attention that came with it impacted on our own lives. Because Carol and I were older and could remember a time before the house was a magnet for fans and reporters, it was, as I say, quite a novelty at first. George was a local hero and the things being said and written about him were all very positive and flattering.

True, there was a downside. For example, we often had to sit with the blinds shut because there would be so many people standing outside in the street staring into the house. But at the beginning that was about the worst of it.

While we were all terribly proud of George and his achievements, it was not something we talked about much to other people. Our parents had brought us up not to be boastful, so we didn't go out of our way to tell people who our famous brother was. In fact, when I met new people, I would deliberately avoid telling them of the connection. (This would later include keeping my future husband Norman in the dark!) Real friends just took it in their stride. But I seldom spoke about George even to them. I was really quite shy and reluctant to make a big deal about it. At times, if I had to give my surname, and people asked if I was related to George, I just said 'no'.

Even so, some people, for whatever reason, would occasionally make it clear that they knew of my connection with George and they would be quite difficult about it. Even in the Cregagh Estate, a number of local girls always seemed to have a problem with me, and went out of their way to pick fights. I generally tried not to become involved but on one occasion, a girl who was a notorious bully started to hurl abuse at me when I was in a phone box trying to make a call. It was one of the rare occasions when I reacted. Eventually, when I couldn't take her nastiness any longer, I gave her a couple of slaps where it hurt. The look on her face was something I'll never forget. She couldn't believe that I had turned on her, but I never had another bit of trouble from her.

The worst example, however, occurred when I was a teenager out for the evening at a disco. I was minding my own business, dancing with friends, but a couple of people kept bumping into me. At first, I thought nothing of it. But suddenly they started sneering and saying, 'You're George Best's sister. You think you're something. But you're nothing but an Orange bastard.'

It came totally from out of the blue. Being very shy and nervous, as I was, I didn't respond. I just kept my head down and hoped they'd leave it at that. And everything seemed fine until the disco ended.

We went outside and suddenly I heard someone shouting: 'There she is!' With that, there was a bang and I felt this horrendous pain in the inside of my right leg. I remember getting home and just sitting at the top of the stairs calling out for Mum and Dad. By this time, I had a massive bruise about six inches in diameter on my leg. The police reckoned I'd been shot with an air rifle.

I was so shocked. Not just by that attack itself. But also to think that this had happened simply because I was George's sister.

The growing interest of the press was easier to fathom — although it was also becoming harder to deal with. George was big news and, just like the celebrities of today, fair game for the media. The only difference is that back then he was one of the first superstars of the game so it wasn't like it is today where people know to expect that press intrusion goes with the territory. Back then, it was all very new and there was no real precedent to prepare us for what was about to engulf us as a family.

At the beginning, George was in the papers for all the right reasons — everybody just wanted a little piece of George Best. It didn't matter what he did. Whether he'd had a particularly good game or had been seen out with a new girlfriend, the media wanted a story about it and basically they would have gone to any lengths to get that story. They would show up at the house and question us children. The younger ones, Grace, Julie and Ian, were growing up with this constant attention all around them. For example, when the twins were about five, George was asked to do a television commercial for a local brand of sausages. It was a far cry from David Beckham and his multimillion-pound sponsorship deals, but back then, when celebrity endorsement was still fairly new in television advertising, it was impressive stuff to us.

Not that Mum (who also had to appear in the ad) was terribly impressed. Being a shy woman, she found the filming very difficult and just wanted it over as quickly as possible. Dad was also in the commercial, along with the twins. It is one of Grace's earliest memories. In fact, her earliest memory is of sitting on George's knee during one of his visits home, surrounded by reporters and cameras all snapping away.

Grace says: 'I hated that. Julie always posed for the cameras but I was more reluctant. I really did not like it.'

The filming of the television ad wasn't a picnic either, she recalls. 'We were all shown sitting round the table as dinner was being served. It consisted of sausages (obviously), peas and potatoes. George would look into the camera and utter the immortal phrase, "Cookstown are the Best family sausages."

'As the food came out, I lifted my knife and fork to get stuck in, only to be told firmly the food wasn't there to be eaten. I was five years old and not too happy to be told not to eat food placed in front of me. So I huffed!

'George brought me round by throwing a handful of money on the table which I quickly scooped up. It took forever but eventually we got the thing done.'

For the family, the bonus in George doing the Cookstown commercial was that on a regular basis they sent us hampers with all sorts of their products, like bacon, pies and sausages. And, needless to say, they scored too, thanks to their connection with George — sales of Cookstown products increased by 800 per cent within a few weeks of the advertisement.

In the early years, George used to love coming home as often as he could. He would meet up with his old friends like Robin McCabe, Uncle George and our cousin Louis. And, of course, our family, our parents in particular, just adored having him back.

One thing that stands out in Carol's memory is that as soon as he got home, he used to dump his suitcase and head straight out to see his girlfriend at the time who lived just two streets away in Shimna Close. She was called Kay Williamson and we were all really fond of her. She was a stunning girl and, to us, very sophisticated.

Robin remembers clearly that in the beginning when George came home, they just did simple things like listening to music and drinking lots of tea. They didn't really go to pubs much. On occasion, George would drive Robin down to the shipyard to meet his dad who would have been working overtime. Louis recalls that George and he used to go down to Eddie Spence's for a fish supper and, within minutes of their arrival, all the kids in the area would have gathered, clamouring to speak to him.

They also used to go to the local pub called The Farmer's Rest, where our Aunt Margaret, Louis' mum, worked. Inevitably even during the week when the pub would have been really quiet, as soon as the locals heard that George was there, the place would be doing a roaring trade.

I remember getting so excited when he came home. He seemed to be so grown up and wore fabulous clothes. He used to take me on the bus into town and people would be looking at him, and nudging each other saying, 'That's Geordie Best.' I felt a bit embarrassed but at the same time really proud of him.

He was always generous. I would never have asked for money, even if I was desperate. But I remember on one occasion when he was home, a couple of my friends called round to see if I wanted to go to the local dance. It was midweek and I was broke. Payday was a couple of days away and I knew better than to ask Mum or Dad. I couldn't go and was really upset. I went up to my room. That's where George found me a short while later. When I told him what was wrong, he was angry that I hadn't asked him for the money in the first place. It was only about ten shillings. The next day, he took me into town and bought me a pair of gorgeous black leather boots which I wore for months afterwards. George knew that I would never take advantage of his fame or fortune, and years later it was to become evident how much he appreciated this.

It was the same for Mum and Dad with George when it came to money. They would never ask him for anything. On one occasion, Dad was on strike in the shipyard and obviously not getting any pay. The tabloids had got hold of this and the headline in one of the papers read: 'George Best's Dad on the Dole'. This, of course, was inaccurate. George phoned up as soon as he heard about it. He asked Dad: 'Why didn't you tell me? I could have sent you money.'

Dad explained that, firstly, he wasn't on the dole; he was on strike. And secondly, that was precisely why he wouldn't be able to take any money. As a man of principle, he believed it would be wrong for him to take money from George, knowing that his colleagues were having to get by on next to nothing. He felt that he would be letting his fellow strikers down. But he did demand — and later received — an apology from the offending paper.

As time went on and his fame grew, George was coming home less and less. One reason was that by this stage he had discovered Majorca, then the trendiest of holiday hotspots. He used to go there with a big team of friends, including Mike Summerbee. Obviously the attractions of sunny Cregagh just couldn't compete.

I have very mixed emotions about this period in my brother's life when we began to see less and less of him. I feel sadness and even some anger that I didn't make more of an effort in those days to stay in touch with him. But I accept, too, that it's silly to think that way because I wasn't really in any position to keep up constant contact with him. I was a teenage girl living in Belfast. We were leading very different lives. And although we all made an effort to get over to see him in Manchester, obviously there was a limit to the number of times we had the means to do that.

One of the most important matches that Mum and Dad were able to get to was the famous European Cup Final at Wembley in 1968. Dad had been lucky enough to go to Manchester for the semi-final match against Real Madrid and recalls that most people were not optimistic about United's chances as they had gone into the game with only a one-goal advantage from the first-leg match.

The final was played on a hot and humid May evening in London. Wembley Stadium was packed to the rafters with 100,000 spectators. I remember such excitement in our house. For Sir Matt Busby to have brought Manchester United to the finals was not just an enormous achievement but a poignant one. Everyone remembered the awful tragedy at Munich on 6 February 1958 when so many Busby Babes had perished in the plane crash. To some of the players who had survived, like Bobby Charlton, Bill Foulkes and Denis Law, the 1968 final represented what was probably their last chance to secure a European Cup Winners' Medal. Sadly Denis was unable to play due to injury.

Needless to say, it was a very proud day for Mum and Dad. Carol and I were left back in Belfast looking after Julie, Grace and Ian. Thanks to George, a chip shop had by then become the family business but it was such a special occasion that Mum and Dad even allowed us to close the shop — a treat in itself!

George was closely marked during the game as the Portuguese still remembered his performance against Benfica back in 1966. Meanwhile, Eusebio was tightly marked by Nobby Stiles. I remember it as a dull first half with lots of very hard tackles. Dad recalls vividly Eusebio's attempt at goal in the dying moments of the game. The scores were level at 1-1. Having broken through the United defence, it looked as if the most famous Portuguese player was about to shatter United's dream. All he had to do was beat the goalkeeper. But Stepney read it well and pulled off a magnificent save. The game went into extra time. The excitement in our house was phenomenal.

United went into extra time looking like the weaker team as they were so tired, but within two minutes George had scored and within another few minutes both Brian Kidd and Bobby Charlton had also scored.

United had beaten the great Benfica 4-1 and our brother had contributed to the victory. I was ecstatic, but Carol remembers being annoyed because she'd gone out of the room a couple of times — and each time she did so, United scored! Watching from home as our brother took centre stage at such an important and emotion-filled final was almost surreal. It was hard to believe that that actually was our George out there. How very far he seemed to have come within just a few years!

The images of George and Sir Matt hugging each other were deeply moving. And at the end of the game, George and Eusebio swapped jerseys. To the best of our knowledge, they were the only players to do so — it was Eusebio who approached George to do the swap. That shirt is one of the few items which our family still has from George's playing days. It is a remarkable piece of football history and certainly greatly cherished.

I was very lucky that for a couple of years, between the ages of sixteen and eighteen, I was able to go fairly regularly to Manchester to see George. He used to pay for my flights and then collect me at the airport and drop me off once the weekend was over. More often than not, though, he had a date, and I would be left outside Departures to fend for myself.

It was really exciting to be picked up in his sports cars. I remember especially his little Alfa Romeo. I stayed at Mrs Fullaway's and he used to take me to the matches at Old Trafford. Although I wasn't a big football fan, it was part of my upbringing and it would have been hard not to have been impressed with Old Trafford.

The one thing that will always stay with me was the noise. I have been lucky especially in recent years to have attended many international rugby games at some of the world's greatest grounds, including the historic game at Croke Park in Dublin in March 2007, between Ireland and England, when approximately 82,000 people attended. The noise there was phenomenal, yet still, in my opinion, nothing compared to the roar of the crowds at Old Trafford when George's name was announced as part of the team and every time he touched the ball. Even in one of his first letters home, he describes how, 'The noise kept buzzing in my head.'

I remember him saying that it was the most amazing feeling running through the tunnel on to the pitch at Old Trafford. He said that because the tunnel was on an upward slope, you couldn't actually see the crowd, but it was the noise that gave him that 'buzz' as he called it.

Many years later, during a special Ulster Television show hosted by Gerry Kelly, George was asked by motorcycle rider Robert Dunlop (brother of another Northern Ireland sports legend, the late, great Joey Dunlop) what he missed most about playing.

George instantly replied, 'The buzz. It would be very difficult to find something to replace that — when the whistle blows at 3 p.m. on a Saturday and you have 60,000 fans watching. When you have the ball totally under control and even have control over the crowd. That's the buzz.'

He also told one interviewer in the past: 'I could do something better than most people and I found it so easy. The roar of the crowd gave me such a buzz, and every time I got the ball, I could feel it.'

I remember at Old Trafford being taken into the players' and directors' room after the games, where all of the players and their wives were. It's such a pity that I was so shy in those days. I didn't really talk very much, although I was always made very welcome. I do remember that the wives and girlfriends all looked very sophisticated. I suppose they could be described as the WAGS of the 1960s.

When George left the ground, it was always the same. He was surrounded by the many fans, especially the girls who had waited patiently outside just to get a glimpse of him, or an autograph. He was always very patient, although he had to draw the line somewhere; otherwise he could have been kept there for hours on end.

At times, I actually found it a little bit frightening, as there didn't seem to be much protection for him back then, unlike today at Old Trafford where crash barriers and security staff are in place to protect the players. Generally after the games, George would take me out for a meal, and then take me back to Mrs Fullaway's before he headed out with his friends for the evening. I was very fond of Mrs Fullaway, but sometimes I felt a bit strange that she was looking after George, instead of our mum. And although Mum never ever mentioned it, I often wonder how she felt about it.

I am so pleased that I had those times in Manchester even if it was for a short period. Now that George is no longer here, I do regret deeply that for a period of time we had so little contact. But that is typical of life, isn't it? We all have 'if onlys'. If only I had kept in better contact. However, in fairness to myself, looking back, I wasn't really in a position to do that. George was in a much better position to keep in touch with us all — but his lifestyle was rapidly changing.

One of the last times in that period when I remember spending time with George was in about 1973. It was just before I would marry my first husband, Jim. We were going to Liverpool to visit an old friend of mine and we had decided to call to see George as well. It was at the time when he was living in the very unusual house he'd had built in Cheshire — the one that was likened to a public toilet!

I hadn't told him that we were coming but en route I'd called him from a phone box. Luckily he was at home. We spent a lovely day with him. We had lunch together and he took such pride in showing us around his house. It was ultra-modern with a sunken bath decorated with red mosaic tiles, curtains which closed remotely, and a TV screen that disappeared up the chimney! The windows were huge, with one-way glass that allowed him to see out but stopped others seeing in.

During the entire time that we were there, dozens of people were trying to peer in, and, at one stage, a bus packed with day-trippers even pulled up outside. It was incredible to see people with their faces squashed up against the one-way glass trying to get a glimpse of George. I really don't know how he lived under such constant pressure — in fact, I think that during that period there were times when he didn't cope.

He was quoted as saying of that time: 'Mentally and physically I am a bloody wreck. Not eating or sleeping and drinking heavily.' He added that he had been staying out until four or five in the morning, 'because

I was too frightened to go back to my goldfish bowl of a home.'

Sadly, shortly after that visit, I was to lose touch with George for a bit. Jim and I had married, and because of the constant political conflict in Northern Ireland, we decided to emigrate to South Africa. In 1974, we left Belfast and we didn't return home until 1980. During those years, caught up in my new life, I had little contact with George.

By the early 1970s, the stories about George's drinking, missing training sessions, his playboy lifestyle and, to some extent, his clashes on the pitch, were becoming more common. Not that his skills were in dispute — in February 1970, he had scored six goals for United against Northampton in an FA Cup match — but his drinking and womanising were starting to take a toll.

In January 1971, he was fined £250 and given a suspended six-week ban by the FA for getting three cautions for misconduct in the previous twelve months. George didn't do himself any favours by showing up late for the hearing.

Nor did he show the club and Sir Matt who'd spoken up for him that he'd learned his lesson and felt remorse. A few days later, he again missed his train — this time the one taking United to play against Chelsea in London. When he did finally make it to the capital, instead of reporting back to the team, he showed up at the Islington home of his friend, the actress Sinead Cusack.

What happened next was tabloid manna from heaven, turning what was to be a quiet weekend for Sinead upside down. When she looked out of her window on the Sunday morning, there was a huge commotion. The apartment was besieged by the media and chanting fans. Television news cameras recorded the scene. The newspapers were having a field day. In all, George was to spend four days there. He used to say that Sinead was a great person and that he could talk to her.

While to George's young fans it must all have seemed just a bit of a laugh, to his team-mates and Sir Matt it can't have been quite so funny. For almost a week, the story continued to make headlines everywhere.

Back home in Belfast, our parents were becoming increasingly worried about George and his lifestyle. This was in the days before mobile phones, so getting in touch with George wasn't a simple matter of just picking up the phone. They had to wait until George got in touch.

It was at times like this that the media pressure on our family became even more intense. Reporters would show up at the door at all hours of the day and night. The house was surrounded by cameras. For our neighbours like Mrs Beirne, it must have been quite annoying. The twins were even stopped on their way to and from school by journalists who gave them sweets and got them talking in the hope that they'd get something out of them. It wouldn't happen today — at least, you'd like to think it wouldn't happen today!

When George came back to Belfast, more often than not, reporters would camp outside the house for long periods of time — on some occasions, even overnight, depending on the story.

Carol recalls the time he brought his then fiancée, Eva Haraldsted, back for a visit. They stayed at our house and we were besieged by reporters and cameramen. We had to sit with all of the blinds in the house closed as they were trying to photograph him through the windows. One morning, Carol was going to an early prayer meeting at church and they quizzed her on the way out. When she came back from church, it was the same thing. As if in the interim she'd have come up with some interesting thing to tell them!

The press had become an ever-present feature in our lives. The stories about our family and about George's escapades were often sensationalised and sometimes frankly made up. Our father, not always the most patient man, was plagued by reporters phoning the house at all hours. Obviously over the years he got to know some of the journalists very well and it's important to stress here that not all of them were after sensationalist gossip or were guilty of inventing stories to fill their pages. For example, Dad remembers one night when he took a call from a reporter from the *Daily Express* who warned him that there was a story doing the rounds that George had been killed in a car crash. There was no truth in it, this journalist told Dad so that if other reporters phoned him to 'break' the news, he needn't panic. Dad has never forgotten that man's kindness. But for his thoughtfulness, our parents would have gone through the terrible distress of truly believing, even for a short time, that their son had been killed.

When it came to less kindly media intrusion, though, our family had to put up with a lot over the years. No matter what George did, whether good or bad, the press wanted to know about it. And as the years wore on, and he increasingly appeared in the headlines for the wrong reasons, so our anguish increased. George used to ring up and say, 'Don't believe everything that you read in the press.' But while some of the stories were blatantly made up, others were undoubtedly true and very difficult for our parents in particular to deal with.

There were George's court appearances — in 1973, he was found guilty of assaulting a waitress in a night club; in 1974, he was charged with stealing items including a fur coat from a former girlfriend, Miss World, Marjorie Wallace (all the charges were later dropped); and a decade on, in 1984, he served a short prison sentence for drink driving.

When George was in trouble, Dad always got in touch to let him know of his support. But during even the more difficult times in his private life, it would be true to say that George did not exactly pour his heart out. As Dad says, 'George was always a very independent and private man. You didn't go to him — he came to you.'

Our dad did make clear to George that if he ever needed to talk, he was there. But he didn't push it. George was just not the sort to talk out his problems with someone else.

By the early 1970s, Northern Ireland was facing the horrific onslaught of the Troubles. Life for us back in Belfast was very different and, I think, when George came back to see us, he was genuinely shocked by how bad things had become in the city of his birth. Sectarian killings and bombings were common and indiscriminate. Nightlife in the city had virtually closed down. Even to get into a city-centre street in daytime, you had to queue to be frisked. Hundreds of people were murdered in the early 1970s. Thousands were maimed for life. Belfast back then was truly a city gripped by fear.

Our family was among those touched by tragedy during the years of the Troubles. My dad's nephew, our cousin Gary Reid, was sadly to become one of the victims of the Troubles. He had been leaving his girlfriend to the bus stop, and on the way home he was caught in crossfire and was shot in the back by the army. He died four days after the incident. He was just sixteen years of age.

With a young family growing up in Belfast in the 1970s, our parents, like so many others, were constantly worried that something terrible might happen to any one of us. But at least, they reckoned, George was safely out of it. Until in November 1971 came a reminder that actually he wasn't.

An anonymous caller had telephoned the police to say that if George played for United against Newcastle, he would be shot dead. George insisted on playing — in the event, he scored the only goal during the game. He was collected at the ground by his close friend Malcolm Wagner, and they had to have a police escort throughout the day. The threat was repeated and, because of this, Manchester United made the decision that he would not be allowed to come back to Belfast to play against Spain. In a call home to Dad, he later tried to shrug off the seriousness of the threat, but obviously our parents were both extremely worried that he might be targeted.

Meanwhile, there were rumours in Belfast that George had donated £3,000 to the DUP, the political party led by the Rev. Ian Paisley. This, of course, was totally untrue as George had no interest in politics.

By this time, George was making a considerable amount of money — although not by the standards of the eye-watering sums that footballers are paid today. When George first joined United, he was on a wage of £4 1s 9d a week. Dad says that he phoned the club after George signed professionally and badgered them to give him a pay rise. He was now earning £22 a week. But a couple of years before this, a footballer called Johnny Haynes had become the first to be paid £100 a week. And at that time at Old Trafford there were a number of players on £80–£100 a week. George was playing well and scoring goals so Dad felt that what he was being paid was unfair. As a result of his call, George got a pay rise to £35 a week. The poignant thing is that he never knew about Dad's role in this.

Although Mum and Dad would never have asked for money, George was always generous to us as a family and it was around this time that he decided to buy Mum and Dad their own business. A local chippie had just come on the market and George reckoned that it would be an ideal venture for them. I had previously worked in it at weekends and, for that reason, didn't like it very much. Being a teenager, I really missed out on going out with my friends, and although I gave it my best shot, I eventually told the owners, a Mr and Mrs Brown, that I was leaving. They were fine about it, but one evening I went home to find them in our house. At first, I thought that I had done something wrong but, to my horror, I was told that George had bought the chippie for Mum and Dad. Far from being happy, I was thoroughly fed up. I thought that I had escaped from the place and here I was being told that we now owned it.

Despite having all of us kids to look after, Mum had always managed to work as well, and Dad had never missed a day in the shipyard. So it was fairly obvious that they would both put in the effort to make the business work. The problem in some ways was that they put in too much effort. They refused to cut corners (for example, by using frozen chips) and, although the place did reasonably well, it never really took off for them.

Dad continued to work at the shipyard but he still put in hours every day in the chippie. It was a lot of hard work. Potatoes needed to be peeled and chipped, fish had to be cut, pasties to be made and, of course, there was the never-ending cleaning. Even Granny Withers came around in the mornings to help with the cleaning.

I did try my best and continued working there for Mum and Dad for a few months longer but eventually I found a full-time job elsewhere. It wasn't all bad, though. Boys used to come in every evening, as did a local motorbike crowd, so at least I got a bit of fun from it.

Several years later, Mum and Dad sold the place for a small profit to a Chinese family. The chippie is still going strong, although today it's called the Pharaoh and is owned by an Egyptian family. As well as fish and chips, it now also sells kebabs.

Dealing with the fallout from George's fame affected us all. But understandably it was particularly difficult for our parents. Some of the media comment was extremely vitriolic and hurtful. George himself could possibly shrug it off, but for our mother especially it was not so easy to ignore. A shy, very private woman, she saw not just her son's career but also his private life and that of her family plastered all over the papers.

In today's age of celebrity, the parents of any young boy tipped for football stardom will at least have an inkling of the pressures both he and his family can expect to face. His club too will help prepare and shield him to some extent from the attention. But back then it was all new. The world of football had never had a star like George who had become as famous for his antics off the pitch as he was for his performance on it. Dubbed the Fifth Beatle, he was young and glamorous and stories about him — any stories about him — were selling newspapers. It was truly the beginning of the era of the celebrity footballer.

As we now know, George was already seeking escape through alcohol. But what he saw as a solution was, of course, only increasing the pressure. Sir Matt Busby talked to Dad about George and his problems. In fact, at one point, Mum and Dad were even offered the opportunity to move to Manchester. The club thought that perhaps having his parents and his family close by might help to settle George down a bit. The plan was that we would be set up in a furnished house and, to keep things above board, we would be charged a nominal rent of £1 per week. The club was even going to secure a job for Dad. But in the end our parents decided not to go.

By that stage, Mum was having her own problems with drink. Dad thought about the move long and hard but he knew in his heart that, where Mum was concerned, it would just be moving the problem from one location to another. And there was the rest of the family to consider. Would it be right to uproot the whole family from friends and relatives, school and work in Belfast?

In any case, Carol and I were adamant that we weren't going. We made it clear in no uncertain terms that we wanted to stay in Belfast. Although Carol was the closest to George in age, by this time, their lives had gone in very different directions. Carol recalls that she had her first drink at the age of seventeen. Needless to say, it was George who introduced her to it! But within a couple of years she had become deeply religious. By the age of nineteen, she had been Saved, and from then on never touched another drink in her life.

Although George was close to her and always deeply respected her Christian views, even Carol was unable to persuade him to seek help for his drinking. Back then, George steadfastly refused to acknowledge he had a problem at all. And while we knew from the stories in the press that he was hardly living the life of a choirboy, we didn't at that stage, appreciate just how much alcohol had a grip on him.

He was coming back to Belfast less and less now, missing weddings, christenings, important family occasions. After Julie and Grace were born, George would try to get back home as often as possible, but by the time Ian came along, his visits were becoming much less frequent. By the early 1970s, family visits were a rarity. In fact, from then on, our family can recall only four occasions when all of us were together under one roof.

The first occasion was in 1970, on Mum and Dad's silver wedding anniversary. It was such a fun evening in our house in Burren Way and, as usual, everyone, especially Mum and Dad, was delighted to have George home. His gift to our parents was a large card with twenty-five fifty-pence pieces Sellotaped on to it. Dad still has the card to this day. There's also a beautiful photograph of Mum and George together that evening, which will always be treasured by the family.

Not too long after that occasion, we were all back together again. On 17 November 1971 (just six months after Sir Matt Busby was honoured in the same way), George was caught by Eamonn Andrews and his famous red book for the television programme, *This Is Your Life*.

George often used to boast that he would never be caught out by that particular programme. He used to argue: 'How can someone *not* find out?' In fact, he himself was caught not once, but twice!

That first time, he was lured to the studios on the pretext of doing a fashion show. The entire family had been flown over — and by that I mean the entire family: Mum, Dad, Granny and Granda Best, Granny Withers and, of course, all of us. Carol was twenty-four, I was nineteen, Julie and Grace were eight and Ian just five.

I remember the researcher Jack Crawshaw coming over to Belfast to chat to us all. At first, I didn't want to go. I had just got engaged and didn't want to be separated from my fiancé, Jim. But in the end I gave in as it was such a special occasion.

Carol had to ask for time off from her job, explaining that she had to go to London. When her boss asked her why, Carol, who because of her Christian principles wouldn't lie, just said, 'I can't tell you.'

He replied, 'Well, if I write it down, will that be okay?'

On a piece of paper he wrote the words, 'This is Your Life'. Carol just nodded. He was great about it and promised not to breathe a word, and to his credit he didn't.

To be flown to London and put up in a posh hotel for a couple of nights was quite exciting. We were booked into the hotel under the name of Grant, obviously to try to keep the secret. However, I don't think that it took the staff long to figure it out, especially when my fiancé phoned the hotel and asked to speak to Barbara Best!

The adults were each given £20 expenses, which in those days was a fortune. We weren't really allowed to go very far on our own, though. It was all a bit cloak and dagger. For rehearsals, we were transported to and from the television studios by car, and sneaked in and out, especially on the day of the show when George was in the same building. We even had to be escorted to the toilets.

Anyway, George was caught good and proper. It was such an honour to have been there and so poignant that all of his family were together. That was the last time that he was with us all, together with our grandparents. And after that, it was twenty-eight more years before we were all able to get together again.

During all of those years in between, we had eight family weddings and countless births, christenings and deaths.

I was the first to marry, in May 1973. I married my second husband, Norman, in 1991. Carol was married in June 1974. Mum died in 1978, the same year in which George married Angie.

The family numbers increased with the addition of fifteen nephews and nieces. In May 1996, George's fiftieth birthday tragically coincided with the funeral of one of those nieces — Grace's youngest daughter, Ashleigh, who was just six years old.

The family finally came together again in 1999, on the grand occasion of Dad's eightieth birthday, on 19 November. Carol and I had decided on a simple family get-together with just a few of Dad's close friends. I had phoned George and explained what we were up to and he said that he would definitely be over. I was a little bit worried that he mightn't make it. At that time, he was drinking quite heavily. But my fears were unfounded and he didn't let Dad down.

On the day of Dad's birthday, to our great relief, George and Alex arrived from London, as did Ian who had flown in from Dorset. Carol and I were so paranoid about letting the secret out that we didn't even tell the rest of the family that George would be there.

Dad had been led to believe that just Carol and I, with our husbands, would be taking him for a meal to Carmichael's, a pub/restaurant in Holywood in Co. Down, a few miles from Belfast. When we arrived that evening, the manager came across and said, 'Mr Best, the restaurant downstairs is full but we've got a nice table upstairs for you instead.' Dad was genuinely oblivious to the plot.

We all went up to the function room and opened the door. Dad got the shock of his life when everyone burst into 'For He's a Jolly Good Fellow'. It took him a few seconds to realise that not only was the family there, but also his closest friends.

I said to him, 'Dad, you look as if you could do with a drink. Let's go to the bar.'

Imagine his surprise when George popped up from behind the bar and said, 'Yes, sir, what can I get for you?'

Dad was so pleased to see him and it just finished off the birthday treat in such a special way. The evening was a great success, with a lovely meal. We'd even hired a kissogram — a lovely young lady who came dressed as a policewoman. Dad was a great sport and took it all in his stride. Looking back on that evening, I am just so grateful that Dad was able to celebrate his big day in such a special way, which will hold great memories for him.

I remember making a short speech and finishing off by saying that I hoped to be doing something similar for Dad's ninetieth. Little did we know then what the future held.

The final family reunion came on 25 November 2005, and it was under the most horrendously difficult circumstances — around George's bedside, saying goodbye for the very last time. At least we were all able to make it in time to be with him at the last. In my heart, I believe that George held on until we were all there.

Down through the years, even though in public I always stood up for George, privately at times I was angry and quite fed up with him. I couldn't accept the fact that he didn't come home when he should have. We made excuses for him. We told ourselves it must be so difficult for him to get away.

Looking back now, though, it was clear that he was avoiding coming home — he had new priorities and all too often the priority would be alcohol. George was increasingly seeking solace and support from a bottle. But tragically by then he was not the only one. For the alcoholism that was to blight George's life was already claiming another victim in our family. And it was the one no one would have imagined.

As the pressure mounted on both our parents, our mother — our beautiful, gentle, hardworking mother — had also begun to seek escape through the bottle.

Mum was forty-four years of age when she had her first alcoholic drink. She was to die just a couple of months short of her fifty-sixth birthday.

Chapter 7 ∾

OUR MOTHER'S DEATH

The reporter had been knocking on our door for ages and ages. George was back in the headlines over yet another misdemeanour (I can't even remember what it was) and over the course of that day our house had been more or less under siege from the pressmen who were looking for comments. I was about fifteen at the time and alone in the house with Mum. The blinds were pulled, the door was locked and I had no intention myself of going out to talk to this man. But Mum had other ideas.

It was no secret that Mum was an alcoholic. That particular day, she'd had a few drinks and, unusually for her, was suddenly determined to go out there and tell the reporter what he could do with his story. I was equally determined to keep her indoors.

I tried everything. I pleaded with her. I cajoled her. I pulled her back. I even tried to sit on her. But despite the fact that she was quite a small woman, the drink, as it always did, seemed to give her superhuman strength. She kept trying to push me aside while I tried to keep her behind the door. Eventually she managed to wrench it open.

She told the reporter in no uncertain terms that were quite out of character for her that we would not be commenting on his breaking-news story. I'll never forget the look of sour contempt that came over that arrogant man's face. 'Look at you!' he sneered. 'You're nothing but a drunk and everyone knows it. What's more, without people like me, George wouldn't be where he is today.'

'Without people like George, you wouldn't have a job!' Mum shot back.

I was a shy girl and, like all our family, had been brought up to respect adults and not to give cheek to them. But that night I'd had enough. Listening to this grown man standing there on our doorstep insulting my mother, I let rip. I told him where to go.

But satisfying as it was finally to tell one of our family's tormentors what I really thought of him, inside I felt only despair.

I looked at my mother. My beloved mother who had once taken such pride in her appearance, who had always been so dignified and mild-mannered. To the reporter she was just a drunk.

But what people like him couldn't see was the other side of the story: the pressures that had driven her to drink. And the disease that had so completely taken over her life that even the pleading of those of us who loved her so much made no difference. She just couldn't stop.

George's leaving at such an early age, the pressure from the media — these are among the things to which our mother's drinking has been attributed. And while there is some truth that they may have helped drive her to drink, the fact is that they didn't make her an alcoholic. Alcoholism is a disease, an addiction. But not everyone who drinks becomes an alcoholic. Our belief is that there is a genetic link, that our mother and George and our younger sister Julie, who continues bravely to battle the disease, all shared the same gene that left them vulnerable to this most terrible addiction.

My dad remembers speaking to Mr Moorehead from Belfast's Shafestbury Square Hospital which treated people with addictions. Mr Moorehead told Dad that there were two things to remember: 'Every single one of us is just one drink away from being an alcoholic. And alcohol is a drug.'

As Dad says, 'Don't scorn the alcoholic. Just think to yourself that there, but for the Grace of God, go any of us; because this illness is not selective. Whether you are rich, middle or working class, you can fall victim. It does not care about colour or creed, nor whether you are male or female, young or old.'

Those who criticise alcoholics like George see them as wilful and selfish. They dismiss them as drunkards who don't care about anyone else so long as they are able to satisfy their own cravings. I imagine people with these views have not had any personal experience of living with an alcoholic, and I sincerely hope that they never do.

Those who love or live with an alcoholic will all too often see the other side. The constant battle with the bottle. The truly desperate attempts to stop. George, for example, famously had Antabuse pellets sewn into his stomach. The medication is supposed to make drinkers violently ill if they so much as sip alcohol. But even that didn't work. My brother was an intelligent man. He knew the terrible damage alcohol was wreaking in his life. A man who always took pride in his appearance and his physical fitness, he knew that it was destroying both. Above all, he knew that if he didn't stop drinking, it would eventually kill him.

I used to look at George when he was ill and wonder how anybody could imagine that he put himself through that willingly. How they could think that he reckoned it was a reasonable price to pay so long as he could carry on drinking. Surely they must have seen that if he could stop, he would stop.

Although it was a long time before he acknowledged he had a problem, George did accept that he was an alcoholic, that he had a terrible problem and that he had to stop. But he just couldn't. He tried so very, very hard. Yet in the end it was stronger than he was. And the same was true of our mother.

In our mother's case, the terrible irony is that the disease got a grip on her life only at a time when things were finally becoming a little easier for her and Dad. All her life, she had been such a hard worker. She was totally, utterly devoted to her family. Her husband and her six children were her world and there was nothing she wouldn't do for us. When Carol and I recall our childhood and the days before Mum started drinking, there is one phrase we always come back to which sums her up: our mum was a lady.

Photographs from the time show how she was with her dark hair neatly pinned back and her eyes sparkling with fun and happiness. She was a beautiful woman who took immense pride in not only her own appearance but also that of her children and her home. We never had much materially. I remember in my teens how excited she was the first time she and Dad could afford a carpet for our living room. Before that, the floor was wooden but she kept it so polished and spotless that you could have eaten your dinner off it!

Not that that was a possibility. She instilled good manners in us all. She was loving but firm and we were all expected to pull our weight in the home. But Mum was the real home-maker. She was meticulous about everything she did. I remember her down on her hands and knees scrubbing the concrete front doorstep and path until they were glistening white and her fingers were raw. The brass handles on our windows were always shining. That's what people did back then. Our home, like our neighbours' homes, was kept pristine.

As I mentioned earlier, she, like so many other housewives of the time, had no washing machine. I remember how, during the summer, she used to wash and wring out by hand the big woollen blankets, as there was no way she could have got them dried in the winter months. Mum got her first washing machine only when Julie and Grace were born. It was a single tub with a hand-wringer on it. The 'luxury' model arrived when Ian was born. This was an all-singing, all-dancing twin-tub Hoover with an electric wringer.

She was a great cook and baker even though there never was a lot of money to spare for luxuries. She made great apple tarts and candy apples. And she was a brilliant knitter, extremely fast; often we used to drift off to sleep at night with the 'clickety clack' sound of her knitting needles downstairs. She made most of our clothes herself on a little sewing machine our dad bought her. Many a time, she sat up most of the night to get a garment finished for one of us.

One such occasion was for my local annual Sunday School summer outing. The trip that year was to Ballywalter, a local seaside village. Every year, I used to get new shorts and a T-shirt for the occasion (usually red and white!) But Mum also made sure that I had something pretty to wear for travelling on the bus. She used to go to a local drapery shop called the Paragon, where she bought end pieces of material. She could work wonders with them, which is exactly what she did for my trip to the seaside. She bought a piece of pink chiffon covered with rosebuds, with lining to match, and she sat up all that night making me a fairy-tale dress. When I came down the next morning, she had finished it and I felt really special wearing it.

That was typical of her. She would spend hours lovingly knitting and sewing for us and — when Carol's and my own children were born — for her first grandchildren.

I have to confess that not all her work was appreciated. I remember she used to knit horrible woollen skirts for Carol and me to wear to school. They were done on a circular needle and had hundreds of stitches in them. When they were finished, she put elastic in the waistband, but, being woollen, they were really heavy and Carol and I spent most of the time hauling them up in case they ended up round our ankles! Quite often, to save money, she'd unpick old garments, carefully rewinding the wool into a tight ball. This would then be used to knit something different, so I'm sure that some of George's old jumpers or the awful offending woollen skirts were recycled into another of Mum's great creations. One of my happiest memories is of sitting by the fireside, patiently holding the big skeins of wool you used to get back then, as she wound them into balls.

She was a great singer and she loved Guy Mitchell, Jim Reeves and Bing Crosby. Every time I hear them now, I think of her.

As well as looking after our home, Mum worked as a home help for an old lady called Mrs Patterson who lived close to Granny Withers. Our next-door neighbour, Mrs Imelda Beirne (Melda, we called her) looked after me. But sometimes I had to go with Mum. I remember not liking it as Mrs Patterson seemed to me very old and scary.

It was later, when we were all through primary school, that Mum went to work in the Ulster Creameries which was just a short way from our house. It was great in the summer as we would walk around to the place and sometimes the staff would slip us ice-lollies through the back door. On occasion, Mum would bring home some of the 'misshapen' ones in the saddle bag of her bike, or rather Carol's bike. Carol recalls getting a bicycle for Christmas. However, Mum used to ride that bicycle to work every day and then home again in the evening — just in time for Dad to take it. He then used it to get him to his night shift in the shipyard and then home again in the morning. Carol never got to ride the bike at all!

They were a great team, Mum and Dad. In the summer, when she worked long shifts, Dad used to heat her up one of her favourite Bird's Eye chicken pies, wrap it carefully and take it over to her in work at around tea-time. They worked hard, the pair of them, and every penny they got went to their family.

Mum never forgot her brother and sisters either. As I mentioned earlier, our Granda Withers died just before Christmas when George was about eleven. There weren't the same benefits back then as there are now and Mum knew that her own mother and her young sisters and brother who were still children faced a bleak Christmas. She saved every penny she could and bought presents for the children — Ingersoll watches for the girls and a suit for her brother George. But she made sure that we all got our presents too.

She was kind and loving. To her, family meant everything. And it wouldn't be an exaggeration to say that she idolised George. He was her first-born and she doted on him. Even before he left home, he always got preferential treatment. George was always in the right where Mum was concerned. Carol remembers getting in a play fight with George where he stuck his fingernails in her leg and drew blood.

'Look what's he's done to me!' she cried to Mum.

But Mum just said, 'Come on, you're not that bad. You'll live.'

As Carol says, if it had been the other way round, it would have been a different story!

When George left home for the first time, and Mum went down to see him off at the Heysham boat, it truly broke her heart. In fact, it had such a profound effect on her that for the rest of her life she steadfastly refused to go and see any of her family off when they were leaving home. Only on one poignant occasion, as I will describe later, did she ever break this rule.

George is on record as saying that Mum never saw him play with Manchester United. Carol and I are really baffled about this as Mum and Dad actually got to see him play quite a lot. She used to go over to Manchester with Dad and took great pride in wearing her red suit trimmed with white, with her Manchester United badge in the lapel. In fact, we even have a photograph of her at one of the matches wearing the suit. She was so proud of George. As, of course, was Dad.

When George, Carol and I were small, Mum didn't really go out much. Dad used to go down to the pub or one of the local clubs to meet his mates. He wasn't a big drinker but enjoyed a couple of pints after work on a Friday evening and then sometimes on a Saturday afternoon. Mum was happy to be at home doing her usual cleaning or knitting.

Carol remembers that when she was about seventeen, George, who was back home from Manchester, took her and his then girlfriend Kay Williamson out for the night to a bar in Bangor in Co. Down. Carol had only a couple of drinks but she became very tipsy and George and Kay had to take her back to Kay's parents' house to sober her up before they brought her home. If Dad, but particularly Mum, had found out that Carol had been drinking, they'd have gone mad. That in itself says something about our mum's attitude to drink back then.

Mum was forty-three when Ian was born, and, when he was about eighteen months old, she started going out with Dad at nights, maybe once a week. They would go to local clubs such as the Harland and Wolff staff club, where they'd meet up with friends. Carol and I would look after the three little ones.

At first, Mum would have had very, very little to drink — usually just a Pimm's with lemonade. Generally one drink lasted her all night. Looking back, though, Carol and I can see how she began using drink as a crutch.

Although things were starting to get better for our parents financially, especially after George bought them the chip shop, Mum was finding it hard to cope. She was, we believe, most likely going through the menopause. She had three young children — almost a second family — to look after. Back then, it wasn't the accepted thing for women to talk so much about female problems, and Mum especially would have been mortified talking about such personal matters. So any problems she might have been having as a result of the 'change of life' were never spoken about.

Above all, though, she never, ever got over George leaving home so young. She never said it in so many words. But from the time he left, she changed. The fact that he rocketed to the top so quickly, in terms of fame, put a terrible strain on her. She hated the spotlight being turned on the family. Dealing with reporters, having her picture taken, giving interviews, being pointed out in the street, and even on a number of occasions being insulted by nasty-minded people just because of who she was — some people might have been able to take such things in their stride, but our mum, always a very shy, private woman, found the attention excruciating, even when it was positive and well-intentioned.

It was bad enough having to deal with the media attention, but there were other more sinister pressures. Mum and Dad had been out one evening and Carol was babysitting the younger ones with her then boyfriend, David, a church minister. At about 10 p.m., the local police called at the door and asked to speak to Dad. Carol said that our parents were out so the police said that they would call back later, which they did — a couple of times. Carol was obviously becoming deeply concerned. Eventually the police officers told her that they had received information that Dad was going to be kidnapped.

Mum and he arrived home at about midnight. Dad thought that it was hilarious and asked the police, 'How much am I worth?' The police, however, were taking no chances and made sure that patrols were stepped up around the estate that night. Needless to say, we didn't get rid of Dad that easily! However, while Dad was able to joke about it, Mum was in a terrible state. It really had a profound effect upon her.

She found it very, very difficult to deal with George being criticised in the media or when stories were printed about him that she knew weren't true. She just couldn't shrug it off. Her drinking began slowly, gradually.

One morning, our next-door neighbour and Mum's very close friend, Mrs Beirne, came into the house for a wee cup of tea. This was a regular routine. However, she found Mum pouring herself a glass of sherry.

'Would you like one?' Mum asked her.

'Good God, Annie,' exclaimed Mrs Beirne. 'It's nine o'clock in the morning. What are you doing drinking at this time of the day?'

'I need it to get me through the day,' Mum said simply. And maybe that just about summed it up.

Bit by bit, it now became increasingly obvious that she had a problem. She used to send Carol to the Rosetta Bar for a bottle of wine. She even sent me. And if they wouldn't serve me because I was too young, she'd always find somebody to go for her. Or she'd go herself.

Dad asked local bars and off-licence establishments not to serve her. Some were sympathetic, some were not, but it was pointless as she would just go somewhere else until she got served. Even when she seemingly had no money, the drink always appeared. Alcoholics can be very, very crafty.

Dad tried everything. He pleaded with her to stop. He begged her to see a doctor. He even tried to get a hypnotist to help her. This was all futile. Nothing worked. For years, she steadfastly refused to accept that she had a problem. She never accepted that she was an alcoholic.

The change in her when she took drink was shocking. Before, my mum was a lovely, sweet-natured woman, a woman who never spoke ill of anybody. When she was drunk, she was argumentative and very difficult. She would taunt us and goad us. She knew what was a sore point with each of us, and she'd keep on and on and on about it until it became unbearable.

Carol remembers Ian, who was only a little boy, probably about five or six, sitting on the floor one evening in front of the television, watching his favourite programme. Suddenly Mum switched it off. Ian switched it back on. Mum switched it off. She went on doing it, over and over again, until the child was in tears.

Julie had beautiful hair and was always grooming it, so Mum would taunt her about that. She taunted me about my boyfriend Jim, who was to become my first husband. 'What does a decent boy like that see in someone like you?' she'd say.

She used to pick rows with Dad although he did everything in his power to keep the peace. She would follow him around trying to pick a fight. I remember nights when he came home from work and then just went out and walked the streets for hours and hours to stay out of her way.

She used to go down the town and come home covered in bruises. She had more than enough injuries. Once she ended up with a broken leg. She said that she'd been mugged. She could have been, but God only knows what really happened. On one occasion, after a particularly nasty incident which needed hospital treatment, Dad and Mum came back from the hospital. Carol remembers Mum crying. She was full of remorse.

'I'm sorry, I'm sorry,' she kept saying. 'This is it. No more. I'm going to stop.'

And she did try. There would be weeks at a time when she stopped. During those periods, we didn't talk to her about what she'd done or what she'd been like when she was drinking. In a way, we were afraid to break the spell. It was so good to have our real mum back: happy, singing, looking after and loving us the way she used to. We just wanted the good days back. But instead it was getting worse.

She would be off the drink for a week, and then she'd return to it with a vengeance. Those people who have been there will know what I mean; your emotions in cases like that are all over the place. It turned very quickly into a love-hate relationship and at times I just wanted to slap her. It's a shameful thing to say, but as a teenager it was so difficult to understand it all.

Carol and I remember what it was like coming home from work. The closer we got to the house, the more butterflies we got in our stomachs. We would peek in through the window, and, if she was sitting in her chair, that was bad news as it meant that she had been drinking. Otherwise she would have been up and about getting things done. If you opened the door and there was no smell of food, you knew it was really bad: she'd been drinking all day. Carol was in a church singing quartet at that time and she used to come home at night never knowing what she'd find.

The thing about living with an alcoholic is that you know that that person has a problem and it's not their fault. You love that person. But sometimes it's hard to like them. I left home when I was about sixteen. I couldn't stand it. With a few friends, I shared a grubby bedsit in north Belfast. It was all I could afford.

I remember going to babysit for Aunt Georgie and Uncle Billy who then drove me back to the flat where I'd been living for a few months. I remember the way my uncle looked around the place with such disgust. 'Look at the state of this place,' he said. 'What the hell are you doing living in a place like this when you've a decent home to go to?'

'You've no idea what it's like,' I told him.

However, I did go back home. A lot of people were starting to come round to the flat, smoking 'dope' and taking drugs — something which I was dead against. I wasn't comfortable in that environment, so going back home was the only option.

Meanwhile, back at home, Carol had been bearing the brunt of it all. She wanted to move out too but she said she couldn't leave the three little ones. Even to this day she is the matriarch of the family. Everyone runs to Carol with their problems, and at times I feel really guilty about this.

She recalls on a number of occasions, when things were really unbearable at home, phoning George and pleading with him to come home. Mum idolised George — surely there was something he could say or do that would get through to her. And he always promised he would. 'I'll be right home, darling. I'll be on the first flight back home,' he'd swear.

Only he never was.

Did he not care? Was he really that busy? Was he not allowed? Or was there a simpler reason? Was it that his own drinking was by then already out of control? Was it that he felt that he was in no position to talk to somebody else about alcoholism? Whatever the reason, Carol and I agree that there were times in his lifetime when we were both really angry with our George. And some of those times were when he broke his promises.

Mum never used George as an excuse for her drinking. Nor did she ever suggest that the pressure of dealing with his fame was the reason for her drinking. In fact, just like George, she never used anybody or anything as an excuse for the terrible illness which was to blight the remainder of her life. And despite the fights and the tears and the hard times, the one thing that was obvious through it all was that she and our dad still truly loved each other.

Dad would say to us, 'You know I love your mum.'

And she would say to us, 'You know I love your dad.'

The real tragedy was that Mum's drinking began just when life was beginning to look easier for our parents. Then it just all upended.

I got married to Jim in May 1973 a few months before my twenty-first birthday. I really didn't want a big affair. We had only twenty-five guests and I specifically chose Clanbrassil House Hotel close to Holywood for our reception, as it didn't have a licence to sell alcohol. Even so, I spent the whole day in agony, worrying and wondering, 'Does she have a bottle in her bag?'

Mum didn't drink that day but she was shaking and on edge. The atmosphere was so fraught, I just wanted it all to be over.

George sent Jim and me a very generous cheque as a wedding gift, but he didn't attend the wedding. I was really sad that he wasn't coming home, but at the same time I tried to understand that it probably was better if he didn't attend. Even so, from the outset, we were hounded by the press. They just wouldn't believe us when we explained that George wasn't going to be there. They phoned the house, but that wasn't enough so they turned up at the door. They followed us to the Brannagh Mission Hall where we got married. Still they got no information. They followed some of my friends and tried to interrogate them. One tabloid even offered them a financial incentive to talk about George. By the time we reached our reception, the media were already there. It was as if they thought that we were hiding George and he would turn up at any minute.

I think that the penny finally dropped with the press that George wasn't coming when we sat down for our meal and he was nowhere to be seen. As usual, though, they were determined to get some sort of story out of the occasion. And this was summed up by the headline in that one paper: 'BEST MAN MISSING' it read.

Like any new bride, I was a bundle of nerves. But the worry about Mum and the unwelcome press attention hardly combined to make my special day memorable for the right reasons.

Jim and I moved to live in South Africa, to escape the never-ending political problems and violence in Belfast. At the time, South Africa offered a much more attractive lifestyle, and our first son, Steven, was born there in June 1975.

In 1974, Carol married Allen MacPherson who, throughout the years, has remained such a support to her and to all our family. Their first child, Ann, was born in March 1975, and Stuart followed in June 1976. Carol continued to look after Mum and Julie and Grace and Ian.

It was so hard on the three youngest. We used to say that they never really knew Mum in the good days. We were lucky in that we at least had our memories of the lovely mother that she was. It was the same with Allen and Jim. They never knew Mum when she was sober, although I know that Jim always had a real soft spot for her.

Even now, looking back, the most difficult question to answer is how could someone so ladylike and dignified, who lived for her home and her family — how could she could become what our mum became?

Carol and I hate to read, as we so often do, articles or books saying that our mother died of alcoholism. The fact is that Mum died of heart disease. And, yes, of course, we fully accept that the drink exacerbated the problems she had. But there were other factors in her premature death, too, not least the fact that she smoked like a trooper. And she didn't eat properly when she was drinking. Every now and again, she would take a notion for fried onions which she loved, or Dad would bring her in fish or some chicken from the local chip shop to try to tempt her to eat. But she didn't look after herself at all. We honestly believe that she would probably have died from heart disease anyway — although we don't deny that the drinking did probably hasten her end.

Mum had a heart attack in June 1977, and, when the doctors examined her, they explained that it had, in fact, been her second. She had had another one before without realising it.

After that second attack, she never really made anything of it — over the next few months, she didn't seem able to get her strength back. It was as if she'd lost the will to live.

Carol remembers pleading with her, 'You've got to look after yourself.'

But Mum just shook her head and said, 'No. I don't care any more.'

During the summer of 1978, Carol phoned me in South Africa and told me that Mum was really ill. I didn't have the money to come home but I borrowed it from a close friend, Lorna, so that Jim and I could come back with our son Steven who was then just over three years old. No one at home had seen my little boy.

I remember hugging my mother as soon as I got home and feeling just this little bag of bones. She wasn't a tall woman but she'd always been well built. Now she was just skin and bones. Throughout our stay in Belfast, I grew increasingly concerned about her. She hadn't been drinking for quite some time, but still her health was not good.

Then, during the last week that we were there, she started to drink again. I was devastated. I tried to reason with her, but she just wasn't interested.

We were going to London to spend a week with Jim's brother on our way back to South Africa. Ever since that day she'd left George at the boat for England, Mum had refused to go with any of us to say goodbye at an airport or ferry terminal. When I left to live in South Africa, it was Dad and Carol who came along to see us off at the boat. Carol remembers on that occasion going back home only to find that Mum wasn't in the house. Of course, everyone thought that she was away to get a drink but, dear love her, she had just gone out to get fish and chips for the family to try to cheer everyone up.

Anyway, when we were leaving, Mum, surprisingly, insisted on coming to Aldergrove Airport to see Jim, Steven and me off. She came right to the Departure lounge with us. I put my arms around her as I left, and kissed her. My last words to her were, 'Please look after yourself. I'll see you soon.'

I'll never forget her reply. 'No, you won't,' she said gently.

And I never did.

A week later, on 12 October 1978, as Jim and I got ready for our flight back to South Africa, Jim's dad phoned to tell me that our mum had been found dead in bed.

Jim and his family didn't encourage me to go back home to Belfast for the funeral. I know they did this for the best of reasons. I remember his dad telling me, 'Life is for the living. Your flight to South Africa is waiting. You have to go and get on with your own lives.' But ever since that day, I regretted my decision.

I spoke to Carol and Dad just minutes before getting on to the plane. Everyone was heartbroken. I felt an enormous guilt that I wasn't there, at my own mother's funeral. It was bad enough, I told myself, that Mum and Dad so seldom had all of their children under the one roof, but for me not to have gone home at that time made it worse.

I also remember being really surprised and a bit angry that George had gone home. I remember thinking at the time that he hadn't bothered to come home for anything else, and asking myself why he had chosen now to go. But grief affects people in different ways and I suppose that I was trying to salve my own conscience.

When I came back from South Africa a few years later, it was as if I was going through her death for the first time. It was hard to come home with Mum not there. I wanted to go to the house alone when no one else was there. I just wanted to sit on the bed in their room. It was so hard going to her grave. To me it was as if she had only just died.

We all have regrets in life, however irrational. Dad regrets that in that last week of her life, Mum and he were sleeping apart. Things weren't good between them so he was sleeping on the settee downstairs. He normally took Mum a cup of tea before he set off to work, and then she would rise to get Julie, Grace and Ian ready for school.

That last week, however, he hadn't been doing it. But during the final night of Mum's life, when he couldn't sleep, Dad decided that in the morning he would take up the tea, and get down on his knees and beg her to stop drinking.

In the morning, it was still dark, so he just turned on the light on the landing and left the tea on the bedside table. Mum's arm was out of the bed and he felt it. It was cold, but he didn't immediately think anything was wrong. However, when he came back upstairs before he left for work, and found the tea untouched, he reached across and touched Mum's shoulder which was also cold. Then he realised the truth. Our lovely mum was dead. She had suffered a massive heart attack.

There would have been nothing he could have done to save her but Dad says, 'I have always, always regretted that I wasn't with her that night. That I wasn't with her in the true sense of being a couple, in the last week of her life.'

Dad, of course, has nothing to reproach himself over. In her lifetime, he did everything he could for our mother. And after her death, his children, particularly the twins who were fifteen and Ian who was only twelve, were his priority.

The young police officers who attended our house on the morning of Mum's death remember Dad's desperate efforts to resuscitate Mum. Pauline Matchett, as she then was, recalls that she and her colleague Michael Jenkins were on mobile patrol from the nearby Castlereagh RUC station when they got the call out to Burren Way.

'There was no name given,' she says. 'But as soon as we heard the address, we were thinking, "Hang on, isn't that the Bests' house?"'

'When we arrived and went upstairs, the most distressing scene met us. Mrs Best, who was in bed, was obviously dead. Her arms were cold but her stomach was still warm. Her husband Dickie was in a terrible state trying frantically to bring her back. He was pumping at her chest, crying out to her.

'Apparently he'd come up to waken her and give her a cup of tea and had found her like that. He'd called 999 immediately. The ambulance had arrived. But it was obvious she was gone.

'The youngest child, Ian, was running around asking, "What's wrong, Daddy?" so Michael took him by the hand and said, "Would you like to come outside and have a wee look at our police car?"

'He took Ian out, put him in to the front seat and let him have a look at the instruments to try to distract him from what was going on indoors.'

Looking back, Pauline recalls the shock she felt: 'I grew up in Portadown in Co. Armagh in a very sporty family. There were fourteen of us and we all supported Manchester United but in particular Geordie Best. For example, my late brother Ernest adored George so much that when he applied for university, he chose Manchester just to be near him and the team. George was such a hero to so many people in Northern Ireland.

'And now here I was attending the scene of this terrible tragedy for George and his family.'

A couple of days after Mum's death, Pauline returned to the police station around tea-time. The place, she recalls, was bedlam. The Enquiry Office was packed and the duty officer was trying to attend to members of the public and answer phones at the same time. As she passed one ringing phone, Pauline picked it up only to discover, by sheer coincidence, that it was Dad trying to track her down.

He asked her if she'd spoken to anyone in the media about Mum's death and Pauline confirmed that of course she hadn't. She remembers that Dad was extremely upset.

The media who Mum had found so very difficult to deal with in her lifetime had delivered a final blow in the hours just after her death. The local paper, the *Belfast Telegraph*, had reported that it was the children who had found Mum that morning as Dad had already gone to work. It hurt Dad deeply. In fairness, the paper later carried an apology for the mistake. But by then, of course, the damage had been done.

I have mentioned a number of times how I believe that things don't happen just by chance. On 14 November 2006, just a few days before the first anniversary of George's death, I received a message through the George Best Foundation website. Part of it read:

> I was standing in my garden on the evening of George's funeral. I was looking up at the sky which was star-filled. I was thinking of George and of my brother who passed away to that other horrible disease cancer.
>
> For no particular reason I looked up over my left shoulder and saw a shooting star. I smiled and said, bye bye George.
>
> It was the first time I had smiled peacefully for quite a while. For that's exactly what George was. A shooting star, not often seen but spectacular, majestic, brilliant, special, beautiful….

The message came from Pauline, the policewoman who had been at our house that terrible morning when Mum died.

There is, however, a happy — and romantic — footnote to Pauline's own story. She and her colleague Michael Jenkins, who had accompanied her to our house that day, later married.

Looking back on those years now, I see that there are, of course, parallels between what we went through with Mum and George's fight against alcoholism. There was the same sense of despair. The same desperation to try to help him, to make him stop. The same heartache.

How much of an impact Mum's death had on George is hard to say.

As I've said, he rarely talked about his emotions. But in an interview he gave many years later at our house in France, he did, I believe, reveal something of how very deeply it had affected him.

George had agreed to do a documentary for Channel Five which Norman and I found out about only when my mobile phone rang one day and a female voice said, 'May I speak to Barbara, please? I'm from Channel Five. I'm just calling to confirm the time that we will be arriving in France.'

This was news to me so the caller was met with a wall of silence.

'Oh dear,' she said. 'I take it that you haven't a clue what I'm talking about.'

A couple of days later, the phone rang again.

'Hi, Norm. It's me,' said George. 'Just to let you know that we've arrived.'

'Arrived where?'

'At the airport. Perpignan Airport. I'm here with the crew.'

Needless to say, Norman was wondering: 'What crew? Has he invited the pilot and the flight attendants back? What is he talking about?'

The crew, of course, were from Channel Five and they had found out from George only as they were boarding the flight at Stansted that, despite George's assurances that 'Barbara and Norman won't mind. They're great', we weren't actually expecting them.

And so a very uncomfortable crew arrived with a very drunk brother in tow.

The next few days were hectic. There were cameras in our faces all the time. And George was drinking all the time. I was following him around like a bad smell, trying to protect him against saying anything that he would later regret, but sadly an interview was filmed without my knowledge, when he had a lot of drink taken.

In it he talked about Mum in a way that I'd never heard him talk before. He broke down when he was asked if he felt guilty about not being there for her. I had never seen or heard George bare his soul like this, so it was particularly difficult to watch.

When the interviewer pressed George about how he felt about Mum, he became very emotional. He said that when he was living in the US and in therapy in San Jose, he'd been made to write a letter, supposedly to Mum, as part of his treatment. In the letter, he said, he'd written that he was sorry.

He added: 'I always thought that it [Mum's death] was my fault. I said that I was sorry for the years I wasn't there. It's that simple.

'In hindsight I could have been there. I felt guilty and to a certain extent I still do. But I realise now that there was nothing I could do about it.'

In the end, there was nothing any of us could do about it.

If there is one story that sums up for me the last tragic years of Mum's life, it is a story Carol tells about a haunting incident that stays with my sister from those years. It sums up the grief my sister felt at the loss of our lovely, gentle mum as she succumbed to the disease she simply couldn't overcome.

Carol remembers being on a bus and seeing a woman, around about Mum's age, staggering down the street. The woman was very obviously very drunk. Carol remembers someone behind her on the bus calling out, to the laughter of other passengers: 'Look at the state of that. How would you like that coming home to you? It's disgusting!'

On many occasions, that's exactly what we did have coming home to us. 'Disgusting' was a terrible word to use to describe that poor woman — and it's certainly not one that we would ever have used about our mum. But Carol couldn't turn to the people behind her to tell them that; she was too upset. Staring out the window, she quietly cried all the way home.

All of us in our family have shed many private tears for our mum. We have never forgotten what alcohol made her become. But we have never forgotten either the lovely, gentle, caring mother that she truly was.

And we never will.

Chapter 8

LOVING BROTHER, LOYAL FRIEND

George was living in America when Mum died. Dad had the painful task of ringing him that morning to break the terrible news.

Earlier that same year, on 24 January 1978, when he was thirty-one years old, George had married his first wife, Angela MacDonald Janes, in Las Vegas. By that time, of course, George's career with Manchester United, with all its triumphs and travails, was well over. It had ended on New Year's Day 1974, in a game against Queen's Park Rangers.

The story of George's football career, of his 'retirements', his eventual split with Manchester United, his signing for a number of clubs throughout the British Isles, South Africa and the US has, of course, been endlessly documented in books, newspapers and documentaries.

The move to LA in 1976 offered, George firmly believed, a new beginning — and not just for the American soccer authorities who were trying to promote a sport which had never really caught on in a grand scale in the US. Among other big names who'd been attracted to the North American Soccer League around that time were the likes of Franz Beckenbauer, Johan Cruyff and, of course, the legendary Pelé. As with the recent signing of David Beckham with another LA team, the aim back then was to try to popularise soccer in the US. In the long run, that early attempt failed. But, for a few years, the big names of world football, George among them, injected a new vitality and glamour into the game in the States.

At first, as so often in the past, George met the challenge the US presented with enthusiasm, by training hard, getting fit and even, for a time, laying off the booze. Almost inevitably, though, his addiction to alcohol continued to cause problems, and soon he was back to his old ways. However, on the plus side, now that he was away from the UK, he was no longer quite so firmly in the media spotlight.

By the time of Mum's death, George was playing with the Fort Lauderdale Strikers. He had originally signed with the LA Aztecs and it was in LA that he met the tall blonde woman who would be his first wife.

News of his marriage to Angie took us all by surprise. That's if you could say that anything George did would be a surprise. He simply phoned Mum and Dad in the evening to let them know that he had married Angie earlier that day in Las Vegas.

The twins were by now in their early teens and Grace recalls the disappointment she felt when George phoned home to inform the family that he'd got married — without seeking her services as an attendant! 'I was devastated. I hadn't been a flower girl at my oldest brother's wedding. That's what wee sisters do, I thought. I felt cheated!'

Although no one had been at their wedding, later that same year George invited the whole family out to LA to meet his new wife. I was living in South Africa at this stage and Carol was married with a family of her own. As Mum had already had a heart attack, doctors were advising her not to make the long flight, but she persuaded Dad to go, taking with him the three youngest members of the family — Julie, Grace and Ian. Carol looked after Mum while they were away.

First impressions of George's new life were, Grace recalls, impressive. 'He and Angie lived just beside the ocean. It was amazing. We felt like we were in heaven.'

But even to the younger ones, it soon became clear that there was trouble in paradise. Grace remembers that George would disappear regularly to the bar, returning home later obviously the worse for wear. Then the arguments would begin.

'After a week,' says Grace tellingly, 'I just wanted to go back home to Mum.'

But she also recalls how both George and Angie tried hard to make the visit a success, with days out and a family visit to Disneyland. She adds: 'Best of all there was a trip to the Anaheim Stadium where George was playing football with the LA Aztecs. I have never forgotten that. Watching him play as he took on three, then four, players, I suddenly realised for the first time just how good he was. He *was* special. He was my brother and I was so very proud of him.'

After Mum's death Angie accompanied George back to what was then a very grim Belfast, for the funeral of the mother-in-law she had never even met. Dad and the rest of the family were beside themselves with grief, and it must have been a very difficult experience for Angie as well. George broke down as soon as he arrived home. And no one had warned poor Angie of the normal custom in Northern Ireland when a person dies.

Carol and I often speak about Angie's shocked reaction when she walked straight into the living room that day to find Mum's corpse laid out in her coffin. As Grace who was there at the time recalls: 'I'll never forget Angie's reaction when she saw Mum laid out in her coffin. She was horrified. Obviously they didn't do that in California!'

Despite her shock, Angie quickly regrouped. Carol recalls that she was very supportive and really made an effort for everyone, trying her best to lift their spirits.

As anyone who has seen Angie knows, she was (and still is) a fine-looking woman who has always been extremely aware of and careful about her personal well-being and fitness. At one stage, she was a personal trainer to Cher. Angie insisted during her stay on trying to encourage our not-so-fit family to indulge in a little bit of gentle exercise — especially my Aunt Lily, a sister of Mum's.

Lily was a very glamorous redhead who was always immaculately made up, and festooned in jewellery. She was most embarrassed that Angie kept 'picking' on her. Angie had decided to demonstrate some exercise techniques and she persuaded Aunt Lily to lie on the floor with her feet hooked under a chair to do some sit-ups. Apparently it was a hilarious sight. Even Granny Withers, grief-stricken though she was at losing her daughter, had to smile. She said later to Carol: 'And I thought that I would never laugh again.'

As I was back in South Africa, I missed that chance to meet Angie, and it wasn't until late 1980 that I did meet her. Our first meeting was a strange one. Jim and I had returned to Northern Ireland from South Africa and I was expecting my second child, Jenny, in October. I had gone over to Dad's as George and Angie had arrived in Belfast for a quick visit. We both arrived outside Dad's at the same time. Because of my very large 'bump', I struggled awkwardly out of the car. However, Angie, who was expecting Calum in about four months' time, very elegantly stepped out of the taxi, and the first words that she spoke to me were, 'My God, look at the size of you. You're huge!'

She, of course, looked amazing and I felt like a baby elephant beside her. It certainly wasn't the best introduction in the world, but I didn't hold it against her! When Calum was born, on 6 February 1981, both Carol and I made sure that we recognised the happy event by sending cards and presents. In fact, over the years, even after George and Angie divorced, Carol continued sending gifts to Calum at Christmas and on birthdays.

I seldom saw Angie over the years, the final time being at George's funeral. She has settled back in England now, but as before there is no contact with our family. I was a little surprised and hurt to read comments she was reported to have made after George's death in an interview with a well-known glossy magazine. Asked about our family, she apparently said that she hadn't had much contact with us as 'The Best family aren't the most communicative.'

I couldn't really understand that. It was more down to circumstances, especially after she and George divorced, that there hadn't been much of a relationship between us.

Needless to say, George's return to Belfast for our mother's funeral aroused massive media interest. As the day of the funeral neared, the police asked Dad if he wanted them to keep the reporters and cameramen at bay. At first, Dad turned down the offer but then when he thought about it he remembered that when our Granny Best, his own mother, was being buried, the press had turned the funeral into a circus. That day, they had been everywhere, trying to get a picture of George who, yet again, wasn't actually there. Dad had had to go and tell them to take themselves off.

Now he decided to ask the police for help during Mum's funeral. The police sealed off our street so that only people who lived there could get in and out. They also followed the funeral cortège all the way to the cemetery where, again, they helped ensure that the family had some degree of privacy.

For all of us, the loss of our mother was a terrible blow. But it was particularly hard for the younger ones who had never really known her when she was fit and well and not battling with the bottle. Sadly, the media clamour over her death was what they'd come to expect, even at their young age.

While Carol and I could remember what life was like before George had become a household name, the twins and Ian grew up with media attention as the norm. As Ian recalls, the younger members of the family were always aware of George's fame: 'Every time George came home, our house would be surrounded by the press. I remember being lifted over into the neighbours' garden to go to school as we couldn't open the door without being quizzed. Then it was the same procedure on the way back home from school.'

He adds, 'I remember going to some of the matches that George played at Windsor Park. One incident comes to mind when George was playing and some lad about two seats in front was singing about George (the old song about "Georgie Best, superstar, walks like a woman and wears a bra").

'Being about ten years old at the time, I took this very badly and told the lad to shut up and not to sing rude songs about my brother.'

However, not all of it was bad — it goes without saying that there were advantages to having a brother who was so famous and I don't want to sound as if the press made our lives a constant misery. But there were pressures.

Inevitably, perhaps, Ian, as the only other boy in the family, became the focus of speculation about his own football skills. He recalls: 'When I was at primary school, we started a football team with headmaster Mr Parkinson who was also a referee. I was picked to play and it was the first time in years that the primary school had had a football team.

'We played our first match at home and I think the score was 3-1 to us. I scored two. What a start to the League! We went on to win every game we played. I ended up being joint top goal scorer with a lad called Paul Wilson. I think it was forty-nine goals each we scored. I also played for Cregagh Boys, as did George.

'Then I did my first newspaper interview with the News of the World. But that was enough for me. I knew then that I just didn't want the attention.

'At secondary school, I'd been asked to play for the school team. I was happy enough playing — especially when I was told if I did not go to the football practice, I would be put in detention. However, I didn't play for the school for long.

'And while I also played for Cregagh Boys for a time, I eventually gave that up too even though I was asked to go for trials. Dad left it up to me, but I rejected the offers. I didn't want to be known as George Best's brother. That was the way people treated me when I did play.'

George always said that Ian had real talent and he regretted that he didn't pursue a career in football. Dad was disappointed too. But like George he understood fully what was behind Ian's decision. George also said that he was immensely proud of Ian for sticking to his principles. From the day Ian said he wasn't playing football again, he never did.

Ian was also a good golfer, though, and he recalls one occasion when George landed him in trouble over an impromptu practice session: 'I was about thirteen years old and I was into playing golf. George and I went up to a nearby field to knock a few golf balls about. George had never played golf or swung a club before but he took the club and hit that little white ball with such force it cleared the field.

'He then hit a couple more not knowing where they had landed. That was until this gentleman came storming across the field shouting at me because I now had the club in my hand.

'I got a right mouthful from the man until George stepped in and explained that he was the one who had hit the balls. The gentleman said, "No problem, George. Really that's not a problem."

'As if I could have cleared the field anyway at the age I was then....'

We were quite a sporting family. Julie was very good at Irish dancing and won many medals in competitions. And I mentioned earlier my own interest and success in hockey and netball. However, the one in our family who had the most success in football — apart from George — was actually Grace.

At the time when she took that trip to LA to see George and watched him play at Anaheim, she was playing herself for a team called Post Office Ladies, then top of the women's league. In 1979, she was selected to play for the Northern Ireland Under-18 Ladies' Squad. Grace played in two international matches against the Republic of Ireland, scoring in one of them. And ironically she wore the number 11 green jersey of Northern Ireland — the same as our famous brother!

Apart from having the same blue eyes as George, Grace always felt that this was something unique the two of them shared. Sadly, as she says, her international career ended not so long after that when she got married and had her own family.

On the occasions when George came back to Belfast, he just relaxed at home. He didn't go out much, although at times Dad would take him down to his local social clubs, but this was very difficult, as they didn't get much peace. It was always the same: it was impossible to have a quiet evening out. It wasn't possible for George to have a drink at home either, as Dad refused to have alcohol in the house. To this day, Dad won't drink either alone or at home.

Ian remembers one way in which George used to relax: 'I remember George would sit on the floor and ask any one of us to comb his hair. If you were to do it, you would be there for hours as George used to just love his hair being brushed.'

The family went a couple of times to Manchester for Christmas and would spend some time with George, usually going out together for Christmas dinner to a restaurant. Ian remembers that at Belfast Airport security would insist that all the presents be opened. The younger ones had to turn their backs while the checks were being carried out so that they wouldn't see what Santa had got them.

Our younger brother made the most of his time in Manchester: 'I would ask George to take me with him when he went out. I used to go to his nightclubs Slack Alice and Blondes during the day and stuff myself with crisps and Coke. I used to think it was great being out with George as a young lad. I was always very proud of him.'

He recalls, 'The thing about being with George was that no matter where we went, we were treated as if we were George himself.'

As mentioned earlier, George always had endless patience with fans and autograph hunters. He loved to talk to people — especially about football. It was very rare that he would have been reluctant to make time for anyone who wanted a chat.

Ian says, 'George was always polite to people even when we were trying to eat our meal and fans would come up to ask for an autograph. To me it seemed one of the most annoying things. George could never finish a meal once people started to ask for autographs or his meal would be really cold by the time he'd finished. Yet he had this endless patience. He really did respect the fans and always had time for them.'

Back home in Belfast, George got a marvellous reception. In all, he was to be capped thirty-seven times for Northern Ireland. Ian remembers the typical atmosphere during one international game at Windsor Park: 'Dad and I had gone into the players' lounge to see

George but Dad had asked me to go back out and get Mum. The main entrance at Windsor Park was surrounded by autograph hunters waiting for the players to leave the ground. I found Mum but we then had to fight our way back through, even pushing a policeman out of the way!

'I just got hold of Mum's hand and led the way through the crowd. As you would expect, people were not happy, thinking I was trying to get to best advantage point. However, as we got close to the entrance, the security man recognised us and came to help. "Let Mrs Best through," he said. And as soon as he spoke, it was like the Red Sea parting. Everyone just stepped aside. Needless to say, it was never like that when we were with George. People would just swamp us and it would be impossible to move.'

Ian also remembers another mêlée, this time at the King's Hall in Belfast when George was there to take part in a promotion at a local motor show for the car firm, Saab: 'Grace and I had gone to see George. The place was packed with people who had come to see George, not the motor show. When we got to the Saab stand, people were laying siege to the table where George was to be stationed. But he had not arrived and it was bedlam.

'When he did arrive, he had to be escorted to the table. I got hold of Grace and made our way to the front, calling out to George. He asked people to stand aside to let my sister and me through.'

Ian explains what it's like sharing a surname with George: 'Being George's brother, you always get the same questions. For a start, "Are you really George's brother?"

'People are understandably interested in him. But the questions sometimes just go on and on. "What is the age gap?" "Do you play football yourself?"

'Most people ask out of genuine interest. But there are some who are just damned rude. They have to tell you what they think of George and his battle with alcoholism. Often they say deeply hurtful things. I often wonder how they would like it if I was to hit back about someone in their own family.

'The thing is, and I've always known this because I grew up with it — some people think because they've met George once or even just seen him on TV that they knew him intimately and that this entitles them to ask the most intrusive questions. Most people only ask questions out of genuine interest. But there are some who don't know where to draw the line. There is a stage where I get to and I can't bear the questions so I just don't answer them.'

Grace points out that over the years when people have been told that she's George Best's sister, the usual response has been, 'No, you're not!'

She adds: 'I get bombarded with questions trying to catch me out. "When's his birthday?" "What's his son's name?" "Where does he live?"'

She recalls that when she was in hospital having her second child, Lyndsay, 'the girl in the bed opposite me went through the questioning routine. I told her if she didn't believe me, fine; I was fed up trying to prove it. At visiting time, our dad came up with my eldest child, Andrew. After they'd gone, the girl came over and asked if the "wee man" who'd visited me was Dickie Best. Her mum had recognised him. She believed me after that.

'The next day, a big floral arrangement arrived with a card reading, "Family now complete, love George."

'That night, while I was asleep, the girl pinched one of the flowers. She owned up the next day — but asked if she could keep it because George sent it!'

However, Ian also remembers feeling let down by our brother: 'There were times when George would say he was coming home and then he would not turn up. There were times when he said he would meet up with me somewhere, but again, he'd fail to show. That was infuriating as you just felt he'd let you down. But George was also the most generous and polite person you could meet. He did a lot of good work behind the scenes but that never got the headlines. Over the years it was so hard to read criticism of my brother or to hear other people put him down, knowing it was unfair and that those making the comments didn't know the real George or had never even met him.'

George had his faults and he may occasionally have let some of the family down over the years. But he tried to be loving and supportive to all of us — not least to the younger ones who were born after he'd left for England.

Even though the support may have been sporadic, there were occasions when he turned up when it mattered most. Ian points out: 'My proudest moment was when I was doing my military training in Junior Leaders' Regiment in Bovington, Dorset. When it came to the day of my passing-out parade, George turned up with our dad to see me. True, his being there did take the spotlight off the parade slightly. But hey, I didn't care. My brother was there to see me. That was all that mattered.'

Of all the tragedies to engulf our family, none was more poignant than the sudden death in 1996 of our little niece Ashleigh, the daughter of Grace and her husband David. Ashleigh, who was only six when she died, was born with a condition known as hydrocephalus. This was discovered before her birth, and it was impossible for the medical team to give Grace and David an accurate and honest assessment of what the future held for Ashleigh. It was going to be a matter of time to see how things turned out.

It was very difficult for them. I think that they prepared themselves for the worst. It was a waiting game. However, Ashleigh progressed really well. As the months and years went on, she was leading practically a normal life. She had a slight paralysis on one side and was doing well at school where educationally she was only about six months behind for her age.

She was the most lovable child, affectionate, full of fun, always smiling. We all adored her. Especially George. Grace says: 'Mum never got to meet my own children and that makes me sad. But my children, Andrew, Lyndsay, Ashleigh and Connor, did meet George and Alex, and of them I know that the one who captured George's heart most was our third child, Ashleigh.'

Ashleigh was just full of life and love and her first encounter with Alex, whom she couldn't wait to meet, was just typical of her. Grace recalls: 'George and Alex had just arrived to visit Dad. As soon as school was over, Ashleigh bounded into the house and threw her arms around her Uncle George's neck.

'"Where's Alex?" she cried.

'"Alex is right behind you!" George laughed. "You ran right past her!"

'Ashleigh rushed over to Alex and gave her an enormous hug and told them both that she loved them. Alex just burst into tears.'

My sister adds, 'Ashleigh was such a lovable child and I'm so glad that they got to know and meet her.'

In 1996, Ashleigh was admitted to hospital for routine treatment. As Grace explains: 'On 19 May 1996, our wee angel died suddenly in hospital. She was just six years old. That was by far the worst day of my life. And even now, ten years on, I struggle to come to terms with it.' Her death shocked and devastated the entire family.

By tragic coincidence, her funeral was on 22 May — George's fiftieth birthday. Grace says: 'George called me regularly over the next few days expressing his sorrow, offering his help and assuring us that he would come over for the funeral. But it was already obvious that was not a good idea. The press were gathering outside my home. And on the morning of the funeral itself, George phoned to say that they were camped outside his house too. He thought it best not to come as it would turn what should be Ashleigh's day into a circus. My husband David and I totally agreed with him.

'George and Alex sent a beautiful wreath with a card that read, "A special little lady". And that's exactly what Ashleigh was.

'I was so touched that George recalled her in his autobiography, *Blessed,* where he described her as "the greatest little kid I ever met".'

But George was also to provide Grace with support of a more practical kind, as she explains: 'After Ashleigh died, there was an investigation into the care she'd received in hospital prior to her death. We needed an independent report from a doctor in England but it would cost £1,500 — money which David and I just didn't have. Our dad was always very loath to ask George for money but on that occasion he phoned him and told him about the case. Without hesitation, George said he would pick up the bill.'

Grace tells another story which illustrates George's generosity and thoughtfulness: 'Our youngest son, Connor, is a talented little golfer. He started playing golf when he was eight and for that Christmas he got a half set of junior clubs. He started entering competitions against kids a number of years older and won quite a few.

'In 2002, George was again the subject of the *This Is Your Life* show. At the dinner that followed, he got chatting to Connor about his golf. He asked him what sort of clubs he was using and, when he heard, he said they were much too small. George reached into his inside pocket, produced £300, and told Connor he was to use it to buy himself a new set of clubs. When we arrived back home from the show, we had to drive straight from the airport to the golf shop to buy the clubs for Connor.

'To this day, we are so grateful to George for that. With his new clubs that season, Connor went on to win seven competitions including the

The twins with Mum, Dad and George. George is holding Grace; Dad is holding Julie. This was taken at an event to launch a range of George Best themed products, including footballs with his picture.

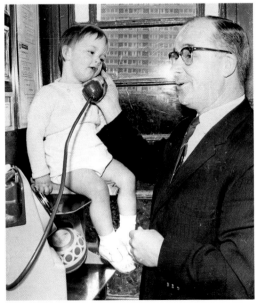

Toddler Ian chats with his big brother, while Dad looks on. We didn't have a phone at home, so we used the local call box to keep in touch.

George arriving with the Manchester
United team for an away game.

The height of fashion: George in the early
1960s. (*Kenneth Wheeler Ltd*)

Big heart: George gave his Northern Ireland shirt from the famous game against Scotland to John Doherty, a young local boy who was ill in hospital. Years later they met up again in a television studio where John told George how much he'd treasured that shirt and how he'd never forgotten his kindness. *(Belfast Telegraph)*

MANCHESTER UNITED FOOTBALL CLUB

European Champion Clubs Cup Final — 1968

Please allow bearer to board the Special Train at EUSTON STATION reserved for the Official Party and leaving at 5-35 p.m.

L. Olive
Secretary.

Just the ticket: Dad's team ticket to the European Cup Final in 1968.

George is honoured at a civic reception in Belfast City Hall in June 1968, following the European Cup success. Looking on is the then Lord Mayor of Belfast, Alderman William Geddes. (*Newsletter*)

Loving mother, loving son: this treasured family picture was taken in the summer of 1970, at Mum and Dad's silver wedding anniversary party. (*Daily Mirror*)

Best on the ball: George confounds the opposition with one of his trademark mazy runs, 9 December 1970. (*Getty Images*)

Pop idol: with his football talent and pop-star looks, no wonder George attracted the girls. This photograph, taken by renowned Manchester photographer Harry Goodwin, the official photographer to *Top of the Pops* between 1964 and 1973, is one of my favourite pictures of George. (*Harry Goodwin*)

My hero: Martina, the little girl in this 1976 photograph, had cerebral palsy, and said she would only walk for George Best. Here, she gets a hug from her hero.

A visit to Millington Primary School in Portadown, Co. Armagh, 1981.

Father and son: George and Calum.

LOVING BROTHER, LOYAL FRIEND   135

Wee Wonders, All-Ireland Final in 2004. His prize was to play in the UK
final at St Andrews in Scotland. In the event, he came third in the
eleven- to twelve-year-old boys' category with a level par round. George
phoned to say that he would pay the cost of our trip to Scotland and
again David and I will always be grateful to him for that.'

It wasn't only for his kindness and generosity that the family
remembers George, though. There was also his great sense of humour.
Grace recalls: 'On one visit home George asked me where he could go
to get something good for a takeaway meal. I told him about our local
Indian restaurant where we go regularly. Fifteen minutes later, the
owner called me in great excitement. "You'll never guess who's in my
restaurant!" he said.

'Dad had driven George down to the place in the car and, while he
was parking, George went on inside. Once inside, George ordered the
takeaway. And a glass of wine. When Dad came in, George quickly hid
the glass of wine behind the counter!

'Once the food was ready, the pair of them left. But George told Dad
he'd forgotten to give the guy a tip. So he went back in and tipped him.
And he also tipped back the glass of wine.

'George wasn't going to leave a glass of wine unfinished!'

Grace says that next to Ashleigh's death, watching George die was
the hardest thing she's ever had to face. But like the rest of our family,
her memories of our brother will always be precious and special: 'I will
always be so proud and count it as a privilege to have had George as my
big brother and to have been a small part of his life.'

It's not only members of our immediate family who recall this private
side of George — the kindness and support he showed down through
the years. Bobby McAlinden paid a very moving tribute, at George's
funeral, to the loyalty and generosity of the man who had been his
friend for over forty-six years.

Bobby and George first met when they were both fifteen. George was
playing outside right for Manchester United B team and Bobby outside
left for Manchester City. After that match, they shook hands, and went
to their respective dressing rooms. But it was to be the start of a long
friendship, which grew over the years. By his own admission, Bobby
recognised that he was never going to be a top-flight footballer but this
never mattered to George, and their friendship blossomed. What made

it even more special was that the two of them shared exactly the same birthday — 22 May 1946.

Bobby recalls the time when George first told him that he had decided to go to the States to play. It was shortly after he'd famously parted company with Manchester United. Bobby told him that he thought it was a great idea but was taken aback when George said, 'I want you to come and play as well.' For a start, Bobby hadn't played for over a year. But that didn't bother George. He told Bobby to go away and over the following couple of months to get as fit as he could. George assured him that he would negotiate a one-year contract for him in the US. At the time, for Bobby, a one-year contract anywhere would have been very welcome. And, true to his word, George secured the contract. Three months later, the pair of them arrived in Los Angeles.

Bobby says, 'Even at this point, I felt that, if George never did anything again for me in his life, I would never be able to repay him.' They shared accommodation together for the first year and Bobby recalls, 'What was his, was mine. If he didn't have it, I had and vice versa.'

Just before the start of their second season in the States, the lease was about to run out on their accommodation and they needed to look for somewhere new. They had gone to see a very nice, two-bedroom apartment which they both really liked. The estate agent suggested that if they liked it that much, they should consider buying it. George instantly thought that this was a great idea.

'We're going to buy it,' he decided. 'Why pay rent when we can own it? Besides it's a good investment which could make us some money.'

Bobby agreed that it would be a good investment. His problem was that he couldn't afford his share of the down-payment. But George told him not to worry, saying that he would pay and Bobby could pay him back when he was able.

Bobby recalls, 'First of all, he made me his team-mate, then his room-mate and now we were equal partners in a really desirable piece of property in one of the nicest areas of California. Another example of how good a man he was. Yet, everything he did, he did in a quiet way. He was never flashy.'

Back then, so many people were trying to get George interested in so many different business ventures, but he was never really interested.

One day, someone came along with a proposal which George liked, but he said he would get involved only on condition that Bobby was also involved. So it was agreed. Bobby says, 'George knew that I loved the American way of life. He knew I wanted to stay and that the football wasn't going to last forever. It was his way of ensuring that once the football finished that I was going to have something with a future.'

George returned to England to live, but Bobby stayed in the US where he still lives. Even though they were leading separate lives again, they spoke regularly on the phone. Bobby remembers one call that came in the middle of the night: it was George ringing to say, 'Happy Birthday'. Every year after that, without fail, George would ring him on his birthday.

In his funeral tribute Bobby pointed out, 'Sadly, I'll not get that call next year. But I've got my memories. I felt especially honoured when George asked me to be his best man when he married Angie. All of those memories are great. No one had a friend as good as George was to me.'

One of the big regrets I have had, as I mentioned before, was that for a number of years I did not keep in regular contact with George. By the 1970s, our lives had literally gone in different directions. He was living in the US and I was living for a time in South Africa. It was perhaps inevitable that we would find it harder and harder to keep in touch. We were caught up with our own lives, and I just picked up whatever news I could about him from back home.

But that situation was to change. Encouraged by my husband Norman, I got back in touch with George. It was a decision that I will always be glad that I made. It gave me back my beloved brother and, for the last two decades of his life, the three of us, Norman, George and I, were to share some very special times.

Chapter 9 ∾

REKINDLING THE
RELATIONSHIP

I had been living in South Africa since 1974, but reluctantly decided to return to Belfast. My first marriage was already strained and, pregnant with my second child, I thought that coming home might help to stabilise the relationship. I arrived back in March 1980, and Jenny was born that October. The following year, my family was complete with the arrival of Paul. Sadly, in the long run, my marriage to Jim did not survive.

We didn't see much of George over the next few years. His own life was quite turbulent. He faced bankruptcy in 1982. But worse was to follow. Arrested for drink driving, he had also been charged with assaulting a police officer. On 17 December 1984, he was sent to Pentonville Prison where he spent that Christmas. Eventually he was transferred to Ford Open Prison until his release in 1985.

I was devastated. I just couldn't take on board that my brother was in prison. Carol and I spoke on the phone the day he was sentenced and we were both tearful. We wrote to him and sent Christmas cards. It was very difficult to know what to say to him, but we tried to keep his spirits up. Deep down, though, I was really worried about where it was all going to end. His marriage to Angie gradually deteriorated, and they finally divorced in 1986.

When I met Norman McNarry in 1984, as with so many other friends and acquaintances previously, it was some time before I told him that George was my brother. Norman and I had actually been seeing each other for a considerable time before I got round to telling him.

One evening, we were sitting quietly watching television. There was a documentary about George on and I really wanted to watch it. Unfortunately there was a rugby match on the other channel at the same time. And Norman is a big rugby fan. Anyway, I said to him, 'Can you switch channels, please? I'd like to watch the programme about George Best.'

Norman looked a bit surprised but he didn't say anything and changed channels. About halfway through the programme, he suddenly said, 'I didn't know that you were so interested in George Best. You seem to know an awful lot about him. Why did you want to watch this programme? I want to see the rugby.'

I was so embarrassed I couldn't even look at Norman. In a small voice, I said, 'I want to watch it because he's my brother.'

I could feel Norman's eyes boring into me but he said nothing as we sat there watching the rest of the programme. I was sure he was thinking to himself: 'I have a right one here.'

And indeed he was. As he explained later, in his own inimitable fashion, what he was actually thinking at the time was: 'She's a nice girl. But obviously barking!'

Later we talked about George and I opened up about the now quite detached relationship I had with him. I explained to Norman that neither I nor indeed any of the family saw very much of him at that time. He was doing his own thing, he had his own problems. From my perspective back in Belfast, I couldn't see that he would really want or need us much in his life.

But over the coming months as we spoke about it more, Norman, realising how much I missed my brother, began to encourage me to consider getting in touch with him again — at least to attempt to re-establish some sort of relationship.

At first, I just flatly refused to do this. I really was convinced that if George wanted to, he would call us. But gradually I began to think that maybe it was up to me, too, to make more of an effort.

Norman and I had been to London on a number of occasions, but I still found it difficult to call George to let him know we were there. I remember thinking, on our way home from one of these trips, how sad it was that I wasn't making any effort to contact my brother and I vowed that the next time that we were going to London, I would definitely call him.

I was really nervous about making that first phone call. Bearing in mind that it was approximately twenty-five years since George had left Belfast, it would be an understatement to say that a lot of water had passed under the bridge since then. If we were to meet up, it would be a case of getting to know each other all over again. And the reality was that, even though he was my brother, I was quite in awe of him — not sure if he would really want to know.

However, I made the call. I explained that Norman and I were coming to London and would love to meet up with him. He was living in a flat in Chelsea just off the King's Road at the time, and so we made arrangements to meet him in his local pub, the Phene Arms.

I was nervous, worrying about what we were going to talk about after such a long time. In fact, I was convinced that he wouldn't even turn up. But as soon as we went into the pub, I spotted him. He was waiting for us with his partner at that time, Mary Shatila. We all had a meal and a few drinks together, and then Mary suggested that we go back to the flat for a coffee.

We had been in the flat for only about ten minutes when, all of a sudden, George stood up and said to Mary: 'Can you get Barbara and Norman a taxi?' With that, he sauntered off to bed.

Mary and I just looked at each other. She was absolutely mortified and started to apologise. Even though I was equally embarrassed, to try to lessen her obvious discomfort, I said, 'Don't you worry about that. I don't mind.'

But I did. I minded deeply.

We left the flat and returned to the hotel. I was feeling hurt and had decided that I had done my bit — that there was no point in trying any more.

However, first thing next morning, the phone rang in our hotel room. It was George. 'Hi there, darlin'. Sorry about last night. Would you and Norman like to meet for lunch today?'

At first I felt like telling him where to go. But again I agreed to meet him. I was so glad that I did. We had a lovely lunch in a very popular Italian restaurant on the King's Road called Pucci's. George was in much better form and, as was to be the pattern with him from then on, I could never stay angry with him for long. We didn't mention the incident from the previous evening.

And Norman and I both got on quite well with Mary although I was never convinced that George was completely serious about their relationship.

Even though Norman was the one who had encouraged me to get in touch with George, he himself hadn't been sure what to expect. In the beginning, he had feared that he was going to meet someone who was full of his own importance — big-headed and arrogant. The incident in the flat seemed to confirm that suspicion. Admittedly it wasn't a great start, but I am thankful that it improved.

Very quickly, Norman realised that George was one of the most down-to-earth people that he had ever met, with absolutely no airs and graces and very easy to get on with. Over the years, the pair of them built up a healthy respect and genuine fondness for each other.

Meanwhile, bit by bit, I was gradually getting to know George again. It wasn't anything spectacular at the start. We just took things very gently. Each time Norman and I went to London, we would meet up for a meal. Sometimes I would ring in advance, and other times we would just turn up at the pub and hope that he would be there. We never had a repeat performance of that first visit.

And then one night in the Phene Arms, as we sat talking, he suddenly put his arms round me in front of everyone and, in a boyish way, proudly announced to the company: 'This is my sister.'

I'll never forget that moment. The years had rolled away. He was no longer George Best, the football superstar. Or George Best, the distant celebrity. He was my brother George.

Inwardly I was so pleased that things were progressing well. Ours was a no-pressure, very relaxed relationship and, over the next twenty-odd years, a close and trusting one. I take great comfort now from the fact that over those years I never did or said anything that would have hurt him. No matter what he did, while sometimes privately I would have been really mad with him, publicly I never let him down.

I never asked for anything from George other than his company and his time. And I'm sure he recognised and appreciated this.

On 8 August 1988, George came back to Belfast for his testimonial match at Windsor Park in Belfast. He brought Calum, who was then just seven and a half years old, over with him. Calum was such a lovely little boy, with a mop of blond hair, and so well-mannered. George had to fly back to London for a meeting, so Calum stayed with Norman and me. He and my son Steven got on really well.

The match was a complete sell-out. The crowd gave George a rousing reception and it was a proud moment for us all to see Calum and George running out on to the pitch where he had shown his superb skills playing for Northern Ireland in the 1960s and 1970s.

Grace has very fond memories of the match. She was sitting beside Sir Matt Busby and Bob Bishop. It was such an honour to have Sir Matt there. Everyone knows of the relationship that George had with him and that he had so much affection and respect for Sir Matt. He once described the man he called the Boss this way: 'He can remain aloof and yet human. He can tear us apart and still command respect. He can praise us and we know he is genuine. He can advise us and we know that there is no dark motive afoot.'

Grace recalls that the match programme had billed an appearance by a mystery guest. This turned out to be Willie Henderson who entertained the crowd by trapping the ball with his bum! An interesting skill.

However, my sister also vividly remembers that George showed a lot of his own unique skills and how the entire crowd rose to applaud him. She says that she cried that evening not just for the pride that she felt for George but also for the one person not there to share it: our mum.

It was a great tribute, and meant much to George that he was given the testimonial at Windsor Park. I have often wondered why the same privilege was not afforded to him by the club which he loved so dearly. Even though some people regard his career to have been relatively short at Manchester United, I believe that the service he gave to that club should have been recognised.

In the run-up to the testimonial match in Belfast, George had stopped drinking for many months. I remember looking at him and thinking how fit and healthy he was. I remember thinking, if only it would last…

Sadly, though, as so often in the past, his addiction to alcohol once again took control. His escapades continued to make the headlines. In a way, we had become used to it. But for me, one of the most awful incidents was an infamous television appearance in September 1990. I remember keenly the horror I felt watching Terry Wogan's prime-time TV chat show that night.

George, as I'm sure many people remember, was very, very drunk. It was obvious from the moment he walked on. And it would be fair to say that he made a complete idiot of himself. However, the embarrassment and the distress that I felt as I watched him were totally eclipsed by my anger. Anger not at George, but at the people in charge of that show who allowed him to go on live television in that state.

Looking back, it is hard to believe that, given George's well-documented drink problem, he was kept in a room with easy access to alcohol for such a long time before the show went on air. I often wonder when I look back at it if the show's organisers have ever felt a twinge of guilt about it. Or did they just think it made for a bit of controversy and publicity for the programme? I felt embarrassed watching my brother that night. But I believe that others have had more reason to feel shame when that clip was shown over the years.

George's relationship with Mary Shatila eventually came to grief. By now, he had met Alex Pursey who, in 1995, became his second wife. Alex was obviously much younger than George, but Norman and I, who met her a few times before their marriage, both got on well with her and didn't see the age gap as a problem. However, we weren't invited to their wedding. No one from our family was. I could never understand that. It just seemed sad that none of us was there for such a special occasion.

But it didn't make any difference to our relationship. We still continued to see each other every time Norman and I were in London. Instead of meeting up with George and Mary, it was now George and Alex. They had moved from the flat in Oakley Street to their new place, a lovely one-bedroom basement apartment in the very up-market Cheyne Walk in Chelsea.

I loved the apartment. One very significant step for me was that George and Alex said that anytime we were in London and they were away (which was quite a lot), we could use the apartment instead of paying for expensive hotels. To me, it wasn't about saving money. It was a sign of George's trust. And that meant more than anything.

In February 2000, George became very ill and had to attend the Cromwell Hospital in London for an appointment. He was so ill by that stage that Professor Roger Williams didn't even have to examine him. He knew to look at him how very sick George was, and he admitted him straight away. Tests were carried out which confirmed just how seriously damaged George's liver was. It was to be a long stay in hospital. And when George was allowed to go home, his liver was only partially working.

The months that followed that spell in hospital were obviously very difficult and testing for both George and Alex. There seemed to be a lot of fall-outs between them. One of these rows resulted in George flying home to see the family. He seemed to me to be very unhappy — unsettled and emotional. He told us that he wanted to get a wee place back in Northern Ireland, possibly a mobile home in Millisle, one of the seaside resorts where we had spent many happy times as children.

Norman and I were a bit taken aback at this. We just couldn't imagine George in a mobile home, especially during the summer months when the site would be crowded with visitors. What privacy would he have when it, and all the campsites in the area, would be jam-packed? Still, if that was what he wanted…

We took him along to view some, which were really lovely. Obviously mobile homes today are quite different from the ones we remembered from our childhood. With every modern convenience imaginable — en suite bathrooms, double glazing, central heating, you name it — it was all a far cry from the days when we had to go to the frog-infested well at Granny's house in the country to fetch water.

George was really excited. Even though he had come back to Northern Ireland because of a row between himself and Alex, he said that he would return to England to talk to her about the possibility of investing in a mobile home in Millisle. I somehow got the impression that he wouldn't win that one! But I was hoping that he would indeed come back to Northern Ireland.

And yet I had the feeling that George was striving to find something other than a place back home. I felt that what he wanted was a project to give him something else to think about. He wasn't at all well by this stage. Perhaps he thought that this could be a way to help him stop drinking. Or maybe by going back to a place which had meant so much to him in those long-distant days of childhood, he was trying to find a peace within himself.

Shortly after this visit, George called us to say that he and Alex had decided to buy, not a mobile home, but a house instead. They were flying over to Northern Ireland to look at properties. They already knew the sort of thing they wanted. It had to be near to the coast, and preferably overlooking the sea.

Carol and I contacted a local estate agent close to where she lives in Co. Down and collected lots of brochures for suitable properties in the area. Norman set up appointments with the owners of the houses, and George and Alex then flew back to Northern Ireland to have a look. In hindsight, it was really quite funny, as we made the appointments in our own name — McNarry. Obviously therefore the owners had no idea that it was George who was coming. Their reactions were a picture, but George, in his usual manner, put everyone at ease.

Having viewed several properties, George and Alex felt that none of them was suitable. There was just one left but we hadn't made an appointment as we thought that it might be a little bit too quiet for them. It was on the outskirts of Portavogie, the fishing village where Carol and Allen were living. From the brochure George and Alex both liked the look of the house, so we decided to take a chance and call without an appointment. Norman went to the door, apologised for the intrusion and asked if it might be possible to view the house. The owner's son seemed about to ask us to make an appointment when George got out of the car, and of course, we were all ushered in.

I knew instantly that both George and Alex had fallen for the place. It was a lovely house — big, bright and beautifully presented. It was on a substantial plot of land and, even better, it had a spectacular site — quite high up with a fabulous view of the sea. Their eyes just lit up. The owner was called George Donnan. We all sat down in the kitchen with his son Colin and, within fifteen minutes, the deal was done.

I was so pleased and really excited about the prospect of having George back home. Deep down, I wasn't honestly sure if it was going to work for them. But if it helped George to stay off the drink, it was worth a try.

Things moved very quickly indeed. I organised a solicitor for them and, within a couple of months, by September 2000, the Bests were resident in the fishing village of Portavogie.

The weeks that followed were just great fun. George was like a child in a toyshop. He was really happy shopping for furniture and carpets, buying knick-knacks, and constantly calling in to the garden centre in Donaghadee. They both loved visiting the village of Greyabbey, which has several quaint antique shops where they picked up many great bits and pieces for their new home. Alex, in particular, was amazed at how reasonably priced things were compared to London.

Auction houses became favourite haunts as well. I remember on one occasion I had to go with Alex to an auction as George had gone back to London for his job — commentating for Sky. George had spotted a lovely old butter churn which he really wanted and I had been nominated to do the bidding. The estimated price was set at £75 but in the end I got into a bidding war with someone else and had to pay over £300 for it. But Alex and I daren't go home without it!

I used to say to George that it wouldn't be safe to let him loose at an auction because of his naturally competitive nature. He wouldn't let anyone outbid him and would probably have ended up paying way over the value of things. Not that I can talk!

The months wore on, and Norman and I spent some great times with George and Alex. We used to eat out a lot together. I don't think that there was a restaurant in the Ards Peninsula or, in fact, the entire Co. Down that didn't get a visit! One of our favourite haunts was a lovely little pub and restaurant in Donaghadee, called Grace Neill's, which is reputedly the oldest pub in Ireland. The owner at the time, Stephen Jeffers, who is an amazing chef, looked after George really well. I remember George telling me that Stephen wouldn't serve him alcohol when he went into the pub on one occasion.

While George and Alex just loved eating out and we loved being with them, it was a costly business. Norman and I always insisted on paying our own way and would only occasionally let them pay if we had done something big to help them out. I didn't care about the money as it was just so good to have George back again. It was special being part of his life.

There was one night which I remember in particular. Ulster were playing Cardiff in a Heineken Cup match. George and Alex had called to see if we wanted to go out for a meal, but we had to say no as we were going to the rugby. We asked them if they'd like to join us, never thinking that they would say yes. But course they did. However, there was one problem: the match was sold out.

Norman phoned Michael Reid (Chief Executive of the Ulster Branch of the IRFU) to try to get two tickets, but no luck. Norman said that they were for my brother — but Michael didn't know that my brother was George Best. Still no luck. Norman finally said that they were for George and instantly things moved. We all got seats in the officials' box. Norman and I passed our tickets on to another couple of fans.

Norman was really taken aback that night when, after it was announced over the speaker system that George Best was in the crowd, people cheered and gave him a standing ovation. For the first time, Norman could understand — could see and hear and feel — just how highly thought of George was. He remembers talking to Michael Reid that night and saying, 'It will give George a chance to meet the players.'

'No, Norman,' Michael replied. 'It's the other way round. It will give the players a chance to meet George Best.'

Cardiff were beaten that night, 32-23. I will never forget the look on Neil Jenkins's face back in the clubhouse after the match when he saw George. He was mesmerised. Unfortunately we had to leave early, though, as George was feeling unwell. David Humphreys was man of the match and I would have loved George to have been able to present him with the award.

Although George wasn't drinking at the time, he loved to go along to a local pub and restaurant called The Quays, to have a game of pool with the locals in the village. The owner, Francis Adair, told us that he will never forget the first day that George walked into the pub. It was about four weeks after he and Alex had arrived in Portavogie and George went over to Francis, shook hands with him and said, 'Hi, I'm George Best. Nice to meet you.'

Francis still smiles at the memory and can't believe that George felt he had to do this. At the start, Francis gave him table number six which was in a quiet corner of the pub. But it was just a bit too quiet so George moved himself to another one where he could see what was going on in the bar. Ironically it was table number 7. And it was close to the fire, which suited George as he was always cold.

He was really loved by the locals who treated him just like one of their own. They didn't make any special allowances for him — he had to wait his turn to play a game just like anyone else. He was very good at pool and, from what I've been told, very hard to beat. That was until the night a girl called Gillian came along. She'd been in the pub one evening and someone said, 'George, Gillian will give you a game.'

'No problem,' said George.

Gillian beat him hands down. George, who was always so

competitive, just couldn't believe it. In the end, the boys had to come clean and tell him that actually Gillian had been the European Ladies' Champion. I think he eventually saw the funny side!

The locals in the pub always respected George's privacy. No one ever took advantage of him. No photographs were ever taken. He was left in peace. As Francis put it, 'The Quays was George's castle because when he was inside it, he was protected.'

Francis says that, at the start, George seldom drank in the pub. He was generally quite happy to wander in and out, have a game with the lads, and have a chicken curry, which he loved. But it didn't last. Once again, his drinking was spiralling out of control. Francis and the rest of the staff tried their best to look after George during this time. But the extent to which they were limited in their attempts to help him had such a darkly familiar ring.

One day, one of the staff said to him gently, 'George, maybe you shouldn't have that drink.'

George shrugged his shoulders and replied, 'No problem. I'll just go to the off-licence, buy a bottle and drink it on the beach.'

What can anyone do in a situation like that? At least if he was in the pub, we knew he was safe. We also knew that in an attempt to lower his consumption, people would water down George's drink. On occasion, it was even poured down the sink when he wasn't looking.

The staff tried so hard to help him. But alcoholics are never stuck for a drink. George consistently pointed out that if one person or pub refused to serve him, he would simply go on to the next one. Sometimes he used to pour his drink in a coffee cup. I suppose that was to disguise it in case Alex came in.

It used to amaze me, though, how many people would actually come up and offer to buy George drink. I remember one bizarre incident in Portavogie when someone left a few bottles of alcohol on their doorstep. I've heard of milk deliveries but that was just ridiculous.

When George was drinking, the staff at the pub always made sure that he was taken home safely. Wherever he needed to go to, they'd see that he got there safely. Francis remembers that quite often George would bring his dog into the pub. He had a beautiful red setter, appropriately called Red, who would be treated to sausages on his arrival. But quite often it was Francis or Davy, the chef in the restaurant, who had to take the dog home.

Everyone in the village looked out for George. A typical incident occurred one cold, bleak winter's evening. A local man had come across George walking along the road in the pitch dark on the way to the pub. He stopped to pick him up to make sure that he was safe. But he wouldn't encourage George's drinking by dropping him off at the pub, so he left him a short distance away, at the garage. The people of the area tried hard to protect George. Our family will always remember what they did for him.

Francis recalls that when George died, everyone in the village was devastated and, on the day of George's funeral, a candle was lit and placed on his favourite table. It burned all day — from the moment the doors were opened in the morning until they were closed again that evening. The pub was packed for most of the day but not one person sat at George's table.

In spite of all the support from the locals, it was obvious that George's drinking was getting worse. Alex and George were not getting on at all well, and she now decided to go back to London for a while. As Norman and I have two dogs of our own, we brought Red to our house to stay. We were worried that George couldn't cope. I felt really guilty as George loved that dog. He used to ring Carol and me and demand to know why Red couldn't come home. It was so sad.

Carol called regularly to make sure that George was okay and to bring him meals. She tried to talk to him about his drinking, reminding him that she was just getting her brother back and that she didn't want to lose him again in the same way that we had lost our mum. But George was defensive, saying that Mum had died suddenly overnight from heart problems and that he was fine and was going nowhere. That was always George's line — 'I'm not going anywhere.'

Eventually Alex came back from London, bringing her mum and dad for a bit of support. I got a call from her one day, begging us to come and try to talk to George. We agreed straight away, but when we got to the house, he had gone, and Alex said that she couldn't persuade him to come home.

It didn't take long to find him. He was in a Chinese restaurant in the village, on his own. Norman went in and sat and had a coffee as he chatted with him. He didn't try to put any pressure on George. That wouldn't have worked. Instead, he told him that I was in the car with our dogs, Duke and Prince, and that I was really worried about him. Norman suggested that we could go for a drive and then take him back home. But George became very agitated and said that he was afraid to go home. Obviously I am not in a position to know exactly what happened. But it was fairly clear that there had been some sort of altercation between the two of them.

We did go for a drive. And then we sat looking out over the sea until we finally talked George into going home. The atmosphere back at the house was frosty, to say the least.

During this period, needless to say, the media were having a field day. The locals in the village did their best to protect George and, it being a small village, they were quick to spot a strange face. Some of the reporters came into the pub, but they were soon ejected by a group of locals who called themselves 'The Press Gang'. George's house was constantly under siege and he couldn't get out. But, once again, the locals stepped in to protect him. To escape, George would phone the Chinese restaurant for a meal to be delivered. When it arrived, he would hide in the back of the van and manage to get out of the house that way. He would go to the pub where he'd be looked after until later, when the coast was clear, and Davy would take him home.

Once, when they got back to the house, they found that a reporter and a photographer were lurking on the doorstep. George was angry and demanded to know what they were doing there, pointing out that they were on private property. Davy says that the reporter became aggressive and tried to goad George, saying: 'Go on then; hit me.' Imagine the headlines if George had retaliated.

It was after that particular bout of drinking that George became quite ill. His immune system had been badly weakened and, having got drenched walking Red one day, he developed pneumonia. He was admitted to the Belfast City Hospital where he spent ten days. Once again, Red came to stay with us for a while to take the pressure off Alex a bit.

Things seemed to calm down after that, George stopped drinking and their lives appeared to get back to some sort of normality. Alex's birthday was approaching. For weeks, George and I had shared the secret of the treat he was planning for her — he was taking Alex on the Orient Express as a surprise. His excitement was infectious.

On the day that they were due to fly off, they stopped off for a cup of tea at our house. I was both shocked and worried when I saw George. Although he seemed to be in high spirits, physically he looked awful. His body was really swollen up — his feet so badly in fact that he couldn't get his shoes on, and Norman had to lend him some open sandals. Nothing, however, was going to stop him from making sure that Alex got her trip. They both thoroughly enjoyed it and I got an Orient Express teddy as a gift. It takes pride of place in our office at home.

When he and Alex returned, George had to go back to the Cromwell Hospital. The fluid was drained off and he phoned to let me know that things were okay. Although I can't remember how much fluid he told me they'd drained off, I remember being shocked that it was such a huge amount.

Obviously George still had to work, which meant travelling back to London quite a bit. And obviously the travelling soon began to take its toll. Alex also had to go back to London quite regularly, so Norman and I would help out by going down to stay in the house to look after Red. We loved staying in that house. Norman and I had on occasion looked at properties in the area ourselves, but because of my job it wasn't practical to travel on a daily basis. So it was always a treat for us to be able to stay in such a beautiful house with its amazing views. It was very peaceful.

For George and Alex, however, it was becoming apparent that living in Portavogie was anything but practical. We had gone out for a meal one evening to the Crawfordsburn Inn, another one of George's favourite restaurants, and suddenly he just casually dropped it in the conversation: 'We're going back to England.'

Although it wasn't a surprise, I was still very sad. We had had a great time and would really miss them both. But they assured us that we'd all keep in touch and that we could come over to visit them anytime.

The house was put on the market in December 2001. In reality, George and Alex had been back in England quite a while before that. It was sold early in the new year of 2002.

Meanwhile, on 13 December 2001, George was presented with an honorary degree by Queen's University in Belfast. Norman and I were invited to the conferring ceremony, and, although we couldn't make it for the lunch beforehand due to work commitments, nothing was going to keep us from supporting George at such a special occasion.

With Alex and Phil Hughes, we sat upstairs in the gallery of the Whitla Hall from where we had a bird's eye view of the academic procession.

I didn't know what to expect but when I saw George in his gown walking in the procession I was really choked up. The citation was extremely moving and I will always have that precious memory of seeing George on the stage with his hands folded in front of him, looking so shy. He had come such a very long way from that little house of ours in Burren Way. I thought of our mother and how very proud she would have been of the son who left to make his way in the world when he was only fifteen.

That evening, we all went out to celebrate at the well-known Cayenne restaurant in Belfast, which is owned by celebrity chef Paul Rankin.

On their return to England, George and Alex quickly found a beautiful house in Reigate in Surrey. Once again, George's enthusiasm in setting up a new home was infectious. He rang to tell us all about 'The Barn', as he called it, and urged us to come over to see it as soon as possible. However, his health had continued to deteriorate and by now he was on the stand-by list for a liver transplant.

Norman and I had gone to London to see a rugby match and, as we didn't have time to get to Surrey, we arranged to meet Alex and George at our hotel for a quick catch-up on the news. George had just come from an appointment with his transplant co-ordinator and he explained to me what the procedure would be. I was amazed how calmly he was able to talk about it. My own stomach was churning just thinking about it.

One of the stipulations of having a transplant was that George stayed off alcohol and this he was managing to do. I say 'managing' but deep down I knew that even though he was so ill, he was finding it a terrible struggle.

In April 2002, George was yet again honoured in Belfast by having the Freedom of the Borough of Castlereagh conferred upon him. It was an unforgettable day with most of the family attending the ceremony at the council offices. And George was thrilled when Denis Law turned up as a surprise guest. We all went to the nearby La Mon House hotel for lunch afterwards. The same hotel was to play a central role on the day of George's funeral.

When I look now at the photographs taken that day, they are a searing reminder of just how ill George was back then. He looked thin and drawn and tired. He seemed to tire very easily. Yet, true to form, he just got on with it all quietly and without complaining. He really enjoyed the day. We all did.

But always at the back of my mind at that time was that haunting fear about George's health. Without a liver transplant, he could not survive. Much as I dreaded the thought of the operation that might lie ahead, the thought of the alternative was unbearable.

Chapter 10 ∾

| TRANSPLANT

W hen George's autobiography, *Blessed*, was published, it was a huge success. Inevitably many people approached us to see if we could get George to sign their copies for them. At first, I was reluctant, as there were so many, but then I figured that if people had been prepared to buy the book, I should make the effort. I asked George if he would mind stopping off at our house one evening as I had a 'few' books to sign.

When he arrived, I was actually embarrassed when I brought him into our dining room. It was like a warehouse, with cardboard boxes piled high with the books.

'Sorry about this,' I mumbled. But he just gave me that cheeky smile and got stuck in to signing every single one of them.

No matter what the press said about him, it was obvious that the fans continued to retain an enormous affection for George. He had good friends too.

In 2002, Norman and I were invited over to 'The Barn' for a joint housewarming and birthday party for George. Although his birthday was on 22 May, it was decided to hold the bash at the weekend, on 25 May. George had been reasonably well for the couple of days before the party. But on the day itself, he wasn't too good at all. Yet he had no intention of postponing the event. Everything had been organised. The marquee was in place, special wines had been chosen and the caterers were organised. It was a beautiful, warm day, but George was so cold he had to have the fire lit in the house.

The guests arrived in the afternoon, and George, even though he felt very low, made such an effort to welcome them all and spend time with them. It was such a great mix of people. I met his doctor, Akeel, for the first time, as well as other old friends like Barbara Windsor and husband Scott, Errol Brown from Hot Chocolate and the actress Susan George with her husband Simon McCorkindale. And it was wonderful to meet up again with Stella and Graham, who had been landlords of George's local pub in Chelsea for many years and had looked after him so well.

Every now and again, George would disappear inside and just sit quietly by the fire. I nipped in to make him some tea and to have a wee chat with him. And that is one of the most cherished memories that I have — that incongruous scene on that lovely summer's day as the pair of us sat there by a roaring fire.

He started to talk to me a bit about the past, about how he once had a real crush on Lulu and how they'd got on really well together. One of the cherished mementoes which our family still has is a telegram sent to him by Lulu and dated 21 October 1967 (the day of the famous Northern Ireland v Scotland game). It reads: 'I know you should win, but against Scotland — are you kidding? Love Lulu.'

But more poignantly, as George talked to me that day, he also opened up to me about the woman who had been the one true love of his life. I didn't push him but just let him talk. After all, as I've mentioned several times, he was never a man to talk easily about his feelings. But sitting there by the fire as his guests milled around outside, he spoke frankly and with great emotion about something which has been rumoured and hinted at in the papers down through the years. He told me that he had a daughter.

She was born in 1969, but George told me that he had never had any contact with her. His eyes clouded with sadness, he explained to me how he had made a promise to the mother of the child that he would not try to get in touch. Listening to him that day, as he talked about the daughter he'd never met, I knew that his heart was aching.

We talked about the transplant, too. I asked him if he was worried about it and he just shrugged his shoulders. Did he miss having a drink?

'Yes I do,' he told me. 'But I have no choice now. I need to get better.'

'Don't worry,' I reassured him. 'You're doing really well, and you will get through this.'

However, when I saw George the next morning, I didn't feel quite so optimistic.

Although the caterers had done a splendid job leaving the kitchen neat and tidy, there was still a bit of clearing up to be done. Black bin bags full of rubbish had to be taken to the back of the house for collection. George was trying to help but he was so ill and weak that he couldn't even manage to lift them. It was one of the rare occasions when I ever heard him complain about feeling unwell. Weary and defeated, he sat at the breakfast bar in the kitchen. I could have cried for him. But of course I couldn't let him see the despair I felt. I just went over and hugged him.

After that, we saw George only once more before his transplant.

Norman, who has a great interest in history and, in particular, the Battle of the Somme, had taken me to Thiepval in 1996 to commemorate the battle on 1 July. That's when my love affair with France began.

We'd had a few more holidays there and, in 2001, we bought a mobile home at St Jeans del Monts in the Vendée region, on the Atlantic coast of France. The easiest way for us to get there was to travel from Belfast to Gatwick and then on to Nantes. George and Alex lived only about twenty minutes from the airport, so George came and collected us and we stayed the night with them before flying off to France the following day.

Just over six weeks later, George got the call to the hospital and, on 30 July 2002, he had his transplant. Dad received the call from Alex to say that George had been admitted. He then phoned me and I spoke very briefly to Alex to ask her to give George my love and let me know as soon as possible how things went.

It was to be a long wait. It was typical of George that nothing was ever straightforward with him. Complications occurred and he needed many pints of blood. The operation took much longer than anticipated. At one stage, the surgeons even 'lost' him. George told us later that he had an out-of-body experience where he was above the operating table looking down on himself.

Fortunately, he survived the operation and, a few days later, Norman, Carol and I flew to London to visit him. I was really nervous, but we were all amazed to see him looking so well. I had the privilege of meeting his surgeon, Nigel Heaton, an amazing and very down-to-earth man.

We all went for lunch together and the London cabbie wouldn't even take the fare. He had obviously recognised Alex.

Carol flew back to Belfast that night, but Norman and I stayed on for a couple of days at 'The Barn'. Alex had been staying in London in a hotel just beside the Cromwell, and was glad to get a couple of days back home. We used George's car to drive up and down to London and, by the time we left for Belfast again, he was looking reassuringly well.

During George's last days, when there was so much controversy over Alex getting in to see him, comments she was reported to have made in one interview saddened and shocked us. She was reported as saying that she couldn't understand why all of a sudden the family was showing concern for George as, according to the report, we hadn't been there when he needed us at the time of his transplant. While I know that she was obviously under a lot of stress throughout the period when George had his transplant, I still found it incredible that she could 'forget' that we were there.

Meanwhile, even before George had had his operation, the debate was raging in the media about whether or nor he, or indeed any alcoholic, should be given a liver transplant. Personally, I find it difficult to understand why anyone should think it appropriate to deny any person a chance of life. Alcoholism is a disease. And no one — not George, not our lovely mum, not the tens of thousands of other people who suffer from that disease, ever sets out to be an alcoholic.

Professor Williams said that, in his opinion, George was entitled to be treated just like any other person. The reality is that there are so many other health problems out there caused by addictions and bad lifestyle habits that it's hard to see how you can argue that one person should be treated and another not. Where do you draw the line? Should smokers also be denied life-saving treatment? Should overweight people?

Of course, I am crucially aware that at the centre of the debate about transplant operations is the enormity of the decision by the donor that, on their own death, the gift of life will be passed on to someone else. It is certainly not something that I or any member of our family takes for granted. We will always be eternally grateful to the donor who made George's transplant possible — as indeed, he was himself. I appreciate very much how difficult it is for bereaved families to make the decision to donate the organs of their loved ones. But I truly believe that organ donation should be done unconditionally.

As a registered organ donor myself, I would have no problem donating to an alcoholic. But that is not to say that I don't recognise the tremendous problems there are in these cases. A liver transplant is not a cure for alcoholism. For the recipient, that particular battle doesn't end with the operation.

It was also hinted in the media at the time of George's transplant that, because of his celebrity, he had been able to jump the queue in the waiting list. Nothing could be further from the truth. In fact, statistics show that he waited a little longer than average.

George's health improved after the transplant and he gradually began to look better. He started getting fit again and was looking really amazingly well. I remember Alex and he went off to the beautiful island of Mustique for a break, and the photographs of the holiday showed a very fit, tanned and handsome-looking George. It was the best I had seen him looking for a very long time.

Over the next year, Norman and I had a few trips to see George and Alex. We always had such a wonderful time. George was looking really well, and seemed to be very positive. He loved showing us around and liked to take me to Fanny's Farm, which was a cross between a garden centre and a produce farm, and sold unusual foods such as imported honey and marinades. He would tend his fish pond and was very proud of his collection of Koi Carp. All in all, he really did seem contented.

Sometimes we would go into Reigate for coffee or to a fabulous restaurant called The Dining Room, owned by chef Tony Tobin from the *Ready Steady Cook* programme. Eating out was a passion and one evening we all set off for a very upmarket restaurant in a hotel about ten miles from 'The Barn'. It was a beautiful place, with prices to match.

We chose the fixed-price menu, which was about £40 per head, but when the bill arrived it was £300. George, who was never mean, nearly had a fit. No one could understand why it was so expensive. But I had noticed that many of the meals carried a supplement. Even the starters all seemed to have a supplement. I was trying hard not to laugh as I had never seen George so taken aback. What made it worse from his point of view was that when we'd arrived at the hotel, because it looked so lovely, he had told Alex to go and reserve a table for the following week. He wanted to take Alex's mum and dad there for a meal. Before we left, however, he got her to cancel the reservation!

To crown things off, on our way back home, we got lost. I said to George, 'Why don't you use your Sat Nav?'

I wasn't too surprised by the reply: 'Because I don't know how to work the bloody thing!'

He was still giving off about the price when we got home and I even overheard him later on ranting and raving down the phone to his friend Bobby McAlinden: 'Bobby, you wouldn't believe it, but we have just paid £65 each for a f****** fish supper!'

One of my favourite memories is of the *This Is Your Life* programme in which George featured, in March 2003. It was the second time that George was caught out by the show.

Norman and I had told him that we were coming over to visit but had given him the date of our arrival as the day after the show was to be recorded. In fact, we were already in London. Apparently he kept saying to Alex things like: 'When are Barbara and Norman coming? I thought it was today. Give them a ring to see what's happening.' And Alex would pretend to ring and then say that our phones must be switched off.

He had been lured to the studio on the pretence of speaking about his transplant with Professor Williams, so you can imagine his complete surprise yet again when he walked out on to the set and we were all there. I'll never forget his face. He just wagged his finger at me, but I think he was really pleased.

The rest of the family were staying in a hotel in London, but Norman and I were going back to stay with George and Alex for a couple of days. When we arrived back at 'The Barn' Alex's mum and dad, Cheryl and Adrian, were there and everyone was in high spirits after such a successful evening. Alex cracked open a bottle of wine. I must admit I was sorely tempted to join her. But Norman and I both thought it wouldn't be fair to George, so instead I made some tea for us and for Cheryl and Adrian.

Unknown to George we had a surprise for him. As he was drinking his tea, Norman said, 'George, I'm sure not many people get presented with two red books in one evening', and handed him the original *This Is Your Life* book from 1971. We had brought it from Belfast. After that first show, our mum and dad had kept it and treasured it. George was like a child leafing through that book, looking at all the photos of the family. Yet another very proud and moving memory etched in my mind.

Sadly, the two *This Is Your Life* books, as well as George's certificate from his honorary doctorate at Queen's University and a beautiful scroll which was commissioned for the Freedom of the Borough of Castlereagh ceremony, have since become part of a legal wrangle. They are such an important part of George's history, especially the original book, which contains lots of very special photos of family, many of whom, like my mum and our grandparents, have passed away. We dearly want to bring them back to Northern Ireland.

In June 2003, Norman and I were once again on our way to France. We had only the morning to spend with George on this trip and, as usual, he collected us from Gatwick Airport. From the moment he met us, though, it was all too apparent that something was very wrong. He seemed agitated and quite angry. It was very unusual to see him like that. Even more unusually, we didn't have to ask him why as he immediately poured it all out.

He was due to go off on holiday to a private villa in Corfu with Alex and her parents. In the past, he had always really enjoyed this. But this time, he said, he just didn't want to go. For a start, he wouldn't be able to lie in the sun — because of the transplant. Alex, he pointed out, would be sunbathing and reading books all day, and he would have nothing to do. As he said, it wasn't as if he could nip off to the local taverna for a drink.

But perhaps what was bothering him more was the thought of what he'd have to forgo back at home. He had been invited to the Special Olympics, which were being hosted in Dublin, and Nelson Mandela was going to be there. George knew that there was a good chance of meeting a man whom he admired greatly. He desperately wanted to be there.

As all this tumbled out, George mentioned something else: lately, he had been feeling very down. This alarmed me. For George, who was such a private person, to admit this was quite out of character. I wondered if it might have been a delayed reaction to the transplant. Before the operation it had been explained to him that he might experience depression or mood swings afterwards. I had discussed this with George a few months after his transplant but he was quite upbeat and said he was lucky that he hadn't experienced anything like that. Could this now be a delayed reaction? Maybe. But in retrospect I also think that it was a sign that the craving for alcohol was taking over again. I have no way of knowing for sure, but to my mind it still seems a distinct possibility.

As soon as we arrived at the house that day, I sensed the atmosphere. George went straight back out, leaving us with Alex. He said that he would be home in time to drop us back at the airport. Alex did not remark on this and carried on as if everything were perfectly normal. When George returned, it was obvious that his mood hadn't improved much. He took us back to the airport and, before I left him, I put my arms around him and hugged him really tightly. 'George,' I said, 'I'm pleading with you, please don't give up.'

He knew what I was taking about, and said quietly, 'I won't, sis.'

But he didn't — or couldn't — look me straight in the eye.

That instant is etched in my memory. Norman and I both felt the same thing — that sudden wave of fear. All the way to France, we agonised about the form George had been in.

As soon as I got to France, I rang him. He tried to tell me he was okay but I wasn't convinced. A few days later, he flew off to Corfu. And in Corfu he started drinking again. It was to be the start of the last thirty months of his life. Thirty months of desperation and constant worry.

When I spoke to George later about what had happened in Corfu, he admitted that he'd done what he'd told me that day he wouldn't do — he had gone to a local taverna. He said that he had been craving drink but had been fighting that craving for ages. And even in the taverna he didn't give in right away. He ordered a white wine spritzer and for a long time just left it sitting on the bar, staring at it, with his mind in complete turmoil. But as we all know, he eventually succumbed.

As he knocked it back, he told me later: 'I wasn't sure what to expect. After the first drink, I knew that I wasn't going to drop down dead and so it just continued.'

In the months that followed, I used to broach the subject of his drinking by asking, 'Well, how are things going?'

He knew what I was referring to and the answer was always the same: 'I'm fine. Don't you worry about me. I'm not going anywhere.'

George is on record as saying: 'They wrote me off when I was thirty, they wrote me off when I was forty and then fifty and I'm still here.'

He often spoke about how he was going to celebrate his sixtieth birthday. He had it all planned. He told us that he was going to have a big bash at the Grosvenor House Hotel in London and then come back to Belfast and have another party there.

Norman and I had gone to London with Dad and Dad's friend Violet to be with George for his fiftieth birthday. It was a really strange, difficult day. That day, we had been with Grace and David as they buried their little girl, our darling little niece, Ashleigh. Now we were flying over to London to be with George. It was a surreal situation. But the BBC had dedicated its whole evening schedule to the event and it was impossible for George to get out of it. Right from the planning stage, we had promised him that we would be there. I think that he would have felt bad if no one from the family had turned up. So we decided to go ahead.

We arrived quite late, after a lot of the events had taken place, so we made our way to a big sports bar called 'Football Football'. All of George's friends were there and it was really quite hectic. After that, we headed back to the Holiday Inn in Mayfair. The place was packed and, as you can imagine, George was attracting a lot of attention. I remember sitting on the stairs surveying the scene. People at the bar were forking out for massive rounds of drink. Glasses were clinking and friends calling out to each other. Everyone laughing and joking. I felt like I was on another planet. I just wasn't in the mood.

Norman and I went over to chat to Diane Law, Denis's wife. She is a lovely person and was a great friend to George. He holidayed with her family on many occasions. There was then some talk of everyone moving on to yet another location, but we had had enough and decided to call it a night.

Prior to the party, Norman and I had phoned Phil a couple of times to find out about the price of a room at the Holiday Inn as everyone else was staying there. He told us that the hotel would do us a special rate of £200 per night. As we were going to be there for two nights, we just couldn't afford that sort of money. We were a little disappointed, as we really wanted to be close to everyone (even Dad and Violet were staying there). However, we made our own arrangements and stayed in another hotel within our budget.

Anyone who knows hotels in central London will know that you generally get what you pay for, and in our case this was very true. Our hotel was basic, to say the least. The rooms, although very clean, had glossy painted walls and no bathroom. You had to walk down a corridor to use the loo. There were no such luxuries as shampoos and body lotion. On our pillow there was just a little bar of soap (unwrapped) which I examined very carefully before I used it. Anyway we managed. But I will never forget the look on Alex's face when she dropped us off there on our second day.

'It's not very grand, is it?' I said.

'Why are you staying here?' she replied. 'You should have been at the hotel with everyone else. After all, it was all sponsored.'

I just said that we had tried but it seemed that it wasn't possible, and left it at that. But I did feel very annoyed. It wasn't about the money, as Norman and I always paid our way. I just felt a bit hurt and slightly angry with George. I thought that he should have looked after us. However, it transpired that actually George wasn't involved in that part of the planning so he had no idea what was going on.

A few years later, I jokingly told him how I felt. He hadn't been aware of any of this and said, 'Don't you worry. It won't be like that at my sixtieth. You and Norman will be right there with me at the top table and we'll all stay in the Grosvenor House Hotel.'

We never got to that top table. But because George had wanted so much to celebrate his sixtieth, we made an enormous effort on 22 May 2006 — although he was no longer with us — to make that day special.

Of course, once George had fallen off the wagon, some sections of the press had a field day. They absolutely hounded him. The papers and television were full of his escapades. What hurt me very much during this time and still makes me feel angry today is that many of the so-called interviews with him published over this period were conducted when George was very obviously extremely drunk. They were little more than the ravings of a drunk man. If these were 'interviews', surely it was apparent that the interviewee was in no fit state to be interviewed.

It brought back to mind that *Wogan* show where George had been allowed to appear live on television despite the fact that he was clearly intoxicated. I wondered how some of the media justified that. I wondered then, and I still do, why papers would, on the one hand, carry features about alcoholism, describing it as a disease and expressing concern for alcoholics and, on the other, publish stories castigating George for something he did or said when he was very obviously out of his mind on drink.

Not all papers and not all columnists were unsympathetic. Not all journalists — and I include here some of those who criticised him — were unfair. They had a right to their opinion. But some of the things written about George during this time were truly savage. Some reporters even bought George drink as they 'interviewed' him. What sort of double standard is that?

By the summer of 2003, coverage seemed to have reached fever pitch. Norman and I had made arrangements to go to France, and had planned to spend a couple of days with George and Alex on our return. By the time we got back from France, all hell had broken loose.

It was reported in the press that George was seeing a young blonde called Paula. Then it was someone else: Gina de Vivo. Alex, understandably, was frantic. We spoke to her as much as possible, trying to keep up to date and to make sense of it all. I couldn't get hold of George himself. He wouldn't answer his phone. I tried to speak to the manager of the pub where he was holed up, but he wouldn't take my calls. I begged the girl who took my call to get George to come to the phone to talk to me. She said that he had left, but I knew this wasn't true. I was watching it live on Sky TV. That in itself is an indication of the sort of intense coverage George was attracting. It was an impossible situation.

When we got back from France, Alex's mum and dad met us at the airport. Apart from anything else, it was all very embarrassing for us. We sat up with Alex until late, trying to work out what to do. We decided that Norman and I would meet George in Reigate the next morning and try to talk to him. When we eventually got hold of him, he agreed to talk. But he was very agitated. His phone never stopped ringing. It was as if he couldn't sit still for a minute. At one point, he went off to the loo and I answered his phone. It was Gina. I said that George would call her back, which he did.

He told us that Gina was being 'held' in a secret place by a well-known Sunday tabloid, which was going to be running a story. Now she was telling him she wanted to leave but didn't know what to do. At one point, I heard George saying: 'If you want to leave, then just get up and go. Jump in a taxi.'

It was a very difficult situation for us. Alex was back at home waiting for news. Gina was on the phone to George constantly. And there we were, stuck in the middle. After about an hour and half, we knew that it was a pointless task. So we took a taxi back to see Alex.

I had such mixed emotions about George at that point. I was annoyed, angry with him. But I was also very worried about him. And we had to go back to Belfast leaving things like that — hoping that somehow it would all sort itself out.

I can't remember how long after that trip it was before I got another phone call from George. The media interest had died down a bit, but there were still problems between George and Alex. Despite this, George sounded remarkably upbeat on the phone: 'Hi, sis,' he said cheerily. 'How are you?'

'I'm fine,' I said. 'How are you? What's happening?'

'Great,' he said. 'We're just going out for lunch.'

I bristled a bit. I didn't approve of what was going on in his private life. 'That's nice,' I replied tartly. 'Am I allowed to ask, with whom?'

'With my missus,' he said, suddenly sounding quite deflated and bashful.

And for the first time with George, I started to cry. I was so relieved. George who was never good with the emotional stuff was trying to calm me down, saying, 'Please don't cry. It will all be okay.'

I fervently hoped that it would.

It was around about this time that Norman and I decided to buy a property in France. We loved our mobile home, but thought that bricks and mortar would be a better investment, so the mobile was sold and we started to house hunt. I spent a few months researching and eventually narrowed our ideal spot down to the region known as the Pyrénées Orientales. It made sense as it ticked all of the right boxes for us, with easy access to the mountains, the Mediterranean and many airports. But most importantly for us, it also had rugby. What we hadn't bargained for was that our ideal home would also have our George!

George knew how much we loved France and was always asking how we were getting on there. He knew that we had sold the mobile and had started to look for a property. Our initial idea was to look for a two-bedroom apartment overlooking the sea — something simple and low maintenance — and we had set up a number of appointments in France for the first week of October, with estate agents who had sourced a number of properties within our price range.

Shortly before we were due to leave, George called us. He suggested that we buy a house instead of an apartment, but we explained that they were too expensive for us.

Later, he called back. 'I'll give you the money you need to help buy the house,' he said. 'And then, if it's okay with you, I can use it as well. It will be my bolt-hole when I need a break.'

Initially I was delighted. But then I began to think long and hard about it. Norman and I discussed it at length as it was a big step. We could see how it could all go wrong. But equally we both got on so well with George. And the idea that he could have a place to go to, to get away from the pressure, made considerable sense. I talked it over with George quite a few times before we left for France and each time he was adamant that this was what he wanted to do.

So, we decided to go ahead. Norman and I flew over on 1 October, and George and Alex were to join us at the weekend. When we arrived, we stayed with some friends in a beautiful little medieval village called Laroque-des-Albères. Our initial idea was to find a property overlooking the sea, but as the resorts of the area are seasonal, it was already very quiet at the beginning of October. Meanwhile, every time we drove back into the village, we fell in love with it a little bit more.

Norman and I viewed quite a number of properties, but nothing was really suitable. Finally the agent said to us: 'I have one more property for you to see and I have kept it to the last. I think it may be what you are looking for.'

The house was in the village of Laroque-des-Albères. As soon as we walked into the gardens and around the back of the house, we were hooked. It was a beautiful, sunny and extremely warm day. The gardens were magnificent, overlooking the mountains, and the sun was reflecting off the sparkling swimming pool.

It was an instant decision. I couldn't wait for George and Alex to see it. But on the day they were due to fly, they had yet another argument, and so arrived twenty-four hours after they were supposed to. We all went to view the property together. I was standing in the garden beside the pool, looking out over the mountains. George came up behind me, put his arms around me, and said, 'Go for it.'

Looking back, I had very mixed feeling about the whole thing. I was really excited, but at the same time had niggling worries that we might be making a mistake. Although George and Alex were together, I detected tensions. But I was so keen for everything to work out for them that I tried to bury my doubts. I just kept hoping that in this beautiful area, and given the close proximity to London, they would use the house to escape to, from the stress and publicity.

We flew back to London together to be met by the usual press stampede. It made me think that I had done the right thing. At least in France they would be away from all this.

With all that in mind, in December that year, Norman and I signed the final papers and became the proud owners of a house in France. I spent the next four months lovingly furnishing the house. I bought everything in Northern Ireland, and Norman and I hired a lorry and drove it all out to France. The place was immaculate and we couldn't wait for George and Alex to come out.

Sadly, however, their relationship deteriorated even further, and they eventually separated. And George found a new love in Ros Hollidge.

Norman and I went out to France at every opportunity. Each time we were going, I would call George to let him know in case he wanted to join us. In fact, the first visit he was to make was the one where he brought the television crew along with him. To put it mildly, that was a very difficult few days. But we survived it.

As well as trying to watch how much he was now drinking, I had to make sure that George didn't get sunburnt. I tried not to fuss over him, but would diplomatically say things like 'Here's some sun cream' or 'Why don't you go and have a rest and I'll keep this wine in the fridge until you get up?' Thank goodness it worked remarkably well. George never liked being told what to do. But by working with him I did feel that I was able to curtail his drinking a fair bit.

One evening, Norman and I were having a couple of friends around for a barbecue. George had said that he was nipping up to the village for a drink, but would be back at 8.30 for the meal. Our friends arrived, half past eight came, nine o'clock came, half past nine — still no sign of George. By this stage, I was starting to get worried, but I didn't want to phone him in case he thought that I was checking up on him.

At ten o'clock, I decided that we should go into the village and try to find him. We tried the bar in the village square. Caroline, the owner, said, 'Oh, yes, George was here. But he only had one drink. He said that he was going home to have a barbecue.'

We checked the other places in the village but had no success there either. By now, we were very concerned. We drove around the nearest three villages, but again, no luck. Distraught and running out of ideas, we headed for home. George, we realised, could be anywhere. He had obviously met up with someone and was probably drunk by now.

Back at the house, we were in for a surprise. There was George, huddled up on a seat in the back garden, trying to keep warm. I could have cried. I imagine he could have too! For he was, in fact, stone-cold sober. He was also very tired and very hungry. He had left the bar as promised to come home for the meal but had taken a wrong turn in the village, and had then spent the next two hours wandering round the roads, totally lost. At one stage, he'd even ended up in the vineyards. He had come across guard dogs and one or two irate owners who thought that he was trespassing.

He had phoned Ros and Phil, but they didn't know our phone number at the house. Eventually he had managed to make it to the next village where the TV crew was staying. But they were out having a meal, so he had to wait for them. When they returned, they dropped him back to the house.

He was so tired that he had a quick supper of cold chicken and one glass of wine and went straight to bed. For a long time afterwards we were to take the mickey out of him about that particular adventure — the day he got lost in France.

George's turbulent and complicated private life continued to attract headlines. Alex and he had started divorce proceedings. He was now in a relationship with Ros. But Gina de Vivo was also still on the scene. And, of course, he was still drinking. I called him frequently or he would call me to make arrangements to go to France.

In the early summer of 2004, he came out for a break with Ros and her daughter, Emma. I had met Ros on a couple of occasions beforehand and was quite looking forward to the break with them all.

The first time I met her was when George had brought her over to Belfast and we had all gone out for a meal. At the time, Norman and I were both very conscious about not having a drink in front of George. In the past, this hadn't been an issue. George had always assured us that it didn't bother him. He used to say that he wasn't trying to stop the world from drinking. Just himself.

However, as time wore on, he finally admitted that he did find it very difficult to watch other people drinking when he was trying to abstain himself. So, from that point on, Norman and I made the decision not to drink in front of him when he was obviously trying to stay sober.

At the restaurant, the waiter arrived to take our drinks order. Ros ordered a soft drink, and Norman and I, feeling duty bound, ordered a Diet Coke each.

'And what can I get for you, Mr Best?' asked the young waiter.

'Make mine a large glass of wine, please,' said George. The air was blue but he just laughed at us.

The visit to the house in France went quite well. Everyone enjoyed the warm weather. We had a couple of meals out but were mostly content to sit around the table in the evenings, having some food with a few drinks. During the day, George would wander into the village with Ros for a drink or a snack, or we would drop them off in the beautiful fishing village of Collioure and then collect them later.

On one occasion, George wanted to go to the pub but had no money with him so I lent him €50. He came back after spending the evening in the village with his, or rather my, €50 still in his pocket. He was amazed. He said that no one would take money from him for a drink.

I panicked a bit, as in France you pay the bill at the end of the evening. I had visions of the local gendarme calling at our house to arrest him! But when I spoke discreetly to a couple of the bar owners about this, they assured me that George didn't owe them money. Everyone had just wanted to buy him a drink. (Despite this, I never did get my €50 back!) It was an illustration of how, even in France, he was recognised. And how, even in France — although they meant well — he was still faced with the problem of people wanting to buy him alcohol.

Overall during this break it was clear just how much worse George's drinking was becoming. After one of his sessions, he ended up with a black eye. And of course that would be the day when Michel, one of our French neighbours, called to see if he could have a photo of George to give to his daughter who was leaving the village to go to work in Paris.

It was a bit awkward as George had the bruises on his face. But equally he didn't have the heart to say no. Emma, Ros's daughter, tried to cover it up as best she could with make-up and Michel took the photo.

As he was focusing his camera, George muttered through clenched teeth, 'When his daughter sees this, she'll be saying, "I thought he was a footballer — not a f*****g boxer!"'

I worried about him constantly. Every now and again, I would hear him open another wine bottle. It made no difference if I didn't buy any. He'd go out and get it himself.

One morning, he got up and poured himself his usual breakfast glass of wine. I had been up early and had gone into the village to buy some fresh bread and croissants. Although George wouldn't normally eat anything, I was trying to get him to have something before his wine. He didn't want any of it. So I suggested: 'Would you like some grapefruit instead?'

'That's one of the things I'm not allowed to eat because of the transplant,' he replied. At first, I thought that he was having a laugh. But when I looked at him, I realised that he was deadly serious.

I didn't say a word. I just looked at the glass of wine and then back up at him. He gave me a helpless shrug as if to say, 'I know.' It was 7.30 in the morning.

It saddened me so much and it brought back what George had said during the making of that documentary at the house a short while previously: 'By the time it gets to 7 a.m. I'm gasping. I love company but sometimes drink is my company. It makes me feel confident. It cheers me up when I'm down. I just can't get it out of my system.'

George and Alex's divorce was a very acrimonious one. It saddened me deeply that their marriage had ended as it did. Throughout the years, we had come to know and like Alex. As I said before, I have always accepted that she loved George and that he loved her. She looked after him throughout the most trying times and I know that it can't have been easy for her. Anyone who has ever lived with an alcoholic will know how very hard it must have been. There were very definitely times over the years when I would have sided with Alex against George. He admitted hitting her and I accept totally that that was wrong. But I also know that theirs was a complex and tempestuous relationship.

What I found very hard to cope with were some of the things Alex said and did during the divorce battle. There were many arguments and debates over the settlement, which I can understand to a certain extent. What I cannot and will never accept is that, because of this, George never got back to his flat in Cheyne Walk, especially for the final part of his life, when he needed it most.

Instead, he went to live at the beautiful Champney's Forest Mere Health Resort, which is in Liphook in Hampshire, which is actually where he met Ros. The owner, Stephen Purdew, an old friend of George's, ensured that he was well taken care of. He had the best suite at the resort, with an enormous balcony and a beautiful view over the lake. Everyone at some stage in their life dreams of a pampering weekend away at such an upmarket establishment, but no matter how good it is, it's not home. George moved in during the divorce for what was to be a few days. He was to spend the last year of his life there.

By the time the divorce was finalised and financial arrangements had been put in place for Cheyne Walk, George had fallen seriously ill and, as I said, was never to live in the apartment again.

During his time at the health farm, George had good spells and bad spells. He was still drinking, but at times he seemed to have it under control. When he was like this, he loved to go to the gym. But as with many aspects of his life, it became an obsession. He was so very competitive. He told me that he would always try to position himself beside someone on the running machine (preferably female) and try to outrun them. If they did thirty minutes, he did thirty-five. If they did forty, he did forty-five. He wouldn't give in.

In my opinion, that couldn't possibly have been good for him. Not with the lifestyle he was leading. I remember asking him once why he was so competitive and he said that when he was young he really wasn't confident that he would make it in the football world, and that is what made him work so hard.

During his stay at Forest Mere, he met Mavis and Denis. Mavis is in charge of Guest Relations at the Health Farm and both she and Denis treated George like a son. They are two of the most lovable people, and their honesty and common sense were to prove an invaluable support to me after George died.

Mavis adored George and every morning he would call into her office and have a coffee with her. They would sit there, chatting and planning the day ahead. On many occasions, she would have things for him to autograph. Quite often, she would ask, 'Now, George, what are you going to do today?'

His standard reply was: 'Oh, I just have to go to the bank.'

It took Mavis a long time to realise that 'the bank' was in fact the pub or the bookmaker's. Gambling was another of George's weaknesses. He always placed a bet on anything that had the word 'red' or the number '7' associated with it.

Mavis ensured that he did eat proper meals and, on more than one occasion, Denis had to nip down to the local optician's to collect some reading glasses for George. He was always losing them. It happened so frequently that the optician kept spare ones and Denis would ring up and say: 'I'll be down later for a pair of glasses for George.' On one occasion, he got a frantic call from George saying that, yet again, he'd lost his specs. Denis made a 100-mile round trip to take a pair to him.

Denis and Mavis made sure that George always had clean shirts and suits for his appearances on Sky or for any other work he was doing. He would often pop in to ask Mavis, 'Well, how do I look?'

Sometimes Forest Mere had quiz evenings, which George just loved. One evening, he teamed up with a couple of ladies and they won. The problem was that the prize was two bottles of wine. Mavis's daughter, who ran the quizzes, said, 'Sorry, George. I'm afraid you can't claim your prize.'

He laughed and said, 'No problem. I'll just sign them and give them to the ladies.' His two quiz team-mates were delighted.

Since George's death, Norman and I have been to Liphook to spend some time with Mavis and Denis, and to see where George spent so much of his last months. The suite where he stayed has been totally refurbished and has been named 'The George Best Suite' in his honour.

It was a very emotional experience, but Mavis and Denis went out of their way to make it easier for us. They couldn't do enough for us. They come from a large close-knit family and I will always be grateful to them for bringing George into that family and treating him as one of their own at a time in his life when it mattered most. And also, of course, I am grateful to Stephen Purdew for giving George somewhere special to live and making his life that little bit easier.

At Liphook, we met with a chap called Dave who drove George quite a lot, especially up and down to London. He gave us back a small bag of George's possessions which he had safely stored. He said that he wanted to hand them directly to me. In the bag was the paperwork from the little black mini that was George's pride and joy, plus a commemorative medal from the Freedom of Castlereagh ceremony. But for me the most moving thing was that among some music CDs also in the bag was one on 'How to teach yourself French'.

When I saw it, I broke down. I remembered that on one occasion in France, when we were in a restaurant where very little English was spoken, George had turned to me with a mischievous grin on his face and said, 'You know, I understand more French than you think.' Maybe he was going to startle us one day with his fluent French! We'll never know.

Another friend of George's whom we met only after his death was a chap called Gordon who had got to know George quite well during those last couple of years, as he ran a pub in Petersfield where George spent a lot of time. He was extremely fond of George and spoke very highly of him. In fact, George had spent the weekend with Gordon before being admitted for that final time to the Cromwell Hospital. It was heartbreaking listening to Gordon describing to us how ill George was over that weekend. He said that he was terribly worried about him and spent most of those few days without sleep, as he was afraid to leave George alone.

Although I found listening to all this very upsetting, it was something that I had to do. I just needed to piece together as much as possible of George's last few months. It was also comforting to hear from all of these people that George had talked fondly of Norman and me and had described how he put great trust in us. He said that he knew we were friends for the right reasons; he knew that we didn't take advantage.

And it is for that reason, I believe, that he left me with one last, but very important, task.

| THE FUNERAL

Like George, my husband Norman is not a man given to public displays of emotion. It was just one of the many reasons, I believe, why the pair of them got on so well together. There was a genuine bond between them — a bond of mutual understanding and respect. They didn't go in for showy gestures, but each of them had a real affection for the other. Norman was never judgmental with George. He was patient and supportive and George responded to that. He would have listened to Norman when he listened to no one else.

Like the rest of our family, Norman was devastated by George's death. But as the end drew near, he was determined to set his grief aside and to perform one last task for his brother-in-law and friend. He was determined to ensure that George's funeral would be a fitting tribute.

As I described earlier in this book, immediately after George's death when our family had faced the gathered media outside the Cromwell Hospital, our dad had appealed for privacy. It was, he said, 'a normal, human thing to ask'. And, in fairness, I think that all the media there that day sympathised with the sentiment. But they also doubtless realised that the chances of keeping such a funeral a quiet family affair were remote.

My dad, however, saw it simply. He was going to bring his son back home to Belfast for a 'normal' funeral. There was never any question that George would be buried anywhere else other than in Belfast. We would bring him back to his home city, back to be buried beside the mother who had loved him so much and who had never got over being parted from him. That's what George himself had wanted. Calum knew that this was his dad's wish and he was entirely in agreement.

It soon became apparent, though, that organising the funeral for a man who was being mourned by millions worldwide was going to be a complex affair. We could never have prepared ourselves for how things were going to turn out over the next week.

As I mentioned earlier, Norman and I had met Adrian Donaldson, the chief executive of Castlereagh Borough Council, at the airport as we flew back to London for that final vigil by George's bedside. On the Thursday evening before George died, Norman had spoken on the phone to Edel Patterson, who is Events Manager with the council. We got to know Edel around the time that George was honoured as a Freeman of the Borough. Edel had helped to organise the ceremony. We had also socialised with her and her husband Clive at the christening of a friend's baby a few months before. As Norman brought her up to date about George's condition, she assured him that Castlereagh Borough Council would be happy to help in any way it could.

It just happened that the council's monthly meeting was being held that evening, and it was readily agreed that it would be honoured to assist in organising the funeral of Dr George Best. Norman would act as the family's representative at all the meetings with the various bodies, which would, we now realised, have to be involved in co-ordinating such a massive public event. He was totally dedicated to getting it all right. But the next week was to bring many emotional challenges not just for him but for the entire family.

Back at the Cromwell Hospital, shortly after George died, the staff from ICU had called the room where we had been waiting to say that all of the machinery that had been attached to his body had now been removed. Anyone who wished could come back down to see him. I wanted to go, but Norman thought that it would be too much for me. However, I insisted, so he came to support me. We went in along with Carol and Julie. I stayed for a minute or two but I found the experience so distressing that I had to leave again. I wanted to remember George as the handsome man that he had always been.

One of the first things we now discussed as a family was the issue of organ donation. Before George died, we had already talked this over. We knew that it was what George had wanted. Yvonne, the nurse who had been with us when the machines were switched off, worked with the family and the transplant co-ordinators. Initially we had felt that we couldn't bear for George's eyes to be donated. Those sparkling blue eyes were so much a part of his charm and good looks that we found it difficult to think of them being donated. But after much soul-searching we agreed that, in all conscience, we couldn't refuse.

While we had unanimously agreed to organ donation, we had been told that it was doubtful that any of George's organs would be suitable. And, sadly, because of the huge quantity of drugs that had been administered to George during his illness, none of his organs was suitable for transplant. Even his beautiful blue eyes could not be used.

In the meantime, plans for his funeral were beginning to come together. It had already been agreed by Castlereagh Council that its offices would be made available for the funeral service. The plan was to use the main building and then to have an elaborate marquee outside to accommodate the overspill. Initially this seemed like a viable option and the family was very grateful for the offer. Deep down, though, I had reservations about whether it was a suitable venue. Phil also voiced his concerns. He wasn't sure that it was fitting to bury George from a council office, albeit a rather grand council office. I was also worried that it would simply not be big enough. I had thought that St Anne's Cathedral in Belfast might be a better location.

St Anne's, which belongs to the Church of Ireland, is an historic and beautiful place of worship situated right in the heart of Belfast. It is an imposing building that could accommodate, I thought, the number of mourners who would want to attend the service. It just seemed to me so much more appropriate. However, I didn't want to appear ungrateful to Castlereagh Council.

I am a great believer in the idea that things have a way of working themselves out. So, although I had concerns about the location of the funeral, I was determined not to let it become a major concern. Plus we had so many other things to organise.

We needed a minister to conduct the service, and Carol knew just the man. An old friend of hers, Pastor Roy Gordon, was the obvious choice. Roy and his wife Patsy have been friends of Carol's for many years. They all used to attend the same church in Belfast until Carol married and moved away to Portavogie, in Co. Down. The rest of the family also knew Roy well and we were confident that he would conduct the service in the spirit we wanted. We didn't want a stranger officiating and we felt that Roy would ensure that the core of the ceremony would be the 'normal, family funeral' our father so wanted for his son.

However, even on that first day, we were starting to get word back that, in Northern Ireland, George's death had sparked a massive public response. Tributes were flooding in. Crowds were starting to gather outside Dad's house. They were leaving flowers, cards, letters, even football shirts and scarves. And the same thing was happening at other locations — at Windsor Park where George had played for Northern Ireland and in front of Belfast City Hall. A book of condolence had been opened there soon after George's death was announced. Within a very short space of time, hundreds of people were already arriving to pay their respects and write their heartfelt messages. One person who was interviewed at the City Hall described George in words that still echo in my memory: 'He was part of my childhood. There were The Beatles. There was the first man on the moon. And there was George Best.'

At Old Trafford and at other locations in Manchester, crowds were gathering too. Even outside the Cromwell Hospital, streams of people were arriving to pay their respects and lay their tributes. There were flowers, pictures of George, footballs, little angels and teddy bears. (We later requested that these would go to a children's hospice.)

It was clear that the funeral was going to be enormous. I still could not imagine how grand it would turn out to be.

By early evening, George had been taken to the funeral parlour in London, and we had started to plan how we were going to get him back to Belfast. Finally we all decided to call it a day.

Norman and I left to return to our hotel. We were tired, emotionally wiped out — but beyond sleep. We just wanted to sit down somewhere together and talk it all through so we walked down to a local pub, around the corner from our hotel.

What a surreal experience! Here we were in the middle of London on a busy Friday evening. Office workers on their way home had dropped in to the pub, joining those who were obviously locals. And everyone was riveted to the television screens in the bar, watching the news which was now dominated by the report of George's death.

There were four large wide-screen televisions around the pub and everywhere we looked, we just couldn't get away from it. Throughout the bar, customers were reading newspapers with banner headlines announcing George's death. I sat there clutching my glass of wine while all around me grown men read their newspapers or watched the television screens with tears coursing down their faces.

For a bizarre moment I wanted to stand up and shout out: 'That's my brother and I am so proud that he was.' But I just sat quietly taking it all in — this sincere, heartfelt sorrow being expressed by perfect strangers for our George.

We stayed for just one drink and then went back to the hotel to make more phone calls home to our children and a couple of close friends. And then I finally broke down. By now, Norman was also in a terrible state. I remember speaking to my close friend Alex and her sister Janice and I don't know how on earth they understood a word I said. I was inconsolable. It was to be a very long, sleepless night.

The following day, Saturday, at about ten o'clock, our family met up again at the hospital. We were all booked on the same flight back to Belfast. It's strange how certain images stay with us, but what I am about to describe will remain with me for the rest of my days. We were all in such a state at the time, but looking back now I find what happened quite amusing.

At the hospital, there was much debate about how we were all going to get to the airport. The consensus was that taxi would be a good idea. There were eight of us travelling, with quite a bit of luggage. So we had the choice of either two taxis or a large seven-seater one. Two taxis would be expensive. The seven-seater was better value — but someone would still have to go by the Tube.

Norman volunteered. He said that he'd go on by himself and then meet up with us at the airport. However, I wanted him with me. I know that it seems bizarre now but no one was able to make a rational decision. So in the end we decided that we would all go from Earl's Court station to Heathrow by Tube!

Imagine the scene — eight people, all with luggage, including two huge plastic hospital bags full of get-well cards and letters that had been sent to George. Carol and I had one each. As we set off for the ten-minute walk to the station, Norman and I were bringing up the rear. There we were — all eight of us sadly trudging in line along a little cobbled street with our suitcases trailing behind.

As I have mentioned before, our family has always kept its feet firmly on the ground and would never have used George's name to obtain special treatment. I am quite certain that, had we asked, any number of people would have been only too willing to transport us to the airport.

Even when we were sitting on the train, all I could see were images of George on the front of the newspapers. To make matters worse, when we arrived at the airport, when Carol was going through security, her bag 'bleeped'. She was asked to open it and, of course, it had to be the one with all the hundreds of get-well cards inside. Carol was mortified and kept apologising to the man who was searching. Every single card had to be removed to get to the bottom of the case. And there was a small pair of scissors which Carol had forgotten to take out.

The man must have recognised who we were. He said kindly to Carol, 'Don't worry, it's okay', and then re-packed all of the cards and waved her through.

We didn't know it, but already on that Saturday the staff from Castlereagh had begun to make provisional arrangements for the funeral. Marquee companies had been contacted and some of the people they thought might be available to participate in the funeral had also been phoned. But they were acutely aware at the council that the wishes of the family should be paramount.

George's death dominated the television and radio news and the press. The media were hungry for any little bits of information, and contacted anyone and everyone they thought could add something to the story. In fairness, the coverage was very positive. George was being remembered just the way he had wanted to be. He was being remembered for his football.

It was early on the Sunday morning when we received the most astonishing news. Adrian Donaldson from the council had phoned to bring us up to date on arrangements. After a short while, he said to me, 'Barbara, how do you really feel about the funeral being held at the council offices?'

For a few seconds I was silent, but I felt that I had to tell him the truth. I explained that everyone else was very happy, but that I didn't think it was going to be suitable. I stressed that I didn't wish to appear to be ungrateful.

'What would you think about Stormont?' he asked.

Stormont is the seat of the Northern Ireland Assembly. Built in the early 1920s in white Portland stone, it is a dramatic and majestic building, approached by a grand tree-lined driveway. Like our family home, it's situated in East Belfast. It is, in fact, only a couple of miles from the Cregagh Estate where we were brought up. But the two places are worlds apart.

For a boy from working-class Cregagh to be buried from Stormont was a unique honour. It was recognition of the very special place George had in the hearts of the people of Northern Ireland. It was also too much for me to take in. I started to cry and had to hand the phone to Norman.

We learned later that the initial suggestion had come from Joan McCoy who works with Castlereagh Council. That morning, she had been discussing the funeral with her husband, Robert, in the kitchen of their home high in the Castlereagh Hills. Like me, Joan was not convinced that the council offices were suitable. She had a number of concerns. The council offices are situated near a large shopping centre. How would the traffic be controlled? Nor could she imagine George's coffin resting in a marquee, no matter how grand it was!

As she outlined her concerns to Robert, he looked out of their kitchen window and said simply: 'That's where he should be buried from', his gaze resting on the Stormont building in the distance.

Events moved quickly after that. Joan phoned Adrian Donaldson to put the idea to him. Adrian in turn phoned Peter Robinson, the MP for East Belfast. And Peter immediately contacted the Secretary of State for Northern Ireland, Peter Hain, who would obviously have the final say on the matter. Not only did Mr Hain give his personal approval and support, but he also said that the staff of the Northern Ireland Office would be fully available to work alongside the staff from Castlereagh and our family.

Adrian explained to us that it could take some time for approval to be obtained for the use of Stormont. You can imagine how difficult it was for Norman and me not to say anything about the plan to a soul — especially Dad. But within one hour of Joan's inspired idea, permission was granted that the funeral service of Dr George Best could be conducted in Stormont.

To the best of my knowledge, that privilege had never been afforded to anyone else. Viscount James Craig, who was the Prime Minister of Northern Ireland from 1921 until his death in 1940, is buried in the grounds of the Stormont Estate, but no funeral service had been conducted there. What a mammoth task now lay ahead.

Yet, within five days, the staffs of Castlereagh Borough Council, the Northern Ireland Office and many other diverse organisations were to pull together the equivalent of a state funeral. Bearing in mind that generally state funerals for dignitaries are planned years in advance, what these people achieved in such a short time was miraculous. Their dedication, professionalism and sensitivity will never be forgotten by our family.

After it was confirmed that Stormont would be the venue for the funeral, it was decided to have a meeting on the Sunday afternoon to get things moving. Adrian was aware of how emotional it would be for Norman and me so he thought that it would be more relaxed if we met at his home. At five o'clock on the Sunday afternoon, the first of many meetings together took place. Those present were Norman and I, Adrian, Joan and Edel. We were kept well supplied with very welcome tea and sandwiches by Adrian's wife, Pamela.

What happened at that first meeting was the first of many startling 'coincidences' of the sort that continue to convince me that things which are meant to be will happen.

On the Saturday, Edel had already started to make a few preliminary enquiries. One of her first calls was to Peter Corry, a well-known local singer and West End actor who had starred in *Les Misérables*. Peter has known our family for many years, mainly through his connection with the Salvation Army on the Cregagh Road not far from our house. This is where my sisters Julie and Grace and brother Ian worshipped. Peter readily agreed to sing at the funeral and, over the next days, was to be a great support.

He also said that, if necessary, he would be able to get in touch with Brian Kennedy, another well-known national and international star who is also a Belfast boy. Edel had thought that it would be very fitting for Peter to sing 'Bring Him Home', the song he sings so movingly from *Les Misérables*. It just seemed so appropriate.

On that Sunday evening, she was on her way to pick up Joan and turned on the radio. 'You Raise Me Up' was playing and she instantly thought it would be another perfect choice of music. She says that she was thinking to herself: 'I'll try to get Westlife. I'll get in touch somehow with Louis Walsh.'

Anyway, when we arrived at Adrian's house, she explained that she had been making some general enquiries and had a few ideas, but obviously wouldn't do anything without our approval. She gently asked, 'Have you any thoughts yourself?'

And so, entirely unaware of what she'd been considering, I outlined my own ideas: 'What I would love is that Peter Corry would take part. I'd really like him to sing "Bring Him Home". I know that George would have liked that. Also I know that he loved "You Raise Me Up". I was thinking about perhaps, trying to get in touch with Louis Walsh to ask Westlife. But on reflection I think that it would be more appropriate to keep it local and I think that Brian Kennedy should be asked.'

When I had finished, Edel and Joan just sat there looking at me and then at each other in total amazement. Within seconds, we were all crying our eyes out. It was meant to be.

Other songs we decided on were 'Vincent', which was one of George's favourites, and 'The Long and Winding Road'. Again, this was to have a special significance on the day of the funeral.

It was suggested that we have a choir which could stand on the steps sweeping majestically upwards from the Great Hall to the Gallery. Adrian said, 'Okay, get a choir. No ... don't. Get two choirs.' I just smiled. I couldn't believe that this was all happening for our George. The two choirs chosen were the Grosvenor Chorale and the Methodist College Choir.

When Edel and Joan headed off to set the wheels in motion, one of the first things that had to be done was to postpone the switching on of the Christmas-tree lights at the council offices. This had been scheduled for Wednesday of that week. The staff at the offices then divided into five teams, each with its own particular role to play. They would be working with the staff from Stormont, but the main responsibility for the organisation lay with the council. The more that I have spoken to Joan and Edel since, the more I learn about how everyone worked tirelessly to make the funeral the memorable event it turned out to be. It is so comforting to know that our George did something very special in Northern Ireland. He brought the people together. All religious and political differences were set aside to pay tribute to him. Doors were opened. Seemingly impossible tasks were achieved. Everyone pulled together.

Edel knew that someone was needed to anchor the proceedings at

Free man: George and Carol at the ceremony where he was awarded Freedom of the Borough of Castlereagh.

Dr George Best: George after being awarded an honorary degree at Queen's University, Belfast.

George and me. This photograph was taken at George's home, 'The Barn', in May 2002, just two weeks before he underwent his transplant operation. It was one of only two photographs to survive the fire that destroyed mine and Norman's house in France.

Happier times: me, George and Alex at 'The Barn'.

France, October 2003. Alex, Norman, George and me, after finding the house there that was to provide a bolt-hole for George. This is the other special photograph that survived the fire in France.

United in grief: after George's death, fans gather outside Old Trafford where a sea of jerseys, scarves, flowers and cards have been laid in tribute. Many of these jerseys have since been laundered and sent to deprived children all around the world.

You'll never walk alone — one of the poignant tributes left outside Old Trafford.

The first intake of male students at Ekwendeni Nursing College in Malawi proudly display their 'new' strips.

This shirt was left at Dad's house by Norman Millar. It had such a lovely message on it that I decided to track him down and return it. (*Diane Magill/ Newsletter*)

Me, Dad and Norman at Áras an Uachtaráin, with President Mary McAleese, centre, and other guests.

A legend remembered: on a very proud day for our family, me and Dad with Chief Executive Brian Ambrose, a dedicated fan of George's, at the George Best Belfast City Airport, during the renaming ceremony on 22 May 2006. It would have been his 60th birthday.

Norman, Sir Alex Ferguson and me at a very successful fundraising gala dinner for the George Best Foundation, on the evening following the airport renaming ceremony. (*Harrison Photography, Belfast*)

The George Best Foundation aims to provide funds for research into liver disease and to encourage a healthy lifestyle for young people through participation in football. The shirts left in tribute following George's death were collected, cleaned and printed with the Foundation's name. They've since been distributed to needy children all over the world — children like this little girl in Sierra Leone. (*Debi Topping*)

the funeral, someone who could hold it all together on such an emotional occasion. It was a simple choice — Eamonn Holmes.

Like George, Eamonn is Belfast born and bred — another boy from a humble working-class background who became a household name. He's one of the most successful presenters on British television. And fittingly, Eamonn is also a fanatical Manchester United supporter. A lifelong admirer of George, he had appeared in March 2003 as a guest on the second *This Is Your Life* programme that featured George.

Eamonn immediately agreed to take part. So did Brian Kennedy. The flautist Sir James Galway, also originally from Belfast, was contacted but sadly he wasn't available on the day. Instead a young flautist called Richard Douglas stepped in. He was absolutely brilliant.

It was decided that Peter would sing 'Bring Him Home' and 'The Long and Winding Road'. Brian would sing 'Vincent' and 'You Raise Me Up'. Peter was happy enough with 'Bring Him Home' but didn't know the other song. However, like the true professional he is, he quickly learnt it and performed it perfectly.

The next step was to find a musical director, and an outstanding Northern Irish musician called Frank Gallagher kindly agreed to take on this task. Frank thought that 'The Long and Winding Road' was too 'bouncy' for the occasion but he knew that it was what the family wanted. It was just a question of getting it right.

He called a musician friend in America to 're-score' the music. Taking into consideration the time difference (it was the middle of the night in America), this was a big request. Frank apologised to his friend, explaining that he had been asked to direct the music at the funeral of a guy called George Best. His friend stopped him. 'I know who George Best is,' he said. 'I'll do whatever you need.' He worked through the remainder of the night and phoned Frank the following morning. The 'gentler' version of the song was ready in time.

Some changes were made to the words of some of the songs, and publishers had to be contacted to obtain permission to do this. One such person was Cameron Mackintosh, the famous producer behind such musicals as *Phantom of the Opera, Miss Saigon* and of course *Les Misérables* from which the song 'Bring Him Home' came. The Orders of Service also had to be printed. A lifelong friend of Norman's, Bill Campbell, who is a publisher, took on that job and sorted any problems with copyright issues.

More coincidence — Bill is actually the next-door neighbour of Edel Patterson. It was at the christening of his daughter Holly that we first met Edel!

By Monday, plans were beginning to gather momentum. The BBC had been in touch with Norman to say that they would like to televise the funeral live. In its history, the BBC has only ever televised three other funerals live: the Queen Mother's, Princess Diana's and Pope John Paul's.

Each time we updated Dad on what was happening, he just shook his head in amazement. At times, it was all a bit too much for him. He had been through so much already, and we tried to protect him as much as possible. But it was now apparent that George's funeral was going to be a major event.

In fact, it was starting to cause some concern with the PSNI from a security and crowd-control point of view. Norman attended all of the planning meetings on these matters. The logistics were enormous. Over 370 officers, ranging from the rank of Constable to Assistant Chief Constable, would be involved. Many factors had to be taken into consideration — from risk assessment to ensuring that road signs were in place on the day. Park-and-ride facilities had to be set up, motorcycle outriders had to be briefed, and crash barriers had to be put in place. Actually there weren't enough barriers available in the area and some had to be borrowed from other locations.

Security had to be put in place for crowd control. A local company, Eventsec, was employed for this task. Once again, Norman and I knew the owner, as he has a property in France in the next village to where we have our house. I remember asking his partner many months later what was the biggest and most prestigious event they had worked on. She instantly replied, 'George's funeral.'

Norman was very surprised to find when he went to one of the planning meetings that he knew well two of the inspectors, Nigel L and Billy D, who were to play pivotal roles in the funeral. He had known them for many years since they had been young constables in the police. The pattern of coincidences continued.

The police had genuine concerns about bringing George's body home. They were worried that the airport could be brought to a standstill. They also were concerned about how they would protect George's body back in Belfast, so reluctantly it was agreed that this saddest of homecomings would be delayed for as long as possible.

My dad, who wanted his son back in Belfast, had to be told, and Carol gently explained to him that he would not be brought back until Friday, the day before the funeral itself. Dad was terribly sad, but typically accepted that it had to be done that way.

The Ministry of Defence was approached and it was agreed with the RAF that George could be flown from RAF Northolt into RAF Aldergrove. The RAF phoned Norman to explain what would happen — and again it turned out that the co-ordinating officer was another old friend of Norman's. We had first met Squadron Leader Jim McG many years ago during one of our regular visits to the Battlefields of the Somme. We'd kept in touch with him and his wife Elizabeth ever since. Dealing with people we knew during this traumatic period made things so much easier for us.

Now that it had been established where George was being flown to, we then had to work out how his body would be transported. At one of the many meetings, I casually mentioned, 'I don't suppose anyone knows somebody who owns a private jet?' Silly question!

Sheila from the Northern Ireland Office said, 'Leave that one with me.' And two hours later a private jet had been tracked down and the owners were more than willing to allow it to be used to bring George home. They are two Northern Ireland businessmen, one of whom is an old friend of Sheila's and they have never sought publicity for this. They simply wanted to do it for George.

It was the same with the funeral cars. Another couple of Belfast-based businessmen contacted the funeral directors who were responsible for the funeral and told them that the invoice for the hearse and other cars should be sent to them. Again, they didn't want any public recognition for this, although many months later we were able to thank them in our own way.

We were faced with a further problem. It was being reported in the press that the funeral would take place in Belfast on the Friday, and we were being put under enormous pressure to have it then. It was argued that some VIPs, for example representatives from the football world, would not be able to attend on the Saturday, due to league fixtures. We understood this. But we were still adamant that the funeral would be held on the Saturday.

Norman phoned his press contacts to let them know this. And to let them know why: it was so important to us as a family to ensure that this funeral was for the people and the fans. In Norman's words: 'George's funeral was not for the great and the good but for the ordinary people, the people who had supported him through thick and thin — the fans.'

In order to attend on a Friday, as Norman pointed out, many of these fans would have had to give up at least a day's pay. For a working man or woman, that's quite a bit. Some would want to travel from elsewhere in Ireland and Britain. In that case, it would cost them even more. Whilst it was obviously important that the VIPs be present, it was, as I say, vitally important to the entire family that the 'ordinary' people had the chance to say goodbye to their hero. We were also aware at this time that many children wanted to attend or at least watch the funeral on television. This would not have been possible if they had been at school.

Yet it was still being reported that George would be buried on Friday. It was even being reported that one of the biggest employers in East Belfast, Bombardier (formerly known as Shorts), was going to close on the Friday, as it was assumed that most employees would simply take the day off anyway.

People were booking flights to come to Belfast, hotels were filling up — we were later to learn that some fans actually missed the funeral as they believed the reports that it would be Friday. They had come over from England but had to fly back home on the Friday evening.

Eventually Norman spoke to the Sky TV representative in Belfast, Gary Honeyford, stressing that the funeral was, without a shadow of a doubt, going to be on the Saturday. He asked Gary to try to convey this to other media, which Gary did. Finally it was established that Saturday was the day when George would be laid to rest.

And of course, in the event, many of the big names of the sporting world were able to attend. They included (to name just a few) Sir Alex Ferguson; Sven-Göran Eriksson, the then England football-team manager; Pat Jennings, a lifelong friend of George's; Martin O'Neill, another friend from the world of football; Barry McGuigan, the former world champion boxer from Clones; racing driver Eddie Irvine; Alex 'Hurricane' Higgins and Dennis Taylor, both champion snooker players from Northern Ireland; and Robert Dunlop, the brother of motorcycling legend Joey who had been killed in a tragic accident in July 2000.

I had specifically asked that the Dunlop family be invited as they had gone through such similar sad circumstances after the death of Joey. Again, Joey was a local hero who had captured hearts everywhere. Tens of thousands of people had attended his funeral. He was a modest, self-effacing man for whom I personally had great admiration — even though I know nothing about motorbike racing!

All of the political parties were represented and it was amazing to see representatives with totally opposing political opinions sitting side by side in Stormont, chatting amicably about George and his life. Over the dark years of the Troubles, he had illuminated the lives of so many people here in Northern Ireland. Dr Martin McAleese attended as a representative of the Irish President, Mary McAleese.

As the pressure before the funeral was building, though, the stress was taking its toll on all of us. At one of the meetings at Stormont, Sheila insisted that Norman, who hadn't eaten a proper meal for about three days, go with her to have some lunch in the dining room. He agreed, only to be violently ill shortly afterwards.

To be truthful, we hadn't had a decent meal for a couple of weeks. We just snacked if and when we could. Proper meals were a rarity. Even weeks after the funeral, I still wasn't able to eat properly, and really couldn't be bothered to cook. It got so bad that Norman, with his typical sense of humour, said to me one evening, 'I want to introduce you to someone, Barbara. Someone you haven't seen for a while. Cooker, this is Barbara. Barbara, this is the cooker.' How sexist is that? And it still didn't work!

The meetings continued. The pressure mounted. The team that was looking after the guest list for the funeral was being inundated with calls. Although Stormont is a large building for public gatherings, it can accommodate only a limited number of people. Obviously the family had the majority of places, with the remainder going to the council and the NIO.

On the subject of guests, we were being hounded by the press wanting to establish whether or not Alex was coming to the funeral. There was never any question that Alex would be excluded from the funeral. In fact, we were acutely aware of how difficult it would be for her to attend on her own, so we asked that invitations be extended through Phil to her mum and dad as well.

Ros was also attending, and, a couple of days before the funeral, I had a call from Mary Shatila, George's partner from approximately twenty years ago. Obviously Angie, George's first wife and Calum's mum, had to be there as well. I'm sure between them they would have a host of stories they could tell. How George would have loved it!

Meanwhile, Dad's garden was rapidly being turned into a shrine by the fans. Castlereagh Council had covered the lawn with green imitation grass to try to protect it. By the day of the funeral, there wasn't a bit of green to be seen, such was the number of tributes that had been left — everything from flowers, scarves, jerseys and footballs to pictures and teddies. Even the hedges were groaning under the weight of tributes placed there. One of the most poignant things was to see so many different football jerseys side by side. All of the old rivals were represented — Manchester United and Manchester City, Liverpool and Everton, Linfield and Glentoran. Their shirts lay intertwined. Most moving of all was the sight of Rangers and Celtic shirts lying side by side. The two Old Firm Glasgow teams traditionally draw much of their support from the Protestant and Catholic communities respectively in Northern Ireland. Shirts which would often be regarded as a mark of division now represented a coming together of all the people in grief.

I mentioned earlier a young boy called Kyle who played football and had written to George when he was in the Cromwell Hospital. I had kept his card with me. Norman and I now felt that it would be very special for him, and fitting, if he could attend the funeral. All we had, though, was an address in the Poleglass area of West Belfast, but no phone number. When we rang the operator, we were told that the number was ex-directory. However, we were not going to be beaten. Norman contacted the PSNI closest to Kyle's house and explained who we were and what we needed. They were, quite naturally, suspicious of the story and rang our liaison officer, Ricky, to confirm that our request was, in fact, serious. Once they were convinced, they sent a patrol car to Kyle's house. No one was at home. We asked could they please go back again and leave a note for someone to call us.

The next morning, Kyle's mum, Geraldine, phoned. She was absolutely overwhelmed, but assured us that both she and Kyle would be honoured to come to the funeral and to the meal that had been organised for afterwards. We had also invited a schoolgirl from East

Belfast, a young girl called Demi Vance who played football for the Bloomfield Football Club, to attend. The way it worked out, there was a young person there representing each side of the community. George would have liked that.

The tributes were pouring in. Hundreds of sympathy cards were arriving daily, from so many different people, from all over the world. Even young children were taking the time to write to us. One of my favourites was passed to me by my friend Alex. It was from a young boy, James Byers, who was just nine years old. It was very moving and read:

> Dear George Best,
> I hope you have a nice time in heaven. You were a legend and a good footballer too. You were loved by everyone. Here is a prayer for you. Dear God. Please give George Best a good time in heaven and let him be treated like a king. Amen.

I find it incredible that so many children wrote to us. That so many children stood with their dads or grandads on that cold, wet day to say their goodbyes.

On Friday, we finally brought George home. We all travelled together to RAF Aldergrove and, again, it was a surreal scene. The PSNI had provided outriders to escort the cars from Dad's house to the RAF base. We didn't have to stop once as we were escorted through major road junctions, where all traffic had been stopped to allow us through.

As we got closer to the base, we could already see people gathering at the roadside and on motorway bridges. When we arrived, we were shown to the VIP suite to wait. The time seemed to drag. Finally the plane which was bringing our beloved George back to us emerged through the clouds. As the plane landed and taxied to a halt, I was shaking, not just because it was a bitterly cold and windy day, but from emotion.

Of all of the memories that I have of that incredible week, one that I will never forget is that first sight of George's coffin. When the plane landed, it had been taken from the far side of the plane. Now, escorted by a lone piper, it was being carried across the tarmac.

As the first notes of the lament filled the air, I began to cry, and then, as the coffin itself appeared, I just broke down. I looked at Dad, trying so hard to maintain his composure, and my heart ached for him.

The coffin was placed gently in the hearse and I placed a single red rose on top of it. I hugged Dad so hard afterwards, and apologised to him for breaking down. But I think he understood that that was one of the most difficult moments for me. Seeing the coffin had brought it home that George was no longer with us. That he really had begun his final journey.

Driving out of RAF Aldergrove was very emotional. RAF members and their families, along with civilians employed at the base, had gathered along the roadside, many just bowing their heads, but the majority applauding as the hearse which held George's body passed by. As the cars drove the twenty miles from Aldergrove to Belfast, the crowds increased dramatically.

I was sitting beside Calum who was already very moved by the numbers of people who had turned out. 'Wait until tomorrow,' I told him. 'You've seen nothing yet.'

As we drew nearer to Dad's house, for whatever reason, I grew increasingly nervous. When we got to Burren Way, many hundreds of people had turned out. It's strange how silence can be so overwhelming. When George died, I was so aware of it, and once again, as he was gently removed from the hearse that day, it was all-enveloping. Apart from the odd sniff or someone blowing their nose, that street packed with hundreds of onlookers was completely quiet. People seemed to be numb with grief.

Two memories are quite clear in my mind. The first one is of Ted Beckham, the father of David Beckham, standing there, quietly watching this very sad scene. And the second one is the face of our neighbour Mrs Beirne, who looked devastated. She had been our neighbour for over fifty years and had watched George grow up. Together with two of her daughters, she would be among the mourners at Stormont.

Once the coffin was in the house, Dad sent someone out to bring Ted Beckham inside for a cup of tea but he had already gone. Something that we noticed over the next twenty-four hours was the amount of respect and privacy which was afforded to us. This was so comforting as we had a mammoth task ahead. The entire family was going to be thrust into the public eye not just at home in Northern Ireland, but around the world.

Just a couple of hours after George was brought home, there was a knock on the door. When I opened it, a poor man, who was very drunk and sobbing uncontrollably, lurched into the hallway. His arms laden with bunches of flowers, he was crying so much it was heartbreaking. He said he wanted to pay his respects. I took his flowers and thanked him, and he left.

Norman and I went to Stormont in the afternoon to see how things were progressing. It was very difficult. Peter Corry was there practising with the choirs and the musicians. Brian Kennedy had just finished his rehearsal of 'You Raise Me Up', but the choir wanted to run through it again so one of the choir members took the leading role. When I heard them all singing together, I just broke down again and sobbed. I was really beginning to worry now how on earth the family would get through the funeral itself on Saturday morning. I looked at Norman who by this stage was pale and haggard; I was worried sick about him.

I was also concerned that we shouldn't lose sight of our aim to make it a day for the fans, not the big names. We were standing on the steps of Stormont with some of the staff, who were discussing where the car carrying George's body would arrive. I was looking past the statue of Sir Edward Carson which faces down the 'mile', as the Stormont driveway is known. Tens of thousands of people would be allowed into the grounds on the day. But still I wanted to make a gesture that would bring the fans — even if only a small number of them — closer still.

A couple of minutes later, Phil telephoned to see how things were going. We discussed this and between us came up with the idea of bringing in to the service itself a symbolic group of fans — ten members of the public picked at random from the crowd on the day. As Phil said, 'George would have wanted that.'

It was decided by those organising the funeral that our plan wouldn't be announced, as it had the potential to cause major crowd-control problems. Instead, Sheila from the NIO, together with Paul from security, would quietly and simply go into the crowd just before the service and select ten people.

Having sorted arrangements for this aspect of the service, I was beginning to feel the emotion get the better of me again. Norman could see that I was struggling, so he insisted that I leave Stormont. I felt guilty at leaving him, but I just needed to get away. I drove the short distance to our house just to spend some time quietly and check on our two lovely golden retriever dogs, Duke and Prince. Friends had been round regularly to keep an eye on them and take them for a walk. But the dogs seemed to know that things weren't right and when I got home they came over and each one put his head on my knees. That made me even worse. Even our dogs were broken-hearted.

I worked for a while on what I was going to say at the funeral service the next day and then headed back to Dad's to bring everyone up to date on what was happening. When I arrived at Dad's, there were so many people there. The garden was now a sea of colour from the hundreds of floral tributes, jerseys and scarves. I was chatting to a few people outside, thanking them for coming, when I spotted a priest. I went over to shake hands with him and he was very upset. He said that he had met George ten years previously and had never forgotten it. That day he had been standing outside Dad's for about two hours. It was as if he couldn't move. I remember him saying to me that he couldn't believe that he, a priest from Coalisland (a staunchly republican village in Tyrone), was standing in the predominantly Protestant Cregagh Estate in East Belfast. I assured him that he was very welcome at our house. Back inside, when I told Dad about him, he immediately said, 'Go and bring him in for a cup of tea.' But sadly when I went out to call the man, he had already left.

Meanwhile, those coincidences I mentioned just continued.

In Northern Ireland, when someone dies, it is quite usual to bring the body home for the wake, where friends and neighbours call to pay their respects. Everyone generally brings gifts of food, such as biscuits, cakes, sandwiches or tea bags. It goes back to the days when money was scarce and the neighbours would all help out to ensure that guests were fed. But we now had so much food in the house, as even the local shopkeepers had sent round bags of groceries. The local battalion of the Royal Irish Regiment had also kept up an endless supply of snacks and sandwiches.

The evening before the funeral, Carol and I discussed what we were going to do with the food that was left over, as it would be such a shame to waste it. I asked if anyone had a number or contact for the Salvation Army, as we could perhaps send something down to the local hostel for the homeless in Belfast. Grace said that she knew a girl called Iris Corry but she would have to go home to get the phone number. Iris is married to a cousin of Peter Corry's, and had been responsible for the organisation of the funeral of Grace's daughter, Ashleigh. But Grace hadn't seen her for a long time.

I said that I would drive Grace home to get the phone number. We opened the front door and, believe it or not, Iris was actually standing on Dad's doorstep! And yes, she was able to organise that the food be taken down to a local hostel so that none of it went to waste.

Norman was still at Stormont going through the last-minute rehearsals. One thing which had to be practised to perfection was the carrying of George's coffin up the sixty steps to the front doors of Stormont. This required a certain expertise and precision. It was not going to be an easy task. After all, it would be seen across the world so it was essential it went well. Friends of Norman's who had previous training in this discipline agreed to take on this role.

Norman felt that he couldn't leave until he was satisfied that he had a thorough understanding of the sequence of events that were to take place the next day. However, it was hard for him to stand to the side and act the role of a dispassionate observer. It was difficult for him to watch a 'dress rehearsal' of a coffin being carried up the steps.

By this stage, all of the staff involved in the organisation of the funeral were exhausted. Joan McCoy became so upset at one stage, that she started to cry. She was worried that it wouldn't all come together. We had a bit of a laugh many months later when Peter Robinson, our local MP, said that things must have been bad as Joan had no make-up on! Anyone who knows Joan will know that she is rarely seen without her lipstick.

Everyone left Stormont very late that evening but hardly anyone slept. Joan said that throughout the night, certain things would pop into her head and she would send a text to people to ensure that, whatever the problem was, it had been attended to. And without fail, no matter what time it was, she got a reply.

Dad spent the night at a friend's house, secure in the knowledge that his house was under constant police guard. People still arrived late into the night to leave their tributes.

It was a long night for everyone. I don't think that one person had a decent sleep. At one point, I did doze off but then I awoke suddenly and sat bolt upright in the bed in a bit of a panic, thinking, 'What will we do if nobody turns up tomorrow?' I believe that George would have wondered about that as well. He knew of course, that he was popular. But did he realise just how popular?

Saturday, 3 December, brought the most appalling weather. It was bitterly cold, windy and raining, but that didn't stop the crowds from turning up. They came from all over. I know of one person who flew in from Geneva. Another man travelled from Wicklow by bus and train, and then walked to Dad's from Belfast city centre. Another couple of men came from Galway, which is a six-hour drive, just to say a final farewell — I'm told one of them actually missed the funeral of a good friend to come up to Belfast. Crowds of people came across from Manchester. In fact, they came from all over the world, united in their feeling of loss, bringing and sharing a warmth that made the inclement weather seem immaterial.

By now, every part of this colossal operation had been put in place. The people already beginning to gather along the route would have no idea of the lengths the staff of Castlereagh Council had gone to, to ensure perfection. The streets of East Belfast had been swept during the night, and buses and taxis were on standby at both airports, with dedicated staff in place to direct any last-minute latecomers. Arrangements were in place to ask everyone attending the service, without exception, to hand in their mobile telephones, which would then be sealed in envelopes and returned after the service. The VIP mourners were to be transported from La Mon House Hotel by bus, but there were helicopters on standby to transport them if the roads became blocked. Staff from the council had even spoken to the local paramilitaries who voluntarily and personally removed their flags from the Cregagh Estate to ensure that visitors from other traditions would not feel intimidated.

The buses which would carry the main body of mourners to Stormont had to pass by a very large paramilitary wall mural in the Tullycarnet estate which was en route to Stormont. Once again, when asked to co-operate, paramilitary leaders had agreed to cover it up. It seemed that every element of society wanted to pay its respects in whatever way possible.

Norman and I drove to my father's house. We had to park in a street around the corner as the police had sealed off Burren Way. As soon as we turned into Dad's street, the first thing that I saw was the hearse with the rest of the funeral cars behind it. I don't know why this had such an impact on me, but I instantly started to cry. It was so final.

The street was lined five or six deep with people who had come to pay their respects. Professor Williams, Dr Alisa and Phil Hughes were the only non-family members who were invited to the house for the private service. That may seem a bit harsh, but the police were very concerned about crowd control and traffic issues and consequently the only cars permitted in the cortège would be the official cars. The remainder of the wider family and close friends were invited instead to attend the private service at the graveside after the service in Stormont, and would be transported there by coach. Calum preferred to have his mum travel with him and, after he attended the service in the house, instead of joining the rest of the family in the official cars, he travelled in a separate hire car.

People have often said to me that the day of the funeral must have been a bit of a blur, but it is quite the opposite. I remember very clearly everything that happened.

The first car was a hearse containing some of the many floral tributes. The second car contained George. Dad, Carol and Allen, Norman and I, and Phil were in the third car. The rest of the cars carried the remainder of the family. The cars had to travel at a specific speed with a specific distance between them. This was to ensure that the crowds did not close in behind the cars and try to show their respects by following the hearse on the funeral route. In Northern Ireland, it is normal for mourners to walk behind the funeral cortège.

The journey to Stormont was incredibly moving. From the minute that George's body came out of Dad's house, until it reached Stormont approximately four miles away, the crowds applauded. I felt it was such a moving but fitting gesture. George loved to hear the applause of the fans when he was dazzling them with his brilliance on the pitch and he would have truly appreciated this final gesture.

To see so many people, men women and children, standing in the pouring rain, many of them weeping bitterly, was very touching. On their banners and placards, held aloft, there were messages that were obviously heartfelt. One that sticks with me was a slogan which was eventually to be painted as a wall mural in Belfast: 'Maradona — good. Pelé — better. George — Best'.

The closer we got to Stormont, the more nervous I became. The scene which met us when we arrived there will be etched on my mind forever. Thousands of people now lined 'the mile' or the Prince of Wales Avenue, to give it its proper name. They applauded as the hearse carrying the coffin draped in the Northern Ireland football flag passed by. They bombarded the cars with flowers, and football scarves, and I smiled to myself as the cars turned into the beautiful grounds of Stormont, and thought: 'GB, imagine us thinking that no one would turn up.'

As with so many events held in his honour since, how he would have loved it all! So many times since he has died, I've said to myself: 'If only he could have seen this!' The loyal fans were determined to give him the send-off he deserved. And as the veteran sports journalist and broadcaster Jackie Fullerton, a long-time friend of George's, remarked with a smile that day: 'George can still sell tickets!'

Many people were obviously deeply affected. Some were crying, some stood with their heads bowed, some clapped and waved flags. All paid homage in their own way. Yet again, I was genuinely touched by the number of children, both boys and girls, who had turned up. One mother told an interviewer that she wanted her children to be part of such an historic occasion and to impress upon them the important part in Northern Ireland's sporting history that George had played.

When the funeral cortège arrived at the bottom of the steep steps leading up to the ornate entrance of Stormont, we were more than a little worried about how Dad would handle it. He was determined to walk up those steps following behind his son's coffin. But we feared that it could be all too much for him, at eighty-six years of age. As we began to climb, Norman said to Dad, 'Take my arm.' Together they began the steep climb.

The coffin itself was being carried by six pall-bearers, stepping slowly and carefully upwards. Despite our worries, Dad very obviously soon got into his step. In fact, about halfway up he suddenly nudged Norman. 'Is there any chance those buggers could get a move on?' he demanded.

The steps of Stormont were lined with hundreds of beautiful floral tributes. Once again, it was deeply moving that so many people had thought so highly of George. Flowers came from HRH The Duke of York who wrote 'George Best was an inspirational footballer from Northern Ireland whose skills captured the imagination of fans around the world.' There were flowers, too, from Tony Blair, the British Prime Minister; Bertie Ahern, the Irish Taoiseach; actor Micky Rourke; Sir Elton John; and Van Morrison; as well as many of the teams that he played for, such as Hibs and Fulham.

One sight which greatly touched me was the boys from Cregagh Rangers Football Club who had formed a guard of honour, together with the councillors from Castlereagh. Everyone was immaculately turned out — the councillors in their robes and the little boys in their pristine new football strips. I felt bad that they had all been standing in the rain for such a long time. One wee boy stands out in my mind. He was so overcome with emotion, the tears were running down his face. Calum made a special point of going across to speak to him.

I have mentioned a number of times just how much thought was put into the organisation of the funeral by Castlereagh Council. The smallest details had been taken into consideration. They had even arranged towels to dry the young boys who had formed the guard of honour!

I was dreading entering the Great Hall at Stormont, but Carol and I held hands really tightly and set off behind Dad who was just behind George's coffin. I couldn't help thinking that even though it was a very sad and difficult task for Akeel, Norman, Allen, Calum, Ian and Phil to carry George's body, it must have been a very proud moment for every single one of them.

I knew that Peter Corry would be singing 'Bring Him Home' as George's body was carried shoulder high down the aisle and I was so worried that if I broke down at that stage, I might not have been able to carry on with my personal tribute to George. I knew that Peter was also very worried. To ensure that he didn't break down, he had earlier asked the lighting engineers for what I believe is called 'moonlighting' — in other words, shining a spotlight directly in the performer's eyes. This meant that Peter wasn't actually able to see the coffin as it approached him. All of us felt that Peter did a magnificent job under very difficult and emotional circumstances.

The hour-long service was charged with emotion from start to finish. Eamonn Holmes went over to Dad and put his arm around him before he went to the podium. He told the audience:

A family grieves, football grieves, and a country grieves as well.

In Ulster folklore we have many heroes, many legends and many myths. George Best will pass into that folklore, as mercurial, as magical, as someone who lived his dream and as someone who made our dreams comes true. What mere mortal could do what he did on a pitch?

George would always recognise that however much a genius he may have been, he was also flawed, and maybe that imperfection made us love him more.

In a country that often cannot rise above politics and religion, George Best did more than most to bring us together as a people to make us realise that there is more to unite us than divide us.

George, we mourn your life cut short, but we are proud to welcome you home.

Denis Law spoke fondly of George and said, 'I would like to think that Bestie and I will meet up again one day.' He then added quickly, 'Although I hope not too soon!'

Professor Williams in his tribute said,

I quickly came to realise how much affection George attracted from all around the world. I attend meetings giving lectures on liver disease, but they didn't seem to be a bit interested in what I said. It was always, 'How's George?'

All around the world, in South Africa, in Australia, in the Middle East: 'How's George?'

George mingled easily with people with that lovely smile which seemed to put people at ease. After the transplant there were some very good times and he was very well indeed but the temptations of life overtook him again. Sometimes I think that we made him too well. It has been the last six months which has been such a disaster, and then we finally lost him.

It is said that doctors shouldn't get too close to their patients. It's not that easy when that person is George Best.

'Hi Prof.' 'Hi George.' That's how it was.

Dr Akeel Alisa told mourners:

I would like to express my admiration to the man who gave us George Best, the proud and brave Dickie Best. I believe that George wanted people to remember him as a footballer, and he was truly the most talented footballer Northern Ireland and the world has ever seen.

George Best showed the beautiful side of football and turned it into a living art. He wasn't very tall, he wasn't very large but there was nothing he couldn't do on the pitch. He gave the people of Belfast a sense of pride. When he was alive, he brought Belfast together as one. There were no religious barriers. Everyone cheered him, and driving today through the streets of Belfast, it seems that he has done it again.

What made it hard for the Professor and me was that whilst the eyes and ears of the world were focused on us, we were truly treating a friend. George Best gave so much and took so little in return.

The Beatles sang Imagine. George Best practised Imagine. The Beatles brought music to our ears. George Best brought magic to our eyes. What he has done for the game of football will never be forgotten. On a cold chilly November day, George, the Best left us way too soon. My wish is that you find peace. God Bless you and thank you for being who you were.

Bobby McAlinden, George's life-long friend, also spoke fondly and warmly of him.

I had been determined to speak at the funeral myself. I felt it was my way of telling George that I loved him — something that I hadn't done when he was alive. People have asked me, 'How on earth did you stand up there in front of the whole world and hold it together like that?' But to me, I wasn't speaking in front of the world. I was speaking to just one person and that was George. And yes, of course it was a tremendously emotional moment for me. I found out only afterwards that Norman had asked Eamonn Holmes to take over if he felt it was becoming too much for me. Eamonn told me later that his backside was half off the chair quite a bit. All the way through, he was willing me to finish it. He said that at one stage he wanted to come up and put his arm around me. I am so glad that he didn't as I think that would have completely finished me off emotionally!

In my tribute to my lovely brother, I said:

Today the world is saying goodbye to Dr George Best, superstar, superhero.

Today I am saying goodbye to GB, super brother, my hero. My love and respect for you was unconditional and simple. I will always cherish the memories of the happy times that I was privileged to share with you. I will always be grateful to Norman — or Stormin' as you fondly referred to him — for encouraging me all of those years ago to make more of an effort to become part of your life again.

I was reluctant at first, as I truly was in awe of you. How foolish! Time with you was uncomplicated (generally!) and fun. Your sense of humour was second to none.

When you live your life in the public eye as George was often forced to do from an early age, people can focus on your flaws and weaknesses. In this respect George was not alone. But most people thankfully can deal with their personal problems without the whole world being involved. George did not have this luxury.

George brought people together. He brought people together from all over the world, and he brought people together in Northern Ireland.

George had a colourful life and he enjoyed very much what he was given. He never complained or passed the blame to anyone but himself, and he truly loved living.

We honour George today, and I believe that everyone is so glad that we brought him home, not just to Belfast, but more importantly into all our hearts.

He was an exceptional man. A man of grace both on the field and off. A sportsman of enormous stature and a friend to all, to whom he gave freely of his time and energy. Something which was sadly not always recognised by others.

Most of us know just how exceptional George was because of his incredible skill at football. A gift that he loved and respected and a gift that gave pleasure and thrills to millions over the years. The beautiful boy of the beautiful game.

Do not look on George as gone. He has only stepped off the pitch, and we have his memory that is special in personal and individual ways to us all. The warm feeling that we have of George at this moment is his spirit that is with us all.

Our family is thankful to everyone here today who has in their own way marked the passing of the world's most adored sportsman. What a great tribute to be loved not just by your family, but by the world at large. And to love them in return.

During your last hours, Professor Williams told the world that you were coming to the end of your long road. It was a road that took you from Belfast at the age of fifteen, to what was to be your destiny. It took you to far-off places and glittering heights. At times it was a hard road. But today, George, that road has brought you back to the city, back to the people, and back to the family who loved you most of all.

Today, George, the long road has brought you home.

Goodbye, GB, and thank you.

As I finished, Peter Corry began to sing that beautiful and haunting song, 'The Long and Winding Road'. We hadn't planned it that way. The organisers hadn't seen in advance what I had written. I hadn't known what would immediately follow my tribute in the ceremony. And yet it all fitted so very perfectly.

And so it was at the end of the service, too, when Brian began singing 'You Raise Me Up'. As he reached the chorus and those words, 'You raise me up', the pall-bearers in sync lifted the coffin.

'I am strong when I am on your shoulders,' sang Brian as they raised it on to their shoulders. By the time the last notes of the song faded, George's coffin had been carried to the front door of Stormont. It was sheer perfection.

It was only recently that I was able to watch film footage of the funeral for the first time. I found it unbearably moving.

George had been given the finest possible send off. He had been honoured in a unique ceremony and setting. In the United Kingdom, the live television figures for coverage of the event had reached 4.5 million viewers at one point. Globally 23 million people had watched the funeral.

On the final leg of the journey, travelling back down Prince of Wales Avenue, I looked once again at the sea of faces, and mentally thanked them for their support. 'All this for one person,' I thought proudly to myself. All this for our George.

Chapter 12 ∾

THE GEORGE BEST FOUNDATION

The world had had its chance to say a very public farewell to George and now the family would conduct a very private service to say our own goodbyes. Having left the magnificence of Stormont, we gathered quietly around Mum's graveside in Roselawn Cemetery, where, in compliance with George's own wishes, he was to be finally laid to rest. It was a very short and simple religious service. As a final gesture, the red rose that I had placed on the coffin at Aldergrove, and which had remained there throughout the funeral service, was dropped gently into the grave.

We were, and we remain, extremely grateful that the public respected our wishes and left us in peace for that very final difficult task. The media, however, were not so unanimous in their respect. The following day — Sunday — we were deeply hurt to learn that one newspaper had published shots of George's coffin being lowered into the ground.

As soon as the brief service at Roselawn was over, we all headed back to La Mon House Hotel where a meal had been provided for the mourners. Once again, I was to learn just how much people were prepared to do for George.

It was December and the Christmas season had started. The previous evening, the hotel had had a function for 400 people. That function hadn't finished until one o'clock in the morning. The staff then had to have the room vacated, cleaned and prepared for 6 a.m., in time to be ready for nine coach-loads of invited guests who were attending the funeral. I spoke to Allen Chambers who was the Banqueting Manager on the day of the funeral. He recalls that extra staff had to be called in to ease the workload. And most of them had volunteered to work between twelve- and fourteen-hour shifts to ensure that everything ran smoothly. Allen himself had been on duty since 4.30 a.m.

Each guest had registered on arrival at the hotel, where tea, coffee and breakfast had been served in time to allow the coaches to depart at nine o'clock. Everything had run to a strict deadline. But Allen told me: 'It was an honour to be involved with the funeral. Obviously there was the prestige attached to it, but it was much deeper than that. This one was personal.'

As soon as the coaches had left the hotel, the room had been quickly revamped to welcome everyone back for lunch, and, once that was over, the room had to be prepared for another Christmas function that evening at eight o'clock.

All in all, the hotel catered for 1,500 people throughout the day! They did a remarkable job, and Dad made a special point of personally thanking not just Allen but the General Manager, Denise Maghie, and the Junior Manager, Lloyd Jackson. Calum, much to the delight of the staff — especially the females — specifically went to the Old Mill Suite to thank them and let them get some photos taken.

One of the staff members on duty that day, Michael Dougal, was very touched by this. He said that it brought back memories of the day back in 1978 when Mum had been buried. Michael had been working in the Drumkeen Hotel back then and remembers George chatting with guests in the hotel. Michael was surprised at this, given the tragic circumstances, but remembers George saying that he didn't mind, as it helped him to put to the back of his mind, at least for a short while, the sad events of the day.

Not long after George's funeral, Lloyd Jackson won the prestigious 'Junior Manager of the Year' in the Janus Awards — the 'Oscars' of the catering world. He had to give a ten-minute presentation to an independent panel, with the title: 'Working Under Pressure'. He used 3 December as a very apt example.

During the course of lunch, Norman and I were chatting to Professor Williams and Dr Akeel Alisa, who, like the rest of us, were overwhelmed by the support that had been shown for the family. Just before leaving for London, the Prof took Norman and me aside and said, 'You can't ignore this. You both must do something positive with it.'

He was right. Because there had been such an overwhelming outpouring of support after George died, we really felt that this should be channelled into something constructive and practical. And so we decided to set up a charity in George's memory.

The aims and objectives of the George Best Foundation (www.georgebest.com) are simple and would have had George's full approval: firstly, to raise funds to research liver disease; and secondly, to encourage a healthier lifestyle through playing football. This latter objective is obviously focused on helping young people find an alternative to the drink, drugs and anti-social behaviour which are such a problem in today's society. In theory it sounded like a simple task for novices like ourselves. But in reality it was to be very complicated, and without the expert guidance and service of our solicitors, Johnsons in Belfast, I don't think that it could have been achieved so quickly.

As I mentioned before, Carol and I had taken many of the cards and letters, which had arrived for George before he died. We wanted to reply to them. On top of that, sympathy cards were arriving in large numbers. It was not just a difficult task, but also a very emotional one.

We decided that I would reply to the emails as Carol, at the time, had no computer. I was like someone possessed, but I was determined to make sure that people were thanked for taking the time and trouble to write to us. Meanwhile, Carol replied by hand to people who had sent cards or letters, and as soon as I had waded my way through the emails, I started on the pile I'd brought home. We both worked hard for quite a number of weeks. But it was rewarding when people actually wrote back to thank us. Sometimes their replies were so moving that we felt compelled to reply to those letters as well!

People have said to me that they were amazed that the family had taken the time and trouble to acknowledge letters, emails and cards. But for us it was extremely important to say thank you for the enormous wave of support. I have struck up a couple of lovely friendships with people from as far away as Australia and even Russia.

Initially both Carol and I tried to phone people to say thanks. But we had to abandon that idea when those we called became emotional. That in turn would set us off. It would have taken forever and reduced us to wrecks!

The next task was to gather together all of the tributes that had been left around Belfast. A local cleaning company called Muggins had collected all the jerseys from Dad's garden and had taken them away and laundered them free of charge. A chap called William McDowell collected hundreds of jerseys from various other locations, and his family personally laundered them all over Christmas time. Once laundered, these shirts and scarves were stored free of charge at a warehouse. William McDowell worked very hard to raise funds and, as a result, 500 of the jerseys had 'George Best Foundation' printed on them.

And since the funeral, many hundreds of the shirts have been donated to disadvantaged kids all around the world. South Africa, Sierra Leone, Jamaica, Malawi, Thailand and Kenya — these are just a few of the places to which the shirts have been taken. There are many lovely stories about how and where the jerseys were distributed — but it would take another book to tell them all. Later in this chapter I'll describe some of the projects the shirts were donated to — and the remarkable people behind them.

Even now, we still find it hard to believe just how much George was thought of — and that so many people throughout the world knew of him. I recently met a man who had lived in Johannesburg in South Africa for a long time He ran a small carpet-cleaning company. He cleaned carpets during the week and then at the weekend when people were paid, he returned to collect his money. Much of his work was in non-white neighbourhoods, and in one of these areas one evening, he was on his way back to his van when he was confronted by a group of men, one of whom shouted 'Where are you going to, you white Afrikaner b*****?'

He walked on ignoring the group. But again the man shouted the same thing at him. Although he himself was armed, he knew that the gang would most certainly have been carrying weapons as well. By now, he realised that it was futile to try to get to his van and that he wasn't going to win if he confronted them. So he tried a different tack.

Turning to them, he said in his broadest Northern Irish accent, 'Are yous guys talking to me?'

The gang looked baffled. The one who seemed to be the leader asked: 'Where are you from, man?'

'Northern Ireland,' he said.

'Where in Northern Ireland?'

'Belfast.'

The members of the group all looked at each other. Then one of them asked, 'Do you know of Georgie Best?'

'Of course,' said the guy. 'I was brought up close to where he lived.'

A football discussion ensued. There were smiles all round and handshakes, and he was sent on his way unharmed.

We'll never know for sure — but it's good to think that the power of George's name may have saved this man from a possible beating or perhaps worse.

In February 2005, Norman and I had booked a trip to South Africa. We were due to leave on 20 December and had planned to stay for three weeks. As it was so soon after George's death, we were unsure if we should go. We were emotionally drained and needed a break but somehow a holiday at such a time seemed inappropriate.

On the evening of 13 December, just ten days after George's funeral, we were sitting at home trying to make a decision about whether or not to go. What followed next was a bombshell.

Our house was untidy, with paperwork everywhere. We were worn out. The telephone rang. It was Andrew, our next-door neighbour back in France.

'Hi, Norman,' he said. 'I am so sorry to have to call you with this, but your house is on fire.'

I will never forget the look on Norman's face. When he told me, I just sank on to one of the chairs. It's difficult to explain — but stunned as we were, neither of us was really too worried by this news. The new bathroom, which we had started at the end of September, was nearing completion, and we automatically assumed that it was a small problem. Maybe the plumber or electrician had done something wrong, we reasoned. It would be something minor that could be contained.

But just fifteen minutes later, Andrew called again.

'I am so sorry,' he said. 'There is no easy way to tell you this. Your house has been entirely devastated.'

It seems that his wife had been out bringing in some firewood when she heard an explosion. She ran in and told Andrew to call the fire brigade. The firemen were there within three minutes. But it was too late. The house was indeed devastated.

Shocked as we were, we were also mystified. An explosion? So much damage in such a short period? It all seemed a bit odd.

Norman made arrangements to fly over first thing the following morning. When he arrived, the house, or what was left of it, was completely sealed off by police and army. Obviously they were treating this as something more serious than an accidental house fire. And as it turned out, it had been.

Someone had gone in and planted three, or possibly four, blast incendiary devices in the house, with a petrol accelerant. The force of the explosion was so strong that the roof was not burnt, but blown off. The ensuing fire had swept through the house at an alarming rate. Two of the three bedrooms and the bathroom were totally gutted. The remainder of the house was partially burnt. And what wasn't burnt was ruined when the roof collapsed.

Norman stayed for two days, during which time he was questioned at length by the police. Every single aspect of our private lives was investigated. Was our marriage happy? Was either of us having an affair? Did we have money problems? Did we owe the builder money? Could it be connected to George in any way? It went on and on.

By the second day of the questioning, Norman had built up a slight rapport with one of the investigating police officers, who apparently didn't speak English. Everything was done through an interpreter. One of his closing questions was: 'Can you please ask Mr McNarry is he gay?'

Norman, who has a great sense of humour, said to the interpreter. 'Can you tell Monsieur Daguerre if he gives me a kiss, I'll tell him.'

Everyone including Monsieur Daguerre started to laugh. So he understood English after all!

For us, though, the months that followed were no laughing matter. Media interest in the story both at home and in France was understandably intense. Even now, the French police have still not discovered why our home was targeted, although we do know that one of the main theories is that it was a case of mistaken identity.

When Norman returned from France, we decided after all to go on holiday. We needed to get away from all the madness. But even that wasn't straightforward. The day before we were leaving, I got a call from a solicitor in London, who said that he needed to see me urgently.

Could we come to London? Failing that, he would fly to Belfast. I explained that it wasn't possible as we were going away. However, he was quite insistent, so we arranged to meet at Heathrow Airport before boarding our flight to South Africa.

Looking back, it was a bizarre meeting. Picture the scene: two very weary, emotionally drained people and two London solicitors sitting in a not-very-private coffee shop in a very busy Heathrow Airport.

One of the solicitors said, 'I take it you know why you're here?'

My heart was racing. I couldn't face any more bad news. I said, 'I have no idea.'

He produced some papers, which were actually George's will, and told me that I was the beneficiary of George's estate.

I think the solicitors were taken aback by my response. Let's just say it wasn't one of euphoria! I rolled my eyes heavenwards and said through gritted teeth: 'Thank you, GB.' Of course, deep down I was very, very touched.

However, although I considered it a great honour, I had a sneaking feeling that the estate of George Best wasn't going to be the simplest thing in the world to sort out. What an understatement!

Norman and I set off for South Africa, but it was so difficult to relax. All I seemed to do was cry. I couldn't even think clearly. We tried to relax but with all of the events of the previous months, it was hard.

However, one thing that did cheer us up was the fact that the CD with the music from George's funeral had been released and was rocketing up the charts. This was great news, as all of the profits from the sales of the CD were going to the George Best Foundation. Everyone had given their services free of charge: Peter Corry, Brian Kennedy, the distributors. All that had to be paid were royalties to the BBC. By the time we came back from South Africa, the CD had reached number four in the charts. We believe that it could have made number one if it had been given more airtime on radio and had been allowed on *Top of the Pops*. Nevertheless, number four was great, and the Foundation benefited by over £65,000.

Before we left South Africa, Norman and I visited a local school in a very poor village in the middle of KwaZulu Natal and presented the children with some of the jerseys that we had brought over from Northern Ireland. We then had to leave straightaway to drive to Johannesburg to meet up with a local reporter who was going to take the remainder of the jerseys to an orphanage for children with Aids.

We were already running behind schedule, so had to try to make up for lost time on the motorway. Imagine our horror when halfway there we were stopped for speeding. Normally this wouldn't be a problem, but in South Africa it is widely known that certain members of the police force are not exactly squeaky clean, and in cases like this, they use their authority to frighten the life out of poor, unsuspecting tourists. When we stopped, the police officer asked where we were going, and, when we explained that we were on our way to the airport to catch a flight, he said, 'What time is your flight?'

When we told him, he replied that we would have to go to the local police station to pay a very large fine. If we were really in a hurry, we could pay him on the spot and it would be much easier and cheaper, and then we wouldn't miss our flight.

I must admit, I was in such a panic, I would gladly have paid him, but Norman refused to be blackmailed. Luckily, we had been warned about this practice. He went to the boot of the car and produced one of the football jerseys with 'The George Best Foundation' printed on the back. The officer knew instantly who George was and asked for one for his friend who was skulking a little way up the road. Norman gladly handed over another one, and then the 'bent' copper had the nerve to ask for the fine money. Norman just shook his head and said that he would be able to sell the jerseys for much more than the value of the fine.

Once again, the power of George worked, as this seemed to satisfy the greedy man and he let us continue our journey. We made it to the check-in desk with about seven minutes to spare!

At the time of writing this book, George's estate remains far from settled. We are still trying to track down very important items which cannot be accounted for. My main focus is to ensure that we can safeguard the significant historical memorabilia that are part of George's legacy. Our dream is to see these things displayed in a museum for football fans to enjoy.

On this note, Mavis and Denis from Champney's Health Resort have played an important role in protecting many valuable items. During his stay at Forest Mere, George turned up one day with a couple of hold-alls and said to Mavis, 'Can you keep these somewhere safe for me?'

Inside, as Mavis discovered, was a real treasure trove. In total, eleven items were in the bag, all very precious. There was the beautiful silver presentation trophy, modelled on an original Northern Ireland International cap, which was presented to George during the Freedom of Castlereagh ceremony. There was a BBC Lifetime Achievement award, dated 2002. This was presented to George in December that year, just six months after his transplant. But for me the most important thing was his 1968 European Cup Winners' medal. Mavis and Denis had carefully itemised each piece before packing it and storing it safely in their attic.

Many months later, I was to discover that George's 1968 European Footballer of the Year Trophy had been tracked down. I had actually forgotten about it. I remembered that when George had decided to sell a couple of his trophies, his English Footballer of the Year award had achieved a great price at auction, but the European one had fallen a bit short of the asking price. So he had decided to hold on to it for a while.

All of George's possessions belong to me now: the flat in Chelsea, his much-loved little black mini, his trophies.... But the way I see it, George didn't leave me with just his worldly goods. He left me with an important task. He left me with responsibilities. It is my job to ensure that his legacy is protected and that the really precious and historic awards and memorabilia that he collected during a lifetime are safeguarded for the fans. You can understand why I am so passionate about protecting all of these items. They are part of football history.

The momentary value of the estate is irrelevant to me. It is unlikely to amount to very much anyway when everything is settled. My priority is to ensure that the irreplaceable items do not have to be sold but will be kept together to be enjoyed by future generations of fans. At the moment, it is a very complex and daunting process but I am confident that, with the help of our solicitors, we'll be successful in protecting these items.

There has been much speculation, a lot of psychological pressure and, in the media, plenty of guesswork about George's estate. On a personal level, I've even felt guilty about being the beneficiary. Why did he pick me? But I know in my heart that George trusted me. He has given me a job to do and I will not let him down. People who knew George in the last years of his life say that he spoke fondly of me and he would always tell them that he knew he could trust me. For my part, I want to repay that trust. I want to do the right thing for his memory.

So often, I wish I could turn back the clock and be able to pick up the phone and say, 'Hi, GB. How's things?' But that is not how it is. He is gone and I have been left with this final task. And it will be carried out to the best of my ability and for the right reasons.

Before George died, I was never a great one for visiting graves. But these days when I am under pressure because of commitments I have taken on since his death, I often go to his grave at Roselawn. I talk aloud to him, asking for his help. 'Come on, GB, help me out here,' I'll say.

On occasions, I'll cry. But more often, I leave with a smile, as I have resolved my problem. I imagine that impish grin and those sparkling blue eyes. They are my guidance.

The year after George's death was incredibly hectic. The George Best Foundation was formally recognised and became official on 26 April 2006, just five months after George died.

Just before setting up the charity, I became quite ill. The stress of everything got to me: George's time in hospital, his death, his funeral, the house in France, the will, and now establishing the Foundation. I eventually cracked under the strain and for the first time in my forty-year working career, I was unable to return to work for quite a long time. Norman was terribly worried about me, and was reluctant to leave me alone. I was on medication. And I was drinking too much.

I remember many times meeting people in the street or when I was out shopping. They would be in tears and I would end up comforting them. In public I was strong, but in private I was a mess. I begged and pleaded with Norman to give up the idea of forming the Foundation. I just felt that I couldn't go on.

Our marriage was put under tremendous strain, but Norman wouldn't let me give up on the charity. He worked on alone for a while until I was well enough to cope, and I am so grateful that he did. With the help of my own GP and counselling, I gradually recovered. Apart from Norman's help, I also had enormous support from two friends, Anita and Alex, and I will always appreciate how they helped me.

In that first year, our family was in constant demand for public appearances. Between the Foundation and private functions, our lives were turned upside down. We were approached by many people and organisations. Football supporters' clubs, league teams, fund-raising groups — all wanted to have their names associated with George Best. There was actually nothing to stop them just going ahead, but out of respect the family was almost always consulted.

Belfast City Council proposed erecting a statue in George's memory and, in February 2006, meetings began to plan this. In the same month, the airline Flybe approached us about the possibility of naming a plane after George. I was moved that no matter who we were dealing with, the family's wishes were always taken into consideration. No matter what we asked for or suggested, it was done — although we never asked for anything too much.

Once the Flybe proposal had been agreed in principle, the next issue was a time scale. We were asked if we had any preference. I asked if it would be possible to have the renaming done on 15 March 2006. The family would be going to George's memorial service on 16 March in Manchester Cathedral and I thought that it would be a fitting time to fly on *The George Best*, on its inaugural flight on the newly established Flybe route to Manchester.

I cannot believe that in such a short space of time they pulled it off and the family was able to make that emotional trip on the plane. It was such a lovely tribute, and it was a poignant moment when Calum and Dad unveiled the image of George.

The memorial service in Manchester was another very emotional occasion. All of the family, together with many of George's friends and colleagues, gathered on a very cold spring day (it was actually snowing) to celebrate George's life. Members of the public were of course invited, but they were chosen by ballot. Inevitably this ballot was way oversubscribed — but at least many ordinary fans did get the opportunity to attend.

Another very special date for me that spring was when Norman and I were invited to join the members of the Portstewart Manchester United Supporters' Club at their monthly meeting. They wanted to present our charity with a donation, so we went along and had a chat with them and explained our hopes for the future; the Foundation was still in the very early stages.

We were presented with a very substantial donation. That in itself was great. But I was so pleased and surprised to be introduced to a chap called Ronnie McKee who turned out to be one of the ten members of the public selected, together with his friend Bill Coey, to be brought into Stormont for George's funeral. He spoke very emotionally about what a great honour it had been for him to be part of such a special occasion. It was lovely for me to meet him.

March was to end in a very special way. On 21 March, Norman and I were invited to dine at Westminster as guests of Peter and Iris Robinson. Apart from the extreme honour of such a gesture, it was to be an exceptional evening in more ways than one, as Norman and I were introduced to the two businessmen who had so kindly and generously flown George home to Northern Ireland in a private jet. To meet them personally and to be able to pass on our thanks was very important to us. I was really nervous about the entire evening, but there was no need. They were both easy to talk to and this, coupled with Peter and Iris's hospitality, ensured a very relaxing evening. Not to mention the superb food which we thoroughly enjoyed in those wonderful surroundings!

Three days later, it was down to Dublin, to Áras an Uachtaráin, the home of the President of Ireland, Mary McAleese. The family had been invited to a monthly dinner with approximately sixty other guests. Norman and I were to be there with Julie and her husband Pete and, of course, Dad with his long-time partner Violet Hutchison. Dad has known Violet for well over twenty years, and she has been a great friend to him, bringing companionship during some very difficult times. Yet again, my stomach was in knots at the thought of such a grand occasion, but it turned out to be a remarkable evening, which I will never forget.

Áras an Uachtaráin is a truly magnificent building situated in the Phoenix Park in Dublin. There was a champagne reception before dinner and then we all had a chance to meet the President and her husband, Dr Martin McAleese, who both made us feel instantly relaxed. Before the superb meal, the President made a warm and welcoming speech and afterwards all of the guests were invited to assemble in the drawing room for coffee or drinks. It was Martin's birthday and after the cake ceremony was over, the President asked if anyone would like to sing.

A man called Joe Kennedy who had been at our table during dinner took the floor first. Originally from Mayo, he had gone to live in Manchester at a very young age and had become a successful businessman. He had a lovely tenor voice and kept us all entertained for a while.

'Anyone else?' asked the President. I just held my breath, as I knew what was coming. Norman, who had already had a few glasses of wine and who would be known to sing a song or two when he is 'happy', took the floor and burst into a rousing rendition of the Belfast song, 'I'll tell me Ma when I get home'. How many people can claim to have sung for a president?

Before the evening ended, President McAleese had time for another chat with her guests and took great pride in showing us her private office with its beautiful fireplace. The evening was rounded off by having a lovely happy group photograph taken with us and the President gathered around her desk. Dad has a copy and it takes pride of place in his home beside a photo of George.

In April, Dad and I recorded a special show for UTV with local presenter Gerry Kelly. It was a great success, with the viewing figure on the evening equalling that of the soaps.

Also in April, the family had our first meeting with Brian Ambrose, the Chief Executive of Belfast City Airport, to discuss our views on having the airport renamed in honour of George. The subject of a suitable date came up and, without hesitation, all of us said the same thing — 22 May. George had wanted to celebrate his sixtieth birthday in style. What better way than by having an airport renamed in his honour?

Once again, given the time scale, the staff of the City Airport worked wonders.

There was the inevitable controversy over all of these tributes. Polls were held, and phone-ins to local radio and TV stations. Was George really deserving of such honour, they asked. Fortunately the feedback was extremely positive, but there were people who didn't agree with the decisions. As a family, we totally accept and understand this. Everyone is entitled to their opinion. But one thing which I will never forget is the vicious personal attack on a local radio show by a man who phoned in to give off about George. It was terrible to listen to, and I was completely incensed by the savagery of his comments. My first thoughts were for our dad. I just prayed that he wasn't listening. It was totally out of character for me, but I was so angry that I phoned the station to complain. Of course, this was only music to their ears. A reaction from a member of the Best family. Live on air.

I explained in a cool and dignified manner what I thought of the man's outburst and told the radio presenter: 'I've said my piece. I don't want to communicate with this person any longer.'

Meanwhile, the family continued to be asked to attend special events where George's contribution to sport was acknowledged. It was a hectic schedule. We were invited to Dublin to the TV3/*Irish Daily Star* awards at the Four Seasons Hotel, and eleven days after that it was back to London as guests of the Professional Footballers' Association at their annual awards in London at the Grosvenor House Hotel.

At this stage, discussions were also in progress with a company called Straight Forward Productions who wanted to do a documentary for transmission on BBC in November 2006, to mark the first anniversary of George's death. Dad, Norman and I spent three very emotionally charged sessions filming the programme. But with the expert guidance and the gentle and sympathetic approach of Ian Kennedy and John Nicholson, the end result was a great success. 'To George with Love' received excellent viewing figures.

During this time, Norman and I were also thinking ahead and trying to put the wheels in motion to get some fund-raising into place. As I said, George always spoke about celebrating his sixtieth birthday in great style so I was very keen to ensure that we could do something around this time. The re-naming of the airport would be a major part of it. I also started to email as many Manchester United Supporters' Clubs as possible to see if any of them would be interested in having something around the weekend of 22 May to raise money for the Foundation, using George's birthday as the theme. I had been thinking about something fairly low key like a wee pub quiz.

Instead, in the space of five days, starting on 19 May, Norman and I were to attend nine functions, including a trip to Manchester where the MUST and IMUSU had an amazing fund-raising evening in a pub called Sam Platt's, just across the road from Old Trafford. The theme was '60 of the Best'. It was very important to us to go to Manchester, as it was obviously a place very close to George's heart. The people there never forgot him. To hear 500 people chanting: 'There's only one Georgie Best' brought a lump to my throat.

Earlier in the year, as a result of my emails, Norman and I had also met with the committee members of the Carryduff Manchester United Supporters' Club back home in Northern Ireland. They too wanted to do something to mark George's birthday — but something a bit grander than my pub-quiz idea. By the time the meeting was finished, plans were already under way for a gala dinner! I think at this stage the two Johns, as they are known, had about twelve weeks to pull it all together.

Belfast City Council was approached and the Lord Mayor at the time, Councillor Wallace Browne, gave permission for the Great Hall of the City Hall to be used free of charge. The evening was a resounding success, with a spectacular guest list: Sir Alex Ferguson, David Gill, Martin O'Neill, Paddy Crerand, Pat Jennings, Chris Eubank the boxer, Professor Williams, Dr Akeel Alisa and, of course, our dad. There was a very successful auction. But the main event was undoubtedly the auction of the first Fabergé egg, which was produced in honour of George.

Fabergé eggs were first created in 1884, at Easter, by the Tsar of Russia, as a gift for his wife. They are made from precious metals and encrusted with jewels. Needless to say, they also cost a fortune! Only four westerners have ever had one designed in their honour — Thomas Jefferson, the third President of the United States; Admiral Horatio Nelson; Jimmy Johnstone, one of Celtic's greatest ever footballers; and George. The profits from each egg produced (there will be only sixty-eight of them) will go to the George Best Foundation. The one that was auctioned on the evening made a staggering £28,000, although they can be purchased at a more modest price.

And, of course, another highlight of 22 May was the ceremony for the renaming of the 'George Best Belfast City Airport'. What an amazing and proud event for the entire family that turned out to be. The airport is situated very close to where Norman and I live in East Belfast and every time I drive past it and see the sign with George's signature proudly displayed, especially at night when it is illuminated, I can't help but smile. Each time I fly into the airport, I get that buzz of pride when they announce: 'Welcome to the George Best Belfast City Airport'. It is now possible to fly on the *George Best* aeroplane into the George Best airport. How special is that?

The first anniversary of George's death seemed to arrive very quickly and, far from quietening down, it was as hectic as ever. One reporter I spoke to said that he just couldn't believe how raw the emotion still was, and how much was still being done in George's memory.

By now, the George Best Foundation was well established. It would be impossible to list every single event that we attended over the year, as there were so very many. But I would like to say a huge thanks to every single person who has worked so hard with their fund-raising efforts. To Cracked Flag, Curtis Magee, Paul Bowen, and Laurence John who all produced beautiful songs dedicated to George and donated the profits from their CD sales. To Adrian who successfully stopped drinking for thirty-four days after being sponsored by a friend, and sent the money to our charity. To all of the supporter clubs and other organisations who held dinners for the Foundation. As I said, the list is endless.

The first anniversary was also marked in a particularly 'notable' way. Six months earlier, meetings had started with the Ulster Bank, who wanted to produce a special commemorative £5 note in George's memory. The bank wanted this in circulation for 25 November. The £5 denomination was chosen, as the note would be affordable for everyone. At this point, I have a confession to make. I've never mentioned to anyone at the Ulster Bank (for obvious reasons!) but George didn't actually like £5 notes. He considered them to be too fiddly and treated them as loose change. He liked to use only £10 or £20 notes and would throw the £5 notes in a little bag, in which he kept all of his loose change! However, I know that he would have considered it an honour to be depicted on one.

During those six months planning with the bank, endless meetings were held and many hundreds of hours of legal work took place. Once again, I am deeply grateful for the expert guidance of Sarah Loughran and Paul Tweed from Johnsons solicitors in Belfast. What's more, details had to be kept secret — I could tell no one, not even our dad. I will never forget the day when I first saw what the finished product would look like. I had to leave the room in tears. It was perfect.

Norman and I first met Cormac McCarthy, the Group Chief Executive, in mid-September 2006, and dates were set for both the press launch on 18 October and then the actual launch of the note itself on 13 November. One million £5 notes were printed. A small number of bank employees had been allocated to look after postal applications, with the notes then despatched to all Ulster Bank branches a week after the launch. But there was such demand that the bank hastily had to recruit more staff to the post room. Within forty-eight hours, over 30,000 postal applications had been received, and, within a week, applications had to be suspended.

Meanwhile, on the morning that the notes were to be made available via the branches, long queues formed everywhere. Many bank staff voluntarily went to work early to deal with the madness that ensued. The Foundation website was inundated with requests from all over the world. Within a week, every single £5 note had been snapped up by devoted fans.

Sadly a lot had also been snapped up not by devoted fans but by some individuals who saw George Best, even in death, as a means of making a quick bit of money. I was saddened and angered to see so many of these special notes making their way on to eBay and being sold for ridiculous amounts of money, thus depriving many genuine fans of the chance of owning their own little bit of history.

The Ulster Bank has been a tremendous support to the George Best Foundation and the substantial donation which was received as a result of the special fiver will be put to very good use.

Also put to very good use during the years were the shirts which, as I described earlier, had been left in tribute to George in the immediate aftermath of his death, not just at Dad's house but also at a number of different locations. There were erroneous reports in the press at the time that we had had them destroyed. In fact, they were distributed throughout the world to various deserving causes. The following are just a few of the projects to which they were sent.

The story of Mphatso Nugulwe is such an uplifting one. She is the deputy principal of the Ekwendeni Nursing College in Malawi and was studying for a Master's degree at Queen's University, in Belfast. I was introduced to Mphatso through the Ballygrainey Presbyterian Church in Donaghadee. When I first met her, I felt instantly comfortable. She has such a sunny, infectious personality that it is hard not to be taken with her. Her story is a remarkable one and when I feel down, I think of what she has gone through.

At thirty-eight years of age, she holds down a very busy job at the college. But she is also 'mother' to nine children, none of whom are her own. Some of the children are distant relatives. The others have been abandoned by their parents who perished in the Aids epidemic. Mphatso has selflessly taken on these children and, with the aid of a housekeeper, is bringing them up and educating them. Her wages barely cover the fees, but her strong religious beliefs carry her through.

When I met Mphatso, the Ekwendeni Nursing College had just had its first intake of male students, and they really wanted to get a football team together. But as they have difficulty enough affording the essentials for their studies, football jerseys were a distant dream. When I was approached by the church, I readily agreed to help out and presented Mphatso with enough jerseys for two teams.

I also brought Mphatso to meet our dad and my sister Carol. And recently Carol and I sent off, at our own expense and with the help of the church, six cartons packed full of clothes and essentials for Mphatso's children. She really was an inspiration to me, which I told her as we bade a tearful farewell in Belfast. One day, I would love to surprise her with a visit to her home country.

Keith McClure who comes from Bangor is another remarkable character. He contacted us through the George Best Foundation website after hearing how Norman and I had taken jerseys to South Africa to distribute to some very needy children in KwaZulu Natal. Keith, a keen athlete, was going to Kenya during the summer of 2006 and thought it would be the perfect opportunity to take some of the football shirts with him.

During his visit, he was fortunate to meet up and then stay with Noah Ngeny, the Sydney 2000 Olympic Games 1500-metres champion. He felt that as he was staying with the family it would be fitting to distribute the jerseys to Noah's former school in Eldoret, and so he travelled to Sirikwa Primary School with Noah and his wife. The school has 700 pupils, but Keith was able to bring only fifty jerseys with him, so a list of the most needy children was drawn up by the school staff and the lucky children were called forward to receive their 'gift'.

As Keith said, 'They came forward with ripped and ill-fitting clothes, but they left with a treasured jersey in their hand and I'm sure a good feeling in their hearts.'

Keith, who explained to the children who George was, found the whole experience truly humbling. He felt that in life George had brought so much joy to people with his skills, and now, even in death, he was still helping people in a positive way. Especially children.

It was a privilege for me to meet Noah's wife and three of their beautiful children during a brief trip to Belfast in late 2006.

A couple of months after George's funeral, I met a girl called Debi who had sent a letter via our dad, requesting some of the jerseys, which she wanted to take to Sierra Leone. By the time the letter got to me, sadly Debi had already returned from her trip. I was frustrated that I hadn't been able to help her out, and phoned to apologise for the delay. Debi was so pleased to hear from me and in the end it all worked out well — she was going back out to Sierra Leone in April that year. We agreed to meet up, and I was instantly taken with her enthusiasm and passion.

She explained that her uncle Billy who works for the United Nations had gone out to work in Sierra Leone initially on a six-month contract. But he fell in love with the country and, four years later, he's still there. Billy has been an avid football fan all of his life and helps out at the local school, Cardiff Preparatory in Freetown, teaching the children to play football. The children of Sierra Leone are extremely poor. The country has been torn apart by years of civil war, and many of its people have been left without food, clothing and shelter.

Debi will never forget the day that she took the jerseys to the school. When the back of the Landrover was opened and the children caught a glimpse of the red and white jerseys, she could hear whispers of, 'Manchester, Manchester'.

Debi said that the smiles on their faces were fantastic. Sadly, as the school has so many pupils, it wasn't possible to let each child have a jersey to keep, so the teachers decided that the best solution was to keep the shirts in the school and they would be used on sports days and, of course, football days. At least that way, each child had the chance to wear one, albeit for just a short while.

In May 2006, I received a letter from a girl called Caron Stewart. Caron is part of the Dungannon Thailand team — a group of volunteers who fund-raise for the Christian Care Foundation for children with disabilities. Caron works closely with the Rainbow House Orphanage in Bangkok and has visited there on many occasions. The volunteers were going out to the orphanage in July 2006 and wanted to take some of the jerseys with them, so yet again as many as possible were squeezed into suitcases and started their journey halfway across the world. The jerseys were gratefully received by some very excited children (and adults too, as no one is put out of the orphanage if they have no other place to go).

I met up with Caron on her return from Thailand, and she told me a lovely story. She had been trying to explain to the manager of the orphanage who George Best was, as he didn't know much about him. To Caron's complete surprise, a little boy, who was wheelchair bound and no more than about seven or eight years old, suddenly butted in to tell the manager all about George. Caron said he that he seemed to know everything about his football hero. Stories like that touch me deeply.

I have huge admiration for people like Mphatso, Caron, Debi and Keith who, for no personal gain, do so much to bring a bit of joy to children who have so little in their lives.

—

The time that has elapsed since George's death has been emotionally and sometimes physically tough. But it has given every single member of our family, and in particular our dad, an overwhelming sense of gratitude and pride.

For Dad, of course, it has meant a great deal that George is remembered, as he himself had wished, for his football. For this book, I asked Dad to sum up George. Many glowing tributes have been paid to George down through the years, but I doubt that any has ever been more heartfelt than these words of the father who reared him:

> George's life was blighted in one way but blessed in another. He did not set out to be an alcoholic. Like hundreds of thousands all over the world, he was fated to be so.
>
> His football talent — he was described as a genius — was undeniable. It is generally accepted that he was one of the greatest players of any era. When Jimmy Greaves, a great player himself, was asked, 'Do you think George was the best ever?' he replied, 'I don't know about that — but *I've* never seen better.'

One thing no one can dispute is that George was a complete player. He could use either foot equally well, he had knife-edge balance, he would drop his right shoulder and go left or vice versa ... and all this at an incredible angle.

He also had pace, could pass the ball inch perfect over distance, could tackle and was good in the air — even against taller players. He was brave without resorting to the diving and acting that prevails in the game today.

But George had other qualities which endeared him to people. He was never boastful and accepted he was lucky to be born with a gift.

The impact all over the world of his death and funeral reflected the respect in which he was held. Our home and his grave are still visited today by people from all over the globe and, of course, from here in Northern Ireland.

For us, establishing the George Best Foundation has been a very difficult task. However, it has also been a labour of love. A labour of love for a very special man who couldn't beat the awful illness of alcoholism, which blights and ruins so many lives.

The difficult times have paid off.

We are proud of the money that has been raised in such a short space of time, and the fact that just one year after that awful day in November 2005, the George Best Foundation was in a position to send to the Foundation for Liver Research, headed by Professor Williams, a substantial sum — £100,000. Already a young PhD graduate has some very exciting results regarding research into liver disease. And in January 2007, the first George Best Research Fellow was employed. It is hoped that our contribution will fund this project for at least two years.

Norman and I have had to put our lives on hold for a while. Norman has retired. The plan was for us to go to France to our home (which has now been rebuilt) but that will have to wait for the moment. We will continue to work to the best of our ability to achieve the aims and objectives of the Foundation.

People often ask me what would George think of what we are doing. Although George was a very humble and shy person, he enjoyed and respected the attention of the many genuine fans, who loved him in return. I know that we are doing the right thing in channelling the genuine grief of so many at his death into something practical and positive, which I hope will help transform the lives of others. I know that that would have his full approval.

We can't say what the future holds for the Foundation, but whatever the outcome, we can say, with hand on heart, that we gave it our best shot and did it for the right reasons.

We did it for your memory and we did it to ensure that the wonderful legacy that you left behind will live on.

We did it for you. Our George.

INDEX